Spring Boot 3.0 Crash Course

Mastering Spring Boot, from Application Development to Advanced Security, Data Access, Integration and Deployment

Kit Harrington

Published by: GitforGits

Publisher: Sonal Dhandre

www.gitforgits.com

support@gitforgits.com

Printed in India

First Printing: July 2024

ISBN: 978-81-19177-38-7

Cover Design by: Kitten Publishing

Prologue

Thank you for choosing our Spring Boot 3.0 Crash Course. Hi, I'm Kit Harrington, and I'm really excited to show you how to use Spring Boot 3.0. Allow me to begin by relating a tale that exemplifies why this book is so important.

A fast-growing tech startup had me as their project manager a few years back. The success of the business hinged on creating a safe, scalable, and reliable app that could manage thousands of users with ease. These lofty expectations were squarely on my shoulders as lead developer. The complexity of integrating different technologies, guaranteeing security, and optimizing performance was a challenge for me, even though I have a lot of experience in this area. I started using Spring Boot as my primary tool at that point. An easier way to build apps using the Spring framework was made available by Spring Boot. I was able to focus on creating effective code because it made setting everything up and running much easier. Thanks to Spring Boot's robust capabilities, we were able to build and deploy features at an incredible pace. Mastering Spring Boot, though, necessitated familiarity with its foundational concepts, recommended practices, and more complex features.

That experience is the foundation of this book. I hope that by sharing what I've learned and the solutions I've found, you'll be able to build your Spring Boot applications with ease and confidence. In this book, I'll show you how to build an app using Spring Boot from the ground up, including all the necessary features and making sure it's secure, scalable, and fast. You may find at times repetition of steps while demonstrating practical examples, so apology in advance but the intention is to ensure you dont get stuck in the middle of coding the application.

In this first step, you will build your first Spring Boot app and configure your development environment. The course will teach you the ins and outs of dependency management, application configuration via properties and YAML files, and more. Annotations, data source integration with Spring Data JPA, and RESTful service construction are some of the more advanced topics that we will cover as we go along. I will demonstrate how to incorporate Spring Security authentication and authorization, two essential components of any application. In this lesson, you will find out how to secure your application from intruders by configuring basic authentication, URL authorization, and JWT authentication.

Also covered will be the basics of working with Thymeleaf templates to build dynamic web pages, accept and process form submissions, and check user input. Learn the ins and outs of integrating popular front-end frameworks such as Angular and React to create cutting-edge, mobile-friendly apps. I will show you how to package your app, make Docker images, and deploy them to cloud platforms and Kubernetes—all of which are essential steps in the development process. Managing environment variables and achieving zero downtime during deployments are topics you'll cover in this course. Using JMeter for performance testing, I will demonstrate how to optimize performance, which is essential for delivering an excellent user experience. You will gain knowledge on how to locate performance issues and enhance your application to its full potential.

With the knowledge and skills, you gain from this book, you will be able to confidently construct applications that are strong, secure, and perform well. So that you can put what you learn into practice right away, I want to equip you with practical knowledge and real-world examples.

Come on, let's start making awesome Spring Boot apps!

Content

Preface

This **Spring Boot 3.0 Crash Course** will teach you all you need to know to create powerful Spring applications with the latest version of the framework. You will be able to create any feature that an application may require because this book covers everything from the fundamentals to advanced features.

First things first: get your development environment ready and build your very first Spring Boot App. Data access, security, configuration, and testing are some of the more advanced subjects you'll cover as you go along. This crash course will teach you how to create RESTful services, use Spring Data JPA to integrate different types of data, and work with properties and YAML files to oversee configurations. You practice to manage application properties, get into the application of annotations, and master the Spring MVC architecture. It will teach you to manage form submissions, validate user input, and construct dynamic web pages using Thymeleaf templates. The book also covers topics like integrating front-end frameworks, handling errors, and deploying applications to cloud platforms and Kubernetes.

Issues with configuring URL authorization, implementing JWT authentication, and integrating with OAuth2 and OpenID Connect are some of the critical problems that are being solved in this book. Methods for troubleshooting auto-configuration issues, managing environment variables in Docker, and making use of performance testing tools such as JMeter are all topics that will be covered. Additionally, the book delves into the topic of how to integrate with Active Directory and LDAP for centralized user management and authentication.

By the time you finish this book, you will know everything there is to know about Spring Boot application development, security, and deployment, so you can confidently take on real-world projects.

In this book you will learn how to:

- Discover the ins and outs of efficiently configuring a Spring Boot 3.0 development environment.
- Integrate various data sources and construct strong RESTful services with the help of Spring Data JPA.
- Get to know Spring Boot's properties and YAML files to set up customizable apps.
- Use Spring Security and JWT tokens to implement secure authorization and authentication.
- Use Thymeleaf templates to build interactive websites and easily handle form submissions.
- Use Kubernetes and cloud platforms to effortlessly deploy Spring Boot applications.

- Make your apps more up-to-date and responsive by incorporating front-end frameworks such as Angular and React.
- Put thorough error handling strategies into your applications and handle errors gracefully.
- Use Docker to manage environment variables and JMeter to optimize application performance.

GitforGits

Prerequisites

Whether you're a seasoned developer or just getting started, this book introduces you to geete comfortable with Spring Boot and take the most benefits of its tools to create high-quality apps quickly. All you need is to be just a basic programming experience with any of the languages to get started with.

Codes Usage

Are you in need of some helpful code examples to assist you in your programming and documentation? Look no further! Our book offers a wealth of supplemental material, including code examples and exercises.

Not only is this book here to aid you in getting your job done, but you have our permission to use the example code in your programs and documentation. However, please note that if you are reproducing a significant portion of the code, we do require you to contact us for permission.

But don't worry, using several chunks of code from this book in your program or answering a question by citing our book and quoting example code does not require permission. But if you do choose to give credit, an attribution typically includes the title, author, publisher, and ISBN. For example, "Spring Boot 3.0 Crash Course by Kit Harrington".

If you are unsure whether your intended use of the code examples falls under fair use or the permissions outlined above, please do not hesitate to reach out to us at support@gitforgits.com.

We are happy to assist and clarify any concerns.

Acknowledgement

I owe a tremendous debt of gratitude to GitforGits, for their unflagging enthusiasm and wise counsel throughout the entire process of writing this book. Their knowledge and careful editing helped make sure the piece was useful for people of all reading levels and comprehension skills. In addition, I'd like to thank everyone involved in the publishing process for their efforts in making this book a reality. Their efforts, from copyediting to advertising, made the project what it is today.

Finally, I'd like to express my gratitude to everyone who has shown me unconditional love and encouragement throughout my life. Their support was crucial to the completion of this book. I appreciate your help with this endeavour and your continued interest in my career.

Chapter 1: Up and Running with Spring Boot

Chapter Overview

Let us start with our first chapter, "Up and Running with Spring Boot," which will serve as the foundation for your skill-building transition into Spring Boot. This chapter will walk you through the core concepts and essential features that make Spring Boot a powerful framework for developing robust applications. You'll start by learning about Spring Boot and how it evolved from the Spring Framework, which will help you understand why it's so popular among developers today.

As you progress, you'll discover the key features that set Spring Boot apart from other frameworks. Some of its features include an opinionated approach to configuration, the ability to build standalone apps, and the ability to integrate with different technologies seamlessly. Understanding these features will help you appreciate the efficiency and simplicity that Spring Boot adds to application development. You will then proceed to set up your development environment, ensuring that all required tools are installed and configured. This includes configuring your IDE, JDK, and other essential components. Following that, you will create your first Spring Boot application, giving you hands-on experience with the framework's capabilities. This practical approach will be supplemented by exploring Spring Boot dependencies and starter projects, which make dependency management and project setup easier.

Finally, the chapter will go over Spring Boot annotations and the Spring Boot CLI. By the end of this chapter, you will have a solid understanding of Spring Boot, allowing you to delve deeper into its advanced features and capabilities in the following chapters.

What is Spring Boot?

Spring Boot has gained significant traction among developers for its ability to simplify the creation of stand-alone, production-grade Spring-based applications. It has become synonymous with rapid application development, offering a set of tools and features that streamline the entire development process. The modern developer community appreciates Spring Boot for its minimal setup, reduced boilerplate code, and the seamless integration it provides with other technologies.

Emergence of Spring Boot

Spring Boot emerged as an enhancement to the Spring Framework, addressing some of the complexities and configuration challenges developers faced with traditional Spring applications. The Spring Framework, introduced in 2003, brought a revolutionary approach to Java development by promoting loose coupling through dependency injection and aspect-oriented programming. However, as the Spring ecosystem grew, configuring and deploying Spring applications became increasingly intricate. This is where Spring Boot comes into play.

Spring Boot was introduced to tackle these challenges by providing a convention-over-configuration approach. It simplifies the development process by offering default configurations and sensible defaults, which can be customized as needed. This allows developers to focus more on writing business logic rather than dealing with complex configurations.

Relation to Spring Framework

Spring Boot is essentially built on top of the Spring Framework, leveraging its core principles and components while abstracting much of the boilerplate configuration. This relationship ensures that Spring Boot applications inherit the robust and flexible nature of the Spring Framework but with added ease of use and productivity enhancements.

At its core, Spring Boot provides:

- Pre-configured dependencies for various functionalities, reducing the need for manual dependency management.
- Automatically configures your application based on the dependencies you have added, ensuring minimal configuration effort.
- Enables the creation of stand-alone applications that can run independently without the need for an external web server.
- Integrates features like metrics, health checks, and externalized configuration out of the box.

Recent Version

Spring Boot has evolved significantly across its three major versions, each bringing new features, improvements, and refinements.

Spring Boot 1.x

The first major release focused on establishing the foundation of the framework. It introduced key features like auto-configuration, starter dependencies, and embedded servers. This version laid the groundwork for making Spring applications easier to create and deploy.

Spring Boot 2.x

Building on the success of the 1.x series, Spring Boot 2.0 brought several enhancements. These included improved support for reactive programming with Spring WebFlux, enhanced Actuator endpoints for better monitoring, and integration with newer versions of the Spring Framework and other third-party libraries. The 2.x series also saw a focus on performance improvements and updated default configurations.

Spring Boot 3.x

The latest major release, Spring Boot 3.0, continues to refine the framework with modern features and support for the latest Java versions. It embraces new standards and best practices in the Java ecosystem, such as better support for GraalVM native images, enhanced observability with Micrometer, and further improvements in performance and memory management. Spring Boot 3.x also introduces new tools and integrations that align with contemporary development needs, such as better cloud-native support and advanced security features.

Applications, Programs, and APIs

Spring Boot is widely used for developing robust web applications. Its integration with Spring MVC allows developers to create RESTful services with ease, handling various HTTP methods and providing JSON/XML responses out of the box. The microservices architecture has also gained popularity, and Spring Boot is a natural fit for building microservices. Its lightweight nature and ability to create stand-alone applications make it ideal for developing small, independent services that can be deployed and scaled individually. It is also commonly used to develop APIs that expose business logic and services to other applications. The ease of creating RESTful endpoints, along with features like Spring Security for securing APIs, makes it a preferred choice for API development.

Spring Boot integrates with Spring Batch to facilitate batch processing, allowing for the development of applications that handle large volumes of data processing jobs. This is particularly useful in scenarios like data migration, ETL (Extract, Transform, Load) operations, and periodic tasks. With support for various messaging protocols and technologies like RabbitMQ and Kafka, Spring Boot simplifies the development of messaging-based applications. This is essential for building event-driven architectures and real-time data processing systems.

Spring Boot's compatibility with cloud platforms like AWS, Azure, and Google Cloud Platform makes it an excellent choice for developing cloud-native applications. Features like externalized configuration, seamless integration with cloud services, and support for containerization through Docker make Spring Boot a powerful tool for modern cloud deployments. Spring Boot can also be used to create command-line applications. The Spring Boot CLI (Command Line Interface) allows for rapid prototyping and execution of Spring Boot applications directly from the command line, making it useful for scripting and automation tasks.

Spring Boot supports GraphQL, enabling the development of APIs that allow clients to request exactly the data they need. This is particularly beneficial for applications requiring efficient data retrieval and flexible querying capabilities. And, with the introduction of Spring WebFlux, Spring Boot supports reactive programming, allowing the creation of reactive, non-blocking applications. This is particularly useful for building high-performance, scalable applications that need to handle a large number of concurrent connections.

Key Features of Spring Boot

Spring Boot's widespread adoption and popularity among developers stem from its powerful and efficient features that significantly enhance the development experience. Following are the ost appealing features highlighting how they simplify application development and improve productivity:

Auto-configuration

One of the most acclaimed features of Spring Boot is its auto-configuration capability. Auto-configuration reduces the need for manual setup by automatically configuring Spring applications based on the dependencies present on the classpath. For example, if you include a dependency for a database in your project, Spring Boot will automatically configure a DataSource bean. This feature drastically minimizes boilerplate code and configuration files, allowing developers to focus on writing business logic.

Spring Boot Starters

Spring Boot starters are a set of convenient dependency descriptors that you can include in your project. They aggregate commonly used dependencies into a single dependency, simplifying the process of adding and managing libraries. For instance, the spring-boot-starter-web starter includes dependencies for Spring MVC, Jackson for JSON processing, and an embedded Tomcat server. By using starters, you can easily set up a Spring Boot project without having to manually specify each dependency, thus speeding up development time.

Embedded Servers

Spring Boot allows you to create stand-alone applications by embedding web servers like Tomcat, Jetty, or Undertow directly within the application. This eliminates the need to deploy your application to an external server. By default, Spring Boot uses Tomcat as the embedded server, but you can easily switch to Jetty or Undertow if required. This feature enables rapid development and testing, as you can run your application directly from your IDE or command line without additional server configuration.

Production-Ready Features

Spring Boot comes with a variety of built-in features that help you monitor and manage your application in production environments. The Actuator module provides a range of endpoints that offer insights into the application's health, metrics, and configuration. These endpoints can expose information such as application health status, environment properties, and metrics like memory usage and request counts. Additionally, Spring Boot supports integration with external monitoring tools like Prometheus and Grafana, making it easier to keep an eye on your application's performance and health.

Externalized Configuration

Managing configuration properties in a flexible and efficient manner is crucial for any application. Spring Boot's externalized configuration feature allows you to define configuration properties in various formats, including properties files, YAML files, environment variables, and command-line arguments. This flexibility makes it easier to manage configuration across different environments, such as development, testing, and production. You can use profiles to group configuration properties and switch between them seamlessly, ensuring your application behaves correctly in each environment.

Spring Boot CLI

The Spring Boot Command Line Interface (CLI) is a powerful tool for rapid prototyping and development. It allows you to write Groovy scripts to run Spring Boot applications without requiring a full project setup. The CLI is particularly useful for creating quick prototypes, running small utilities, or testing out new features. With the Spring Boot CLI, you can quickly create and execute Spring Boot applications directly from the command line, making it a handy tool for developers who need to test and experiment rapidly.

DevTools

Spring Boot DevTools is a development-time feature that enhances the developer experience by providing tools and utilities that streamline the development process. One of the key features of DevTools is automatic restart, which reloads the application context whenever there are changes in the classpath. This reduces the time spent restarting the application manually. DevTools also includes features like live reload, which refreshes the browser automatically when resources change, and remote debugging support, allowing you to debug your application running in a remote environment.

Spring Initializr

Spring Initializr is an online tool that helps you bootstrap a new Spring Boot project quickly. It provides a web-based interface where you can select the desired project metadata, dependencies, and other options. Once you specify your preferences, Spring Initializr generates a fully configured Spring Boot project that you can download and import into your IDE. This tool simplifies the initial setup process, enabling developers to start coding their applications immediately.

Actuator

Spring Boot Actuator is a set of production-ready features that help you monitor and manage your Spring Boot application. It provides various endpoints that expose application health, metrics, info, environment properties, and other operational details. These endpoints can be customized to control which information is exposed and who can access it. Actuator is essential for gaining insights into the application's runtime behavior and health, making it easier to detect and diagnose issues in production environments.

Spring Boot DevTools

Spring Boot DevTools is a development-time module that boosts developer productivity by providing features like automatic restarts, live reload, and configurations for debugging. Automatic restarts help reduce the time spent on manual restarts after code changes, while live reload refreshes the browser automatically when static resources are modified. DevTools also simplifies remote debugging, allowing you to connect your debugger to a running application without complex setup.

Simplified Dependency Management

Spring Boot simplifies dependency management by providing a set of starter POMs that bundle commonly used dependencies. These starters reduce the complexity of managing dependencies individually and ensure compatibility between different library versions. For instance, adding the spring-boot-starter-data-jpa starter includes dependencies for Spring Data JPA, Hibernate, and a database connection pool, all of which are tested to work well together.

Simplified Testing

Testing is a crucial part of application development, and Spring Boot makes it easier by providing extensive support for unit and integration testing. Spring Boot integrates seamlessly with testing frameworks like JUnit and TestNG, and it includes specialized test utilities like Spring Boot Test. This module provides annotations and utilities that simplify the setup and execution of tests, such as @SpringBootTest, which loads the complete application context for integration tests, and @WebMvcTest, which focuses on testing the web layer.

Application Metrics and Health Checks

Monitoring application performance and health is vital in production environments. Spring Boot Actuator provides endpoints for gathering various metrics and health information about your application. Metrics include data on memory usage, CPU usage, HTTP request metrics, and more. Health checks provide information about the status of various components, such as databases, message brokers, and external services. This information helps you ensure that your application is running smoothly and efficiently.

Security Integration

Spring Boot seamlessly integrates with Spring Security, providing a robust and flexible security framework for your applications. With minimal configuration, you can secure your applications using various authentication and authorization mechanisms, such as form-based login, OAuth2, and JWT. Spring Boot also supports method-level security, allowing you to enforce security rules on specific methods within your application. This integration ensures that your applications are secure without requiring extensive setup.

Integration with Other Spring Projects

Spring Boot integrates effortlessly with other Spring projects, such as Spring Data, Spring Batch, Spring Integration, and Spring Cloud. This integration allows you to leverage the full power of the Spring ecosystem, building comprehensive and scalable solutions. For instance, you can use Spring Data to simplify database interactions, Spring Batch for batch processing, Spring Integration for messaging and integration, and Spring Cloud for building cloud-native microservices. The seamless integration between these projects ensures that your applications are cohesive and easy to manage.

Reactive Programming Support

With the introduction of Spring WebFlux, Spring Boot now supports reactive programming, enabling you to build reactive, non-blocking applications. Reactive programming is particularly useful for applications that need to handle a large number of concurrent connections, such as real-time messaging systems and streaming applications. Spring WebFlux provides a reactive stack built on Project Reactor, offering a functional programming model that enhances the scalability and performance of your applications.

GraalVM Native Image Support

Spring Boot 3.x introduces support for GraalVM native images, allowing you to compile your Spring Boot applications into native executables. Native images offer several benefits, including faster startup times and reduced memory consumption. This feature is particularly useful for cloud-native applications and serverless environments, where resource efficiency and quick startup are critical. Spring Boot's integration with GraalVM ensures that your applications can take advantage of these benefits with minimal configuration changes.

Spring Boot's such exemplary set of features makes it a reliable platform for developing modern Java applications, with a strong emphasis on convention over configuration, coupled with its production-ready capabilities. Using these features, you can stay focussed on writing business logic, while Spring Boot totally handles the underlying complexities of application development.

Setting up Development Environment

To start developing with Spring Boot, you'll need to set up your development environment. This involves installing necessary software, configuring your Integrated Development Environment (IDE), and creating a basic project structure.

Installing JDK

Spring Boot requires the JDK to compile and run applications. Spring Boot 3.x supports JDK 17 or higher. You can download the latest version of the JDK from the official Oracle website or use an open-source alternative like OpenJDK. Once downloaded, follow the installation instructions specific for Windows:

- Run the JDK installer and follow the prompts to complete the installation.
- Set the **JAVA_HOME** environment variable to point to the JDK installation directory. This can be done through the System Properties > Environment Variables menu.
- Add the JDK's **bin** directory to the **PATH** environment variable to ensure Java commands are accessible from the command line.

Installing IDE

An IDE is essential for efficient coding and project management. IntelliJ IDEA and Eclipse are popular choices for Spring Boot development due to their robust support for Java and Spring projects.

To install IntelliJ IDEA,

- Download and install IntelliJ IDEA from the JetBrains website and remember the Community Edition is freely available to download and considered suitable too for most development tasks.
- Once installed, open IntelliJ IDEA and configure it for Java development by selecting the appropriate JDK.

Installing Apache Maven

Apache Maven is a powerful build automation tool used for managing project dependencies and building Java applications. Spring Boot uses Maven to manage dependencies, build projects, and run applications. You can download Maven from the official Apache Maven website.

To install Maven,

- Download the binary zip archive from the Apache Maven website.
- Extract the archive to a suitable location on your system.
- Add the **bin** directory of the extracted Maven folder to the **PATH** environment variable.

Installing Spring Boot CLI

The Spring Boot Command Line Interface (CLI) is a useful tool for quickly developing Spring applications using Groovy scripts. It simplifies the process of creating and running Spring Boot applications without requiring a full project setup.

To install Spring Boot CLI,

- Download the Spring Boot CLI distribution zip file from the official Spring website.

- Extract the zip file to a directory of your choice.
- Add the **bin** directory of the extracted folder to the **PATH** environment variable.
- Verify the installation by opening a command prompt and typing **spring --version**.

Creating Spring Boot Project

Spring Initializr is a web-based tool that helps you generate a Spring Boot project with a pre-configured structure and dependencies. You can access Spring Initializr at start.spring.io.

To use Spring Initializr,

- Open the Spring Initializr website.
- Fill out the project metadata fields, such as Group, Artifact, and Name.
- Select the desired dependencies for your project, such as Spring Web, Spring Data JPA, or Spring Security.
- Choose the project type (Maven Project) and packaging type (Jar).
- Select the appropriate Java version (e.g., 17) and Spring Boot version (e.g., 3.x).
- Click "Generate" to download the project as a zip file.
- Extract the zip file and open the project in your IDE.

Configuring IDE

After creating your Spring Boot project, you need to configure your IDE to enhance your development experience.

In IntelliJ IDEA,

- Open the project by selecting File > Open and navigating to the extracted project directory.
- IntelliJ IDEA will automatically detect the project structure and import it as a Maven project.
- Ensure the correct JDK is configured for the project by selecting File > Project Structure > Project and setting the Project SDK.
- Install the Spring Boot plugin (if not already installed) to enable additional features like Spring Boot-specific code assistance and configuration.

Running first Spring Boot App

With your development environment set up, you can now run your first Spring Boot application.

Spring Boot applications can be started directly from your IDE or the command line.

From IntelliJ IDEA,

- Locate the main application class, which is annotated with **@SpringBootApplication**. This class typically contains a **main** method that starts the application.
- Right-click the main application class and select Run.

From the Command Line,

- Open a command prompt and navigate to the project directory.
- Run the command **mvn spring-boot:run** to start the application.

Exploring Project Structure

A typical Spring Boot project has a well-defined structure that includes several important directories and files:

- **src/main/java:** Contains the application's main source code. This is where you will write your Java classes and Spring components.
- **src/main/resources:** Contains application resources like configuration files, static assets, and templates.
- **src/test/java:** Contains test classes and test resources.
- **pom.xml:** The Maven build file that specifies project dependencies and build configuration.

Adding Dependencies

Spring Boot uses Maven to manage dependencies. To add a new dependency, you simply update the **pom.xml** file with the desired dependency. For example, to add Spring Web dependency, include the following in the **<dependencies>** section:

```
<dependency>

    <groupId>org.springframework.boot</groupId>

    <artifactId>spring-boot-starter-web</artifactId>

</dependency>
```

After updating the **pom.xml** file, your IDE will automatically download and resolve the new dependencies.

Configuring Application Properties

Spring Boot applications use a configuration file to manage application settings. By default, this file is named **application.properties** and is located in the **src/main/resources** directory. You can use this file to define various properties such as server port, database connection details, and logging settings.

For example, to change the default server port, add the following line to the **application.properties** file:

```
server.port=8081
```

Spring Boot DevTools

Spring Boot DevTools is a useful development-time feature that enhances the developer experience by providing tools like automatic restarts and live reloads. To use DevTools, add the following dependency to your **pom.xml** file:

```
<dependency>

    <groupId>org.springframework.boot</groupId>

    <artifactId>spring-boot-devtools</artifactId>

    <optional>true</optional>

</dependency>
```

DevTools will automatically restart your application whenever you make changes to the classpath, reducing the time spent on manual restarts.

Spring Boot CLI

Spring Boot CLI is a command-line tool that allows you to run Spring Boot applications using Groovy scripts. This tool is particularly useful for prototyping and testing small applications, and to create and run a Spring Boot application with the CLI, you must follow these steps:

- Create a new Groovy file with the **.groovy** extension.
- Write a simple Spring Boot application in Groovy. For example:

```
@RestController
```

```
class HelloController {
    @RequestMapping("/")
    String hello() {
        "Hello, GitforGits Publishing!"
    }
}
```

- Save the file and run it using the Spring Boot CLI by executing the command **`spring run <filename>.groovy`** in the terminal.

This will start the Spring Boot application, and you can access it by navigating to **`http://localhost:8080`** in your web browser. So, you are now ready to start building Spring Boot applications.

Creating First Spring Boot Application

This section will teach and lead you through the steps of building a simple RESTful web service using Spring Boot, along with a hands-on introduction to the framework's capabilities.

Setting up the Project

Start by creating a new Spring Boot project using Spring Initializr, as outlined previously. For this example, select the following dependencies:

- Spring Web
- Spring Boot DevTools

Fill out the project metadata (Group, Artifact, Name, etc.) and download the generated project as we learned in the previous section. Extract the project and open it in your chosen IDE.

The generated Spring Boot project has a well-defined structure:

- **`src/main/java:`** Contains the main application code.
- **`src/main/resources:`** Holds application configuration files and static resources.
- **`src/test/java:`** Contains test classes.
- **`pom.xml:`** The Maven build file that specifies project dependencies and configurations.

Creating Main Application Class

The entry point of a Spring Boot application is a class annotated with **@SpringBootApplication**. This annotation encompasses several other annotations:

- **@Configuration**: Marks the class as a source of bean definitions.
- **@EnableAutoConfiguration**: Enables Spring Boot's auto-configuration mechanism.
- **@ComponentScan**: Scans the package for Spring components.

Locate the main application class, typically named **<YourApplicationName>Application.java**, in the **src/main/java** directory. It should look something like this:

```
package com.example.demo;



import org.springframework.boot.SpringApplication;

import
org.springframework.boot.autoconfigure.SpringBootApplicat
ion;



@SpringBootApplication

public class DemoApplication {

    public static void main(String[] args) {

        SpringApplication.run(DemoApplication.class,
args);

    }

}
```

This class contains a **main** method that launches the Spring Boot application.

Creating a REST Controller

To create a RESTful web service, you need to define a controller. A controller in Spring Boot is a class annotated with **@RestController**, which combines **@Controller** and **@ResponseBody**, indicating that the methods in the class return data directly rather than views.

So, create a new package named **controller** under **src/main/java/com/example/demo**. Then, create a new class named **HelloController.java** in this package as below:

```
package com.example.demo.controller;


import
org.springframework.web.bind.annotation.GetMapping;

import
org.springframework.web.bind.annotation.RequestMapping;

import
org.springframework.web.bind.annotation.RestController;


@RestController

@RequestMapping("/api")

public class HelloController {


    @GetMapping("/hello")

    public String sayHello() {

        return "Hello, GitforGits Publishing!";

    }

}
```

In the above code snippet, the **HelloController** class defines a single endpoint **/api/hello** that responds with the message "Hello, GitforGits Publishing!" when accessed via an HTTP GET request.

Running the Application

You can then run the Spring Boot application directly from your IDE or the command line.

- From IntelliJ IDEA:
    - Locate the main application class **DemoApplication**.
    - Right-click on the class and select **Run 'DemoApplication.main()'**.
- From Command Line:
    - Open a command prompt and navigate to the project directory.
    - Run the command **mvn spring-boot:run**.

Next, open the web browser and navigate to **http://localhost:8080/api/hello**. You should see the message "Hello, GitforGits Publishing!" displayed in the browser. This confirms that your RESTful web service is up and running.

Understanding Auto-configuration

Spring Boot's auto-configuration mechanism simplifies the setup process by automatically configuring beans based on the dependencies you have included. In this example, the presence of the Spring Web dependency triggers the auto-configuration of a web server (Tomcat by default) and configures Spring MVC to handle web requests.

To expand the functionality of your application, you can also add more endpoints to the **HelloController** class or create additional controllers. For example, to add a new endpoint that returns a JSON object,

```
@GetMapping("/greet")

public Map<String, String> greet() {

    Map<String, String> response = new HashMap<>();

    response.put("message", "Greetings from Spring
Boot!");

    return response;
```

```
}
```

This endpoint responds with a JSON object containing a greeting message. Access it by navigating to **http://localhost:8080/api/greet**.

Adding Dependency Injection

Spring Boot uses dependency injection to manage the lifecycle of components and their dependencies. To demonstrate this, create a service class that provides the greeting message. For this, create a new package, **service** under **src/main/java/com/example/demo**.

Then, create a new class named **GreetingService.java** in this package:

```
package com.example.demo.service;


import org.springframework.stereotype.Service;


@Service
public class GreetingService {


    public String getGreeting() {
        return "Greetings from the GreetingService!";
    }
}
```

The **@Service** annotation marks this class as a Spring service component. Now, modify the **HelloController** to use this service:

```
package com.example.demo.controller;
```

```java
import com.example.demo.service.GreetingService;

import
org.springframework.web.bind.annotation.GetMapping;

import
org.springframework.web.bind.annotation.RequestMapping;

import
org.springframework.web.bind.annotation.RestController;


@RestController

@RequestMapping("/api")

public class HelloController {


    private final GreetingService greetingService;


    public HelloController(GreetingService
greetingService) {

        this.greetingService = greetingService;

    }


    @GetMapping("/hello")

    public String sayHello() {

        return "Hello, GitforGits Publishing!";

    }
```

```
    @GetMapping("/greet")
    public String greet() {
        return greetingService.getGreeting();
    }
}
```

With this change, the **/greet** endpoint now uses the **GreetingService** to obtain the greeting message.

Exploring Application Properties

Spring Boot applications are configured using properties files. The default configuration file is **application.properties** located in the **src/main/resources** directory. You can use this file to set various properties for your application.

For instance, to change the server port, add the following line to the **application.properties** file:

```
server.port=9090
```

Restart the application, and it will now run on port 9090. Access the endpoints at **http://localhost:9090/api/hello** and **http://localhost:9090/api/greet**.

You have just completed the first steps of creating, running, and testing a Spring Boot application. You can build upon this practical experience to delve deeper into Spring Boot's features and capabilities.

Understanding Spring Boot Dependencies

Spring Boot simplifies dependency management by providing a set of curated dependencies that work well together. These dependencies, known as Spring Boot Starters, reduce the complexity of managing individual dependencies and ensure compatibility between different libraries.

Spring Boot Starters

Spring Boot Starters are pre-configured dependency descriptors that include a set of commonly used dependencies. These starters allow you to add a group of dependencies to your project with a single entry in your **pom.xml** file. For example, the **spring-boot-starter-web** starter includes dependencies for building web applications using Spring MVC, Jackson for JSON processing, and an embedded Tomcat server.

Given below is an example of how to include the **spring-boot-starter-web** in your **pom.xml**:

```
<dependency>

    <groupId>org.springframework.boot</groupId>

    <artifactId>spring-boot-starter-web</artifactId>

</dependency>
```

Spring Boot provides a wide range of starters for various use cases, such as **spring-boot-starter-data-jpa** for JPA and Hibernate, **spring-boot-starter-security** for Spring Security, and **spring-boot-starter-test** for testing.

Maven

Spring Boot uses Maven as its build tool to manage dependencies, build the project, and run the application. Dependencies are specified in the **pom.xml** file. Maven resolves these dependencies and ensures that the correct versions are used.

Given below is a basic structure of a **pom.xml** file:

```
<project xmlns="http://maven.apache.org/POM/4.0.0"
xmlns:xsi="http://www.w3.org/2001/XMLSchema-instance"

    xsi:schemaLocation="http://maven.apache.org/POM/4.0.0
http://maven.apache.org/xsd/maven-4.0.0.xsd">

    <modelVersion>4.0.0</modelVersion>

    <groupId>com.example</groupId>

    <artifactId>demo</artifactId>
```

```
    <version>0.0.1-SNAPSHOT</version>
    <packaging>jar</packaging>

    <parent>
        <groupId>org.springframework.boot</groupId>
        <artifactId>spring-boot-starter-
parent</artifactId>
        <version>3.0.0</version>
        <relativePath/> <!-- lookup parent from
repository -->
    </parent>

    <dependencies>
        <dependency>
            <groupId>org.springframework.boot</groupId>
            <artifactId>spring-boot-starter-
web</artifactId>
        </dependency>
        <!-- Add other dependencies here -->
    </dependencies>

    <build>
```

```
        <plugins>
            <plugin>

<groupId>org.springframework.boot</groupId>
                <artifactId>spring-boot-maven-
plugin</artifactId>
            </plugin>
        </plugins>
    </build>
</project>
```

The **parent** section specifies the Spring Boot parent POM, which manages dependency versions and ensures compatibility. The **dependencies** section lists the project's dependencies. The **spring-boot-maven-plugin** in the **build** section allows you to package and run the Spring Boot application using Maven.

Dependency Management

Spring Boot's parent POM (**spring-boot-starter-parent**) manages the versions of dependencies. By using the parent POM, you inherit a curated set of dependency versions that are known to work well together. This reduces the risk of version conflicts and ensures stability.

To see the managed versions, you can browse the Spring Boot Dependency Management POM on Maven Central. Given below is how you can override the version of a dependency if needed:

```
<dependencyManagement>
    <dependencies>
        <dependency>
            <groupId>org.springframework.boot</groupId>
            <artifactId>spring-boot-
dependencies</artifactId>
```

```
            <version>3.0.0</version>
            <type>pom</type>
            <scope>import</scope>
        </dependency>
    </dependencies>
</dependencyManagement>

<dependencies>
    <dependency>
        <groupId>com.fasterxml.jackson.core</groupId>
        <artifactId>jackson-databind</artifactId>
        <version>2.12.3</version> <!-- Overriding the
version -->
    </dependency>
</dependencies>
```

Following are the commonly used spring boot starters:

1. **spring-boot-starter-web:** It is used for building web applications, including RESTful services. This starter includes Spring MVC, Jackson for JSON processing, and an embedded Tomcat server.
2. **spring-boot-starter-data-jpa:** Used primarily for working with relational databases using Spring Data JPA and Hibernate. It simplifies database access by providing a repository abstraction layer.
3. **spring-boot-starter-security:** This is required for adding security to your application using Spring Security. It provides authentication and authorization capabilities.
4. **spring-boot-starter-test:** Primarily used in testing Spring Boot applications. It includes dependencies for JUnit, Spring Test, AssertJ, Hamcrest, Mockito, and other

testing libraries.

5. **spring-boot-starter-actuator:** Most commonly used for adding production-ready features to help you monitor and manage your application. It provides endpoints for health checks, metrics, and other monitoring data.

Adding Custom Dependencies

Sometimes you need to add dependencies that are not covered by Spring Boot starters. You can do this by specifying the dependencies in your **pom.xml** file. For example, to add the Apache Commons Lang library:

```
<dependency>

    <groupId>org.apache.commons</groupId>

    <artifactId>commons-lang3</artifactId>

    <version>3.12.0</version>

</dependency>
```

Maven will download and include this dependency in your project.

Using Spring Boot DevTools

Spring Boot DevTools is a module that provides features to enhance the development experience, such as automatic restarts and live reloads. To use DevTools, add the following dependency to your **pom.xml**:

```
<dependency>

    <groupId>org.springframework.boot</groupId>

    <artifactId>spring-boot-devtools</artifactId>

    <optional>true</optional>

</dependency>
```

DevTools will automatically restart your application when classpath files change, reducing the need for manual restarts and speeding up the development process.

Dependency Exclusions

Sometimes, transitive dependencies brought in by another dependency can cause conflicts. Spring Boot allows you to exclude these unwanted transitive dependencies. For example, to exclude a specific version of a dependency:

```
<dependency>

    <groupId>org.springframework.boot</groupId>

    <artifactId>spring-boot-starter-web</artifactId>

    <exclusions>

        <exclusion>

            <groupId>org.springframework.boot</groupId>

            <artifactId>spring-boot-starter-
tomcat</artifactId>

        </exclusion>

    </exclusions>

</dependency>
```

This excludes the embedded Tomcat server from the **spring-boot-starter-web** dependency.

Resolving Dependency Conflicts

Dependency conflicts can arise when different libraries require different versions of the same dependency. Maven resolves these conflicts using a nearest-wins strategy, where the version closest to your project in the dependency tree is used. You can manually resolve conflicts by specifying the desired version in the **dependencyManagement** section.

For example:

```
<dependencyManagement>

    <dependencies>
```

```
        <dependency>
            <groupId>com.fasterxml.jackson.core</groupId>
            <artifactId>jackson-databind</artifactId>
            <version>2.12.3</version>
        </dependency>
    </dependencies>
</dependencyManagement>
```

Using Bill of Materials (BOM)

A Bill of Materials (BOM) is a special POM file that manages versions of a set of related artifacts. Spring Boot provides a BOM to ensure compatibility between different Spring projects. To use the Spring Boot BOM, import it in your **dependencyManagement** section:

```
<dependencyManagement>
    <dependencies>
        <dependency>
            <groupId>org.springframework.boot</groupId>
            <artifactId>spring-boot-
dependencies</artifactId>
            <version>3.0.0</version>
            <type>pom</type>
            <scope>import</scope>
        </dependency>
    </dependencies>
```

```
</dependencyManagement>
```

This ensures that all dependencies within the Spring ecosystem use compatible versions.

Upgrading Dependencies

When upgrading Spring Boot or other dependencies, it's essential to ensure compatibility and stability. Spring Boot's release notes and documentation provide detailed information on changes and potential migration issues. You can update the Spring Boot version in your **pom.xml** by changing the parent version:

```
<parent>

    <groupId>org.springframework.boot</groupId>

    <artifactId>spring-boot-starter-parent</artifactId>

    <version>3.0.0</version>

    <relativePath/>

</parent>
```

After updating, run **mvn clean install** to rebuild the project and verify that everything works correctly.

Maven also provides a command to view the dependency tree, which helps you understand how dependencies are resolved and identify potential conflicts. Run the following command in your project directory:

```
mvn dependency:tree
```

This command generates a tree view of your project's dependencies, showing the hierarchy and transitive dependencies. This information is useful for debugging dependency issues and optimizing your project's dependency management.

Annotations Overview

Spring Boot leverages annotations to simplify the configuration and development process. Annotations in Spring Boot serve as metadata that provides information to the framework about how to configure and handle various components. Understanding these annotations is crucial for effective Spring Boot development.

Core Annotations

@SpringBootApplication

This is the cornerstone annotation of a Spring Boot application. It combines three other important annotations as below:

- **`@Configuration`**: Indicates that the class can be used by the Spring IoC container as a source of bean definitions.
- **`@EnableAutoConfiguration`**: Enables Spring Boot's auto-configuration mechanism, which automatically configures your application based on the dependencies present on the classpath.
- **`@ComponentScan`**: Scans the package for Spring components such as @Controller, @Service, @Repository, and custom beans.

Consider the below example:

```
@SpringBootApplication

public class DemoApplication {

    public static void main(String[] args) {

        SpringApplication.run(DemoApplication.class,
args);

    }

}
```

Stereotype Annotations

@Component

This indicates that a class is a Spring component. Spring will automatically detect such classes and register them as beans in the application context. This is a generic stereotype annotation.

For example:

```
@Component
```

```
public class MyComponent {

    // Class implementation

}
```

@Service

Specifies that a class is a service. It is a specialization of @Component and is typically used in the service layer.

For example:

```
@Service

public class MyService {

    // Service logic

}
```

@Repository

Indicates that a class is a data repository. This annotation is also a specialization of **@Component** and is typically used to indicate that the class provides CRUD operations on a database.

For example:

```
@Repository

public class MyRepository {

    // Data access logic

}
```

@Controller

Specifies that a class is a Spring MVC controller. This annotation is a specialization of **@Component** and is used in the presentation layer to handle web requests.

For example:

```
@Controller
```

```
public class MyController {

    // Request handling methods

}
```

@RestController

A convenience annotation that combines **`@Controller`** and **`@ResponseBody`**. It indicates that the class is a controller where every method returns a domain object instead of a view.

For example:

```
@RestController

public class MyRestController {

    // RESTful request handling methods

}
```

Configuration and Bean Annotations

@Configuration

Indicates that a class can be used as a source of bean definitions. This annotation is typically used on classes that define beans using @Bean methods.

For example:

```
@Configuration

public class AppConfig {

    @Bean

    public MyBean myBean() {

        return new MyBean();

    }

}
```

@Bean

Marks a method as a bean definition method. The returned object will be registered as a bean in the Spring application context.

For example:

```
@Bean

public DataSource dataSource() {

    return new DataSource();

}
```

@Value

Used to inject values into fields from external properties or environment variables.

For example:

```
@Value("${app.name}")

private String appName;
```

@PropertySource

Specifies the location of properties files to be loaded into the Spring environment.

For example:

```
@Configuration

@PropertySource("classpath:application.properties")

public class PropertyConfig {

    // Configuration methods

}
```

Dependency Injection Annotations

@Autowired

Marks a constructor, field, setter method, or config method as to be autowired by Spring's dependency injection facilities.

For example:

```
@Autowired

private MyService myService;
```

@Qualifier

Used alongside **@Autowired** to specify which bean should be injected when multiple candidates are present.

For example:

```
@Autowired

@Qualifier("specificBean")

private MyService myService;
```

Spring MVC Annotations

@RequestMapping

Used to map web requests to specific handler methods or classes. It can map URLs to the controller methods.

For example:

```
@RequestMapping("/home")

public String home() {

    return "home";

}
```

@GetMapping, @PostMapping, @PutMapping, and @DeleteMapping

Shortcut annotations for **`@RequestMapping`** that map specific HTTP methods (GET, POST, PUT, DELETE) to handler methods.

For example:

```
@GetMapping("/users")

public List<User> getUsers() {

    return userService.getAllUsers();

}



@PostMapping("/users")

public User createUser(@RequestBody User user) {

    return userService.createUser(user);

}
```

@PathVariable

Indicates that a method parameter should be bound to a URI template variable.

For example:

```
@GetMapping("/users/{id}")

public User getUserById(@PathVariable("id") Long id) {

    return userService.getUserById(id);

}
```

@RequestParam

Indicates that a method parameter should be bound to a web request parameter.

For example:

```
@GetMapping("/search")

public List<User> searchUsers(@RequestParam("name")
String name) {

    return userService.searchUsersByName(name);

}
```

@RequestBody

Indicates that a method parameter should be bound to the body of the web request.

For example:

```
@PostMapping("/users")

public User createUser(@RequestBody User user) {

    return userService.createUser(user);

}
```

@ResponseBody

Indicates that the return value of a method should be used as the response body of the web request.

For example:

```
@GetMapping("/greeting")

@ResponseBody

public String greeting() {

    return "Hello, World!";

}
```

@ExceptionHandler

Specifies a method to handle exceptions thrown by controller methods.

For example:

```
@ControllerAdvice

public class GlobalExceptionHandler {

    @ExceptionHandler(Exception.class)

    public ResponseEntity<String>
handleException(Exception e) {

        return new ResponseEntity<>(e.getMessage(),
HttpStatus.INTERNAL_SERVER_ERROR);

    }

}
```

Data Access Annotations

@Entity

Marks a class as a JPA entity, which means it is mapped to a database table.

For example:

```
@Entity

public class User {

    @Id

    @GeneratedValue(strategy = GenerationType.IDENTITY)

    private Long id;

    private String name;

    // Other fields and methods

}
```

@Id

Specifies the primary key of an entity.

For example:

```
@Id

@GeneratedValue(strategy = GenerationType.IDENTITY)

private Long id;
```

@GeneratedValue

Specifies the generation strategy for primary key values.

For example:

```
@GeneratedValue(strategy = GenerationType.IDENTITY)

private Long id;
```

@Column

Specifies the mapped column for a persistent property or field.

For example:

```
@Column(name = "username", nullable = false)

private String name;
```

@Repository

Indicates that the class is a repository which performs CRUD operations.

For example:

```
@Repository

public interface UserRepository extends
JpaRepository<User, Long> {

    // Custom query methods
```

```
}
```

Testing Annotations

@SpringBootTest

Indicates that the class is a Spring Boot test class and provides a full application context.

For example:

```
@SpringBootTest
public class DemoApplicationTests {
    @Test
    public void contextLoads() {
    }
}
```

@MockBean

Used to add mock beans to the Spring application context. Useful for replacing real beans with mocks in tests.

For example:

```
@SpringBootTest
public class UserServiceTest {
    @MockBean
    private UserRepository userRepository;
}
```

@WebMvcTest

Used to test the web layer of the application. It disables full auto-configuration and only loads beans relevant to the web layer.

For example:

```
@WebMvcTest(UserController.class)
public class UserControllerTest {
    @Autowired
    private MockMvc mockMvc;
}
```

Actuator Annotations

@Endpoint

Defines a custom actuator endpoint.

For example:

```
@Endpoint(id = "custom")
public class CustomEndpoint {
    @ReadOperation
    public String customEndpoint() {
        return "Custom Actuator Endpoint";
    }
}
```

@ReadOperation, @WriteOperation, and @DeleteOperation

Annotations used within an **`@Endpoint`** to define read, write, and delete operations.

For example:

```
@ReadOperation
public String readOperation() {
```

```
    return "Read Operation";
}


@WriteOperation
public void writeOperation(@Selector String name) {
    // Write operation logic
}


@DeleteOperation
public void deleteOperation(@Selector String name) {
    // Delete operation logic
}
```

These Spring Boot annotations are a powerful and flexible way to configure and manage your application, and hence by understanding these annotations, you can efficiently build, configure, and manage Spring Boot applications.

Overview of Spring Boot CLI

The Spring Boot Command Line Interface (CLI) is a powerful tool that allows you to develop Spring Boot applications using Groovy scripts without the need for a full project setup. The CLI simplifies the development process, enabling rapid prototyping and experimentation. Understanding the capabilities and usage of the Spring Boot CLI can greatly enhance your productivity when developing Spring Boot applications.

Installing Spring Boot CLI

To get started with the Spring Boot CLI, you need to install it on your system as follows:

- Download the Spring Boot CLI distribution zip file from the official Spring website.

- Extract the zip file to a directory of your choice.
- Add the **bin** directory of the extracted folder to the **PATH** environment variable.
- Verify the installation by opening a command prompt and typing **spring --version**.

Creating Simple Web App with CLI

The Spring Boot CLI allows you to create and run Spring Boot applications with minimal setup. You can write Groovy scripts that define your application components and run them directly using the CLI.

Now, to create a simple web application:

- Create a new file named **app.groovy**.
- Add the following code to define a simple RESTful web service:

```
@RestController

class HelloController {

    @RequestMapping("/")

    String home() {

        "Hello, Spring Boot CLI!"

    }

}
```

- Run the application using the Spring Boot CLI:

```
spring run app.groovy
```

This command starts an embedded web server and exposes the **/** endpoint, returning "Hello, Spring Boot CLI!" when accessed.

Using Spring Boot CLI for Dependency Management

The Spring Boot CLI automatically resolves dependencies required for your Groovy scripts. You can specify dependencies directly within your scripts using the **@Grab** annotation. Now, to add a dependency:

- Create a new file named **app.groovy**.
- Add the following code to include a dependency on Jackson:

```
@Grab('com.fasterxml.jackson.core:jackson-
databind:2.12.3')

import com.fasterxml.jackson.databind.ObjectMapper


@RestController

class HelloController {

    @RequestMapping("/")

    String home() {

        def mapper = new ObjectMapper()

        def greeting = [message: "Hello, Spring Boot
CLI!"]

        mapper.writeValueAsString(greeting)

    }

}
```

- Run the application using the Spring Boot CLI:

```
spring run app.groovy
```

This example uses Jackson to return a JSON response from the **/** endpoint.

Packaging Applications with Spring Boot CLI

The Spring Boot CLI can also package your Groovy scripts into executable JAR files, allowing you to distribute and run them as standalone applications. In order to package a groovy script,

- Create a new file named **app.groovy** with the following content:

```
@RestController
class HelloController {
    @RequestMapping("/")
    String home() {
        "Hello, Spring Boot CLI!"
    }
}
```

- Package the application into a JAR file:

```
spring jar app.jar app.groovy
```

- Run the packaged application:

```
java -jar app.jar
```

This creates an executable JAR file that includes all dependencies and runs as a standalone application.

Spring Boot CLI for Existing Projects

The Spring Boot CLI can work with existing Maven or Gradle projects, providing a way to quickly run and test applications. Follow the below steps to run the existing maven and gradle projects:

Running Maven Project

- Navigate to the directory containing the Maven project.
- Use the Spring Boot CLI to run the application:

```
spring run src/main/java/com/example/DemoApplication.java
```

This command compiles and runs the Spring Boot application defined in the specified Java file.

Running Gradle Project

- Navigate to the directory containing the Gradle project.

- Use the Spring Boot CLI to run the application:

```
spring run src/main/java/com/example/DemoApplication.java
```

The CLI compiles and runs the Spring Boot application using the Gradle build configuration.

Prototyping

The Spring Boot CLI is particularly useful for prototyping and experimenting with new ideas. By allowing you to quickly write and run Groovy scripts, the CLI enables rapid iteration and testing of new features.

For example, lets say to prototype a RESTful API:

- Create a new file named **api.groovy**.
- Add the following code to define a simple RESTful API:

```
@RestController

class ApiController {

    @RequestMapping("/api/greet")

    Map<String, String> greet(@RequestParam(value =
"name", defaultValue = "World") String name) {

        [message: "Hello, ${name}!"]

    }

}
```

- Run the script using the Spring Boot CLI:

```
spring run api.groovy
```

This command starts the application, and you can access the **/api/greet** endpoint to test the API.

Spring Boot CLI Configuration

The Spring Boot CLI can be configured using an **application.yml** or

application.properties file located in the same directory as your Groovy scripts. These configuration files allow you to customize the behavior of the CLI and your applications.

Think of a situation wherein you want to customize a server port. To do this:

- Create an **application.yml** file with the following content:

```
server:

  port: 8081
```

- Run your Groovy script:

```
spring run app.groovy
```

The application will start on port 8081 instead of the default port 8080.

Spring Boot CLI with Spring Initializr

The Spring Boot CLI can interact with Spring Initializr to generate project templates quickly. This integration allows you to bootstrap new projects without leaving the command line.

Consider a situation wherein you want to generate a project:

- Use the **init** command to generate a new project:

```
spring init --dependencies=web,data-jpa --name=myproject
myproject
```

This command generates a new Spring Boot project with the specified dependencies and project name.

- Navigate to the generated project directory:

```
cd myproject
```

- Run the project using the Spring Boot CLI:

```
spring run src/main/java/com/example/DemoApplication.java
```

This approach streamlines the process of setting up and running new Spring Boot projects.

Spring Boot CLI with Groovy Templates

The Spring Boot CLI supports Groovy templates, allowing you to create dynamic views using Groovy's templating capabilities. This is useful for building web applications with dynamic content.

For example, if you want to create a groovy template:

- Create a new file named **templates/hello.tpl** with the following content:

```
<!DOCTYPE html>

<html>

<head>

    <title>Hello</title>

</head>

<body>

    <h1>Hello, ${name}!</h1>

</body>

</html>
```

- Create a Groovy script named **app.groovy** to render the template:

```
import
org.springframework.web.servlet.view.groovy.GroovyMarkupC
onfigurer



@Configuration

class WebConfig {

    @Bean

    GroovyMarkupConfigurer groovyMarkupConfigurer() {
```

```
        new GroovyMarkupConfigurer(templateLoaderPath:
'classpath:/templates/')
    }
}


@RestController
class HelloController {
    @RequestMapping("/")
    ModelAndView home() {
        new ModelAndView('hello', [name: 'Spring Boot
CLI'])
    }
}
```

- Run the script using the Spring Boot CLI:

```
spring run app.groovy
```

This example demonstrates how to use Groovy templates with the Spring Boot CLI to create dynamic web pages. By leveraging the capabilities of the CLI, you can streamline your development process and quickly test and deploy Spring Boot applications.

Summary

To summarize, we learned about Spring Boot, its history, and its evolution from the Spring Framework, which simplified the development of stand-alone, production-grade Spring-based applications. The chapter introduced key features such as auto-configuration, Spring Boot starters, embedded servers, production-ready features, externalized configuration, the Spring Boot CLI, DevTools, Spring Initializr, and Actuator. These features helped streamline development by reducing boilerplate code and configuration.

We set up the development environment by installing the JDK, an IDE (IntelliJ IDEA or Eclipse), Apache Maven, and the Spring Boot CLI. The process included creating a Spring Boot project using Spring Initializr and configuring the IDE. We created our first Spring Boot application, a simple RESTful web service, using **`@SpringBootApplication`** and other essential annotations like **`@RestController`** and **`@RequestMapping`**.

We learned about managing dependencies with Maven and using Spring Boot starters to simplify dependency management and also explored various much needed annotations. The chapter also provided an overview of the Spring Boot CLI, highlighting its capabilities for developing Spring Boot applications using Groovy scripts, managing dependencies, packaging applications, and interacting with Spring Initializr.

CHAPTER 2: BUILDING FIRST SPRING BOOT APP

Chapter Overview

This chapter will walk you through the steps of making a fully functional Spring Boot app. To set the stage for learning how to construct and expose APIs, this chapter begins by making a simple RESTful service. You will gain a solid understanding of the many HTTP methods, such as GET, POST, PUT, and DELETE, that are necessary for creating feature-rich web services.

The next step in creating more adaptable APIs is to learn how to use path variables and request parameters. In turn, this will improve your app's ability to respond to user requests. You will also learn about message converters, which let you easily change data formats for better web service interoperability.

From an overview of the Spring MVC architecture, you will acquire a basic understanding of the manner in which Spring Boot manages web requests and responses. Finally, you will gain an understanding of Spring Boot's error handling capabilities, allowing you to handle exceptions with poise.

Creating a Basic RESTful Service

To build a RESTful service with Spring Boot, you need to understand the key components involved. These components include the main application class, a REST controller, and the necessary annotations to map HTTP requests to handler methods.

Now, to dive into the process of creating a basic RESTful service, start by creating a new Spring Boot project using Spring Initializr or your preferred method. Ensure you include the **`Spring Web`** dependency, which provides the necessary components to build web applications.

Main Application Class

Every Spring Boot application has a main application class annotated with **`@SpringBootApplication`**. This class serves as the entry point of the application as below:

```
package com.example.demo;


import org.springframework.boot.SpringApplication;

import
org.springframework.boot.autoconfigure.SpringBootApplication;
```

```
@SpringBootApplication
public class DemoApplication {
    public static void main(String[] args) {
        SpringApplication.run(DemoApplication.class, args);
    }
}
```

Creating a REST Controller

A REST controller handles HTTP requests and returns responses. In Spring Boot, you define a REST controller using the **@RestController** annotation.

- Create a new package named **controller** under **src/main/java/com/example/demo**.
- Create a new class named **HelloController.java** in this package.

```
package com.example.demo.controller;

import org.springframework.web.bind.annotation.GetMapping;
import org.springframework.web.bind.annotation.RequestMapping;
import org.springframework.web.bind.annotation.RestController;

@RestController
@RequestMapping("/api")
public class HelloController {

    @GetMapping("/hello")
```

```
    public String sayHello() {

        return "Hello, GitforGits Publishing!";

    }

}
```

In the above code snippet, **@RestController** marks the class as a REST controller. The **@RequestMapping("/api")** annotation specifies the base URL path for all endpoints in this controller. The **@GetMapping("/hello")** annotation maps HTTP GET requests to the **sayHello** method, which returns a simple string response.

Running the Application

To run your Spring Boot application, perform the following steps:

- Open your IDE and navigate to the main application class (**DemoApplication**).
- Run the **DemoApplication** class as a Java application.

Once the application is running, open a web browser and navigate to **http://localhost:8080/api/hello**. You should see the message "Hello, GitforGits Publishing!" displayed in the browser, confirming that your RESTful service is up and running.

Expanding the REST Controller

To demonstrate the flexibility of RESTful services, we will add a few more endpoints to our **HelloController** as below:

```
package com.example.demo.controller;



import org.springframework.web.bind.annotation.GetMapping;

import org.springframework.web.bind.annotation.PathVariable;

import org.springframework.web.bind.annotation.PostMapping;

import org.springframework.web.bind.annotation.RequestBody;

import org.springframework.web.bind.annotation.RequestMapping;

import org.springframework.web.bind.annotation.RestController;
```

```
@RestController
@RequestMapping("/api")
public class HelloController {

    @GetMapping("/hello")
    public String sayHello() {
        return "Hello, GitforGits Publishing!";
    }

    @GetMapping("/hello/{name}")
    public String greetUser(@PathVariable String name) {
        return "Hello, " + name + "!";
    }

    @PostMapping("/hello")
    public String createGreeting(@RequestBody String greeting)
{
        return "Your greeting is: " + greeting;
    }
}
```

In this updated controller:

- The **@GetMapping("/hello/{name}")** method uses a path variable to greet a user by name.

- The **@PostMapping("/hello")** method accepts a request body and returns a custom greeting.

With these above well defined steps, you shall have now created and expanded a basic RESTful service.

Handling GET and POST Requests

In RESTful web services, HTTP methods define the operations that can be performed on the resources. The most commonly used methods are GET and POST. The GET is used to retrieve information from the server. This method is idempotent, meaning it does not alter the state of the server. GET requests are often used to fetch data, such as retrieving a list of users or a specific user's details. Whereas, the other method POST is used to submit data to the server, often resulting in a change in the server's state. This method is not idempotent, as each request can create or modify resources. POST requests are typically used for creating new resources, such as adding a new user to a database.

Implementing GET Requests

We already have a basic GET request in our **HelloController** from the previous topic. We will expand it to fetch a list of greetings and a specific greeting by ID.

- Add a new class named **Greeting.java** in the **model** package:

```
package com.example.demo.model;


public class Greeting {

    private Long id;

    private String message;


    public Greeting(Long id, String message) {

        this.id = id;

        this.message = message;
```

```
    }

    // Getters and setters
    public Long getId() {
        return id;
    }

    public void setId(Long id) {
        this.id = id;
    }

    public String getMessage() {
        return message;
    }

    public void setMessage(String message) {
        this.message = message;
    }
}
```

- Update **HelloController** to handle GET requests for a list of greetings and a specific greeting by ID:

```
package com.example.demo.controller;
```

```
import com.example.demo.model.Greeting;
import org.springframework.web.bind.annotation.GetMapping;
import org.springframework.web.bind.annotation.PathVariable;
import org.springframework.web.bind.annotation.RequestMapping;
import org.springframework.web.bind.annotation.RestController;

import java.util.ArrayList;
import java.util.List;

@RestController
@RequestMapping("/api")
public class HelloController {

    private List<Greeting> greetings = new ArrayList<>();

    public HelloController() {
        greetings.add(new Greeting(1L, "Hello, GitforGits
Publishing!"));
        greetings.add(new Greeting(2L, "Hello, World!"));
        greetings.add(new Greeting(3L, "Hello, REST!"));
    }

    @GetMapping("/hello")
```

```
    public List<Greeting> getAllGreetings() {

        return greetings;

    }



    @GetMapping("/hello/{id}")

    public Greeting getGreetingById(@PathVariable Long id) {

        return greetings.stream()

                .filter(greeting ->
greeting.getId().equals(id))

                .findFirst()

                .orElse(null);

    }

}
```

In the above script,

- The **getAllGreetings** method returns a list of all greetings.
- The **getGreetingById** method retrieves a specific greeting by its ID using a path variable.

Implementing POST Requests

Next, we will add functionality to create a new greeting using a POST request. Update the **HelloController** as follows:

```
package com.example.demo.controller;



import com.example.demo.model.Greeting;

import org.springframework.web.bind.annotation.*;
```

```
import java.util.ArrayList;

import java.util.List;


@RestController

@RequestMapping("/api")

public class HelloController {


    private List<Greeting> greetings = new ArrayList<>();


    public HelloController() {

        greetings.add(new Greeting(1L, "Hello, GitforGits
Publishing!"));

        greetings.add(new Greeting(2L, "Hello, World!"));

        greetings.add(new Greeting(3L, "Hello, REST!"));

    }


    @GetMapping("/hello")

    public List<Greeting> getAllGreetings() {

        return greetings;

    }


    @GetMapping("/hello/{id}")
```

```
    public Greeting getGreetingById(@PathVariable Long id) {
        return greetings.stream()
                .filter(greeting ->
greeting.getId().equals(id))
                .findFirst()
                .orElse(null);
    }

    @PostMapping("/hello")
    public Greeting createGreeting(@RequestBody Greeting
greeting) {
        greeting.setId((long) (greetings.size() + 1));
        greetings.add(greeting);
        return greeting;
    }
}
```

The **createGreeting** method handles POST requests to create a new greeting. It accepts a **Greeting** object in the request body, assigns a new ID to it, adds it to the list, and returns the created greeting. By doing these steps, you have successfully implemented GET and POST requests in our or any of the spring boot applications.

Handling PUT and DELETE Requests

PUT and DELETE requests are also used to update and delete resources. The PUT is used to update an existing resource. It is idempotent, meaning that multiple identical requests should have the same effect as a single request. PUT requests are often used to update an existing record in the database. And there is also a DELETE request which is used to remove a resource. This method is also idempotent.

Implementing PUT Requests

To handle PUT requests, we will add functionality to update an existing greeting and update the **HelloController** as follows:

```
package com.example.demo.controller;


import com.example.demo.model.Greeting;

import org.springframework.web.bind.annotation.*;


import java.util.ArrayList;

import java.util.List;


@RestController

@RequestMapping("/api")

public class HelloController {


    private List<Greeting> greetings = new ArrayList<>();


    public HelloController() {

        greetings.add(new Greeting(1L, "Hello, GitforGits
Publishing!"));

        greetings.add(new Greeting(2L, "Hello, World!"));

        greetings.add(new Greeting(3L, "Hello, REST!"));
```

```
    }


    @GetMapping("/hello")
    public List<Greeting> getAllGreetings() {
        return greetings;
    }


    @GetMapping("/hello/{id}")
    public Greeting getGreetingById(@PathVariable Long
id) {
        return greetings.stream()
                .filter(greeting ->
greeting.getId().equals(id))
                .findFirst()
                .orElse(null);
    }


    @PostMapping("/hello")
    public Greeting createGreeting(@RequestBody Greeting
greeting) {
        greeting.setId((long) (greetings.size() + 1));
        greetings.add(greeting);
```

```
        return greeting;

    }



    @PutMapping("/hello/{id}")

    public Greeting updateGreeting(@PathVariable Long id,
@RequestBody Greeting newGreeting) {

        Greeting existingGreeting = greetings.stream()

                .filter(greeting ->
greeting.getId().equals(id))

                .findFirst()

                .orElse(null);

        if (existingGreeting != null) {

existingGreeting.setMessage(newGreeting.getMessage());

        }

        return existingGreeting;

    }

}
```

The **updateGreeting** method handles PUT requests to update an existing greeting. It finds the greeting by its ID and updates its message with the new data provided in the request body.

Implementing DELETE Requests

Next, we will add functionality to delete an existing greeting using a DELETE request by updating the **HelloController** as follows:

```
package com.example.demo.controller;


import com.example.demo.model.Greeting;

import org.springframework.web.bind.annotation.*;


import java.util.ArrayList;

import java.util.List;


@RestController

@RequestMapping("/api")

public class HelloController {


    private List<Greeting> greetings = new ArrayList<>();


    public HelloController() {

        greetings.add(new Greeting(1L, "Hello, GitforGits
Publishing!"));

        greetings.add(new Greeting(2L, "Hello, World!"));

        greetings.add(new Greeting(3L, "Hello, REST!"));

    }


    @GetMapping("/hello")
```

```
    public List<Greeting> getAllGreetings() {
        return greetings;
    }

    @GetMapping("/hello/{id}")
    public Greeting getGreetingById(@PathVariable Long
id) {
        return greetings.stream()
                .filter(greeting ->
greeting.getId().equals(id))
                .findFirst()
                .orElse(null);
    }

    @PostMapping("/hello")
    public Greeting createGreeting(@RequestBody Greeting
greeting) {
        greeting.setId((long) (greetings.size() + 1));
        greetings.add(greeting);
        return greeting;
    }
```

```
    @PutMapping("/hello/{id}")

    public Greeting updateGreeting(@PathVariable Long id,
@RequestBody Greeting newGreeting) {

        Greeting existingGreeting = greetings.stream()

                .filter(greeting ->
greeting.getId().equals(id))

                .findFirst()

                .orElse(null);

        if (existingGreeting != null) {

existingGreeting.setMessage(newGreeting.getMessage());

        }

        return existingGreeting;

    }


    @DeleteMapping("/hello/{id}")

    public void deleteGreeting(@PathVariable Long id) {

        greetings.removeIf(greeting ->
greeting.getId().equals(id));

    }

}
```

The **deleteGreeting** method handles DELETE requests to remove a greeting by its ID. It filters the list of greetings and removes the one that matches the specified ID.

This successfully implemented PUT and DELETE requests enhances the functionality of your RESTful service for complete CRUD (Create, Read, Update, Delete) operations.

Using Path Variables and Request Parameters

In RESTful web services, path variables and request parameters play essential roles in making APIs dynamic and interactive:

- Path Variables are placeholders in the URL that capture values passed within the URI path. For example, in the URL **/users/{id}**, the **{id}** is a path variable that represents the unique identifier of a user. This is particularly useful when you need to fetch, update, or delete specific resources based on their identifiers.
- Request Parameters are key-value pairs passed in the URL query string. For instance, in the URL **/users?name=John**, **name** is a request parameter with the value **John**. Request parameters are typically used to filter or modify the response, such as searching for users by name or filtering results based on certain criteria.

Using Path Variables

We shall make this practical. Suppose you want to build an application that manages greetings. You might want to fetch a specific greeting by its ID. This is where path variables shine. To get started, we will extend our **HelloController** to include an endpoint that retrieves a greeting by its ID using a path variable.

To begin with, first ensure you have a **Greeting** class defined as follows:

```
package com.example.demo.model;


public class Greeting {

    private Long id;

    private String message;


    public Greeting(Long id, String message) {

        this.id = id;
```

```
        this.message = message;
    }

    // Getters and setters
    public Long getId() {
        return id;
    }

    public void setId(Long id) {
        this.id = id;
    }

    public String getMessage() {
        return message;
    }

    public void setMessage(String message) {
        this.message = message;
    }
}
```

Now, update your **HelloController** to handle GET requests for specific greetings using path variables:

```
package com.example.demo.controller;

import com.example.demo.model.Greeting;
import org.springframework.web.bind.annotation.*;

import java.util.ArrayList;
import java.util.List;

@RestController
@RequestMapping("/api")
public class HelloController {

    private List<Greeting> greetings = new ArrayList<>();

    public HelloController() {
        greetings.add(new Greeting(1L, "Hello, GitforGits
Publishing!"));
        greetings.add(new Greeting(2L, "Hello, World!"));
        greetings.add(new Greeting(3L, "Hello, REST!"));
    }

    @GetMapping("/hello")
```

```
    public List<Greeting> getAllGreetings() {
        return greetings;
    }

    @GetMapping("/hello/{id}")
    public Greeting getGreetingById(@PathVariable Long
id) {
        return greetings.stream()
                .filter(greeting ->
greeting.getId().equals(id))
                .findFirst()
                .orElse(null);
    }

    @PostMapping("/hello")
    public Greeting createGreeting(@RequestBody Greeting
greeting) {
        greeting.setId((long) (greetings.size() + 1));
        greetings.add(greeting);
        return greeting;
    }
```

```
    @PutMapping("/hello/{id}")

    public Greeting updateGreeting(@PathVariable Long id,
@RequestBody Greeting newGreeting) {

        Greeting existingGreeting = greetings.stream()

                .filter(greeting ->
greeting.getId().equals(id))

                .findFirst()

                .orElse(null);

        if (existingGreeting != null) {

existingGreeting.setMessage(newGreeting.getMessage());

        }

        return existingGreeting;

    }


    @DeleteMapping("/hello/{id}")

    public void deleteGreeting(@PathVariable Long id) {

        greetings.removeIf(greeting ->
greeting.getId().equals(id));

    }

}
```

In this updated controller, the **`@GetMapping("/hello/{id}")`** method uses the **`@PathVariable`** annotation to extract the **`id`** from the URL and uses it to find and return the corresponding greeting. This makes it very intuitive to understand which resource is being targeted just by looking at the URL.

Using Request Parameters

Request parameters are equally powerful and useful. They allow clients to send additional information with their request, often used to filter data or modify the behavior of the API. Here, we add an endpoint to our **HelloController** that allows users to search for greetings based on the message content. This is done by adding a method in **HelloController** to filter greetings by message content using request parameters as below:

```
package com.example.demo.controller;


import com.example.demo.model.Greeting;

import org.springframework.web.bind.annotation.*;


import java.util.ArrayList;

import java.util.List;

import java.util.stream.Collectors;


@RestController

@RequestMapping("/api")

public class HelloController {


    private List<Greeting> greetings = new ArrayList<>();


    public HelloController() {
```

```
        greetings.add(new Greeting(1L, "Hello, GitforGits
Publishing!"));

        greetings.add(new Greeting(2L, "Hello, World!"));

        greetings.add(new Greeting(3L, "Hello, REST!"));

    }


    @GetMapping("/hello")

    public List<Greeting> getAllGreetings() {

        return greetings;

    }


    @GetMapping("/hello/{id}")

    public Greeting getGreetingById(@PathVariable Long
id) {

        return greetings.stream()

                .filter(greeting ->
greeting.getId().equals(id))

                .findFirst()

                .orElse(null);

    }


    @GetMapping("/hello/search")
```

```
    public List<Greeting> searchGreetings(@RequestParam
String message) {

        return greetings.stream()

                .filter(greeting ->
greeting.getMessage().contains(message))

                .collect(Collectors.toList());

    }


    @PostMapping("/hello")

    public Greeting createGreeting(@RequestBody Greeting
greeting) {

        greeting.setId((long) (greetings.size() + 1));

        greetings.add(greeting);

        return greeting;

    }


    @PutMapping("/hello/{id}")

    public Greeting updateGreeting(@PathVariable Long id,
@RequestBody Greeting newGreeting) {

        Greeting existingGreeting = greetings.stream()

                .filter(greeting ->
greeting.getId().equals(id))

                .findFirst()
```

```
                .orElse(null);

        if (existingGreeting != null) {

existingGreeting.setMessage(newGreeting.getMessage());

        }

        return existingGreeting;

    }


    @DeleteMapping("/hello/{id}")

    public void deleteGreeting(@PathVariable Long id) {

        greetings.removeIf(greeting ->
greeting.getId().equals(id));

    }

}
```

In this code, the **@GetMapping("/hello/search")** method uses the **@RequestParam** annotation to capture the **message** parameter from the query string. It then filters the list of greetings to include only those that contain the specified message text.

This approach allows your API to handle a wide variety of client requests efficiently and effectively.

Using Message Converters

To translate between Java objects and HTTP request and response bodies, Spring Boot makes use of message converters. They make it easier to serialize and deserialize Java objects to and from various formats, including plain text, XML, and JSON. Spring Boot makes it easy to work with different content types in your RESTful services by configuring several message converters to handle various data formats by default.

Built-in Message Converters

Spring Boot provides several built-in message converters, including:

1. **MappingJackson2HttpMessageConverter:** Converts JSON request and response bodies using the Jackson library.
2. **StringHttpMessageConverter:** Converts plain text request and response bodies.
3. **MappingJackson2XmlHttpMessageConverter:** Converts XML request and response bodies using the Jackson XML extension.

These above mentioned converters are automatically configured based on the dependencies included in your project. For instance, the **MappingJackson2HttpMessageConverter** is enabled when the Jackson library is on the classpath.

Sample Program: Working of Message Converters

We will continue with our previously demonstrated greeting service example to see how message converters work in practice. Before we do, ensure the **spring-boot-starter-web** dependency, which includes the necessary libraries for JSON conversion is included.

Now, update the **Greeting** class as below:

```
package com.example.demo.model;


public class Greeting {

    private Long id;

    private String message;


    public Greeting(Long id, String message) {

        this.id = id;

        this.message = message;

    }
```

```
    // Getters and setters
    public Long getId() {
        return id;
    }

    public void setId(Long id) {
        this.id = id;
    }

    public String getMessage() {
        return message;
    }

    public void setMessage(String message) {
        this.message = message;
    }
}
```

Now, we will see how the message converters come into play in our **`HelloController`**:

```
package com.example.demo.controller;
```

```java
import com.example.demo.model.Greeting;
import org.springframework.web.bind.annotation.*;

import java.util.ArrayList;
import java.util.List;
import java.util.stream.Collectors;

@RestController
@RequestMapping("/api")
public class HelloController {

    private List<Greeting> greetings = new ArrayList<>();

    public HelloController() {
        greetings.add(new Greeting(1L, "Hello, GitforGits
Publishing!"));
        greetings.add(new Greeting(2L, "Hello, World!"));
        greetings.add(new Greeting(3L, "Hello, REST!"));
    }

    @GetMapping("/hello")
    public List<Greeting> getAllGreetings() {
```

```
        return greetings;
    }

    @GetMapping("/hello/{id}")
    public Greeting getGreetingById(@PathVariable Long
id) {
        return greetings.stream()
                .filter(greeting ->
greeting.getId().equals(id))
                .findFirst()
                .orElse(null);
    }

    @GetMapping("/hello/search")
    public List<Greeting> searchGreetings(@RequestParam
String message) {
        return greetings.stream()
                .filter(greeting ->
greeting.getMessage().contains(message))
                .collect(Collectors.toList());
    }

    @PostMapping("/hello")
```

```
    public Greeting createGreeting(@RequestBody Greeting
greeting) {
        greeting.setId((long) (greetings.size() + 1));
        greetings.add(greeting);
        return greeting;
    }

    @PutMapping("/hello/{id}")
    public Greeting updateGreeting(@PathVariable Long id,
@RequestBody Greeting newGreeting) {
        Greeting existingGreeting = greetings.stream()
                .filter(greeting ->
greeting.getId().equals(id))
                .findFirst()
                .orElse(null);
        if (existingGreeting != null) {

existingGreeting.setMessage(newGreeting.getMessage());
        }
        return existingGreeting;
    }

    @DeleteMapping("/hello/{id}")
```

```
    public void deleteGreeting(@PathVariable Long id) {
        greetings.removeIf(greeting ->
greeting.getId().equals(id));
    }
}
```

In this controller, the **@RequestBody** annotation is used in the **createGreeting** and **updateGreeting** methods to automatically convert the JSON request body into a **Greeting** object. Similarly, the methods return **Greeting** objects, which are automatically converted to JSON responses by the **MappingJackson2HttpMessageConverter**. This message converter allows our application to seamlessly convert between Java objects and various content types for better interoperability and increased usability.

Spring MVC Architecture Overview

Understanding Spring MVC

Spring MVC (Model-View-Controller) is a framework within the Spring ecosystem that facilitates the development of web applications. It follows the MVC design pattern, which separates the application into three interconnected components: Model, View, and Controller. This separation helps in managing complexity and promoting a clean, modular architecture. Following is a quick overview of the components:

- Model represents the application's data and business logic. It is responsible for managing the data and the rules that govern access to and updates of this data.
- View represents the presentation layer. It is responsible for rendering the model data, typically using HTML or other templating engines.
- Controller acts as an intermediary between the Model and the View. It processes user requests, manipulates the model, and returns a view to be rendered as a response.

Spring MVC Core Components

We will delve into the core components of Spring MVC and how they interact with each other to handle web requests.

DispatcherServlet

The **DispatcherServlet** is the front controller in the Spring MVC architecture. It intercepts incoming HTTP requests and delegates them to appropriate handlers based on the request URL. It acts as the central point of coordination, routing requests to controllers and managing the overall workflow.

Controller

Controllers in Spring MVC are annotated with **@Controller** or **@RestController**. They handle web requests, process user inputs, and return responses. The **@RestController** is a convenience annotation that combines **@Controller** and **@ResponseBody**, meaning that the methods return data directly instead of a view.

Handler Mapping

Handler mappings map incoming requests to the appropriate controller methods. Spring MVC uses various handler mapping strategies, such as **RequestMappingHandlerMapping**, to determine which controller method should handle a given request.

View Resolver

The view resolver resolves logical view names returned by the controller into actual view implementations. For example, it can map a logical view name to a specific JSP file or a Thymeleaf template.

ModelAndView

The **ModelAndView** object holds the model data and the view name. The controller can populate the model with data and specify the view to be rendered. Spring MVC uses this object to pass data between the controller and the view.

Sample Program: Inner Workings of MVC Components

We will use our greeting service example to demonstrate how these components work together in a Spring MVC application.

First, ensure we have the necessary dependencies in **pom.xml**:

```
<dependency>

    <groupId>org.springframework.boot</groupId>

    <artifactId>spring-boot-starter-web</artifactId>

</dependency>

<dependency>
```

```
    <groupId>org.springframework.boot</groupId>

    <artifactId>spring-boot-starter-
thymeleaf</artifactId>

</dependency>
```

Now, create a simple Thymeleaf template for the view. Add a file named **greetings.html** in the **src/main/resources/templates** directory:

```
<!DOCTYPE html>

<html xmlns:th="http://www.thymeleaf.org">

<head>

    <title>Greetings</title>

</head>

<body>

    <h1>Greetings</h1>

    <ul>

        <li th:each="greeting : ${greetings}">

            <span th:text="${greeting.message}">Greeting
message</span>

        </li>

    </ul>

</body>

</html>
```

Update **HelloController** to use a traditional MVC approach:

```
package com.example.demo.controller;

import com.example.demo.model.Greeting;
import org.springframework.stereotype.Controller;
import org.springframework.ui.Model;
import org.springframework.web.bind.annotation.GetMapping;
import org.springframework.web.bind.annotation.PathVariable;
import org.springframework.web.bind.annotation.RequestMapping;

import java.util.ArrayList;
import java.util.List;

@Controller
@RequestMapping("/mvc")
public class HelloController {

    private List<Greeting> greetings = new ArrayList<>();

    public HelloController() {
        greetings.add(new Greeting(1L, "Hello, GitforGits
Publishing!"));
        greetings.add(new Greeting(2L, "Hello, World!"));
```

```java
        greetings.add(new Greeting(3L, "Hello, REST!"));
    }

    @GetMapping("/greetings")
    public String getAllGreetings(Model model) {
        model.addAttribute("greetings", greetings);
        return "greetings";
    }

    @GetMapping("/greetings/{id}")
    public String getGreetingById(@PathVariable Long id,
Model model) {
        Greeting greeting = greetings.stream()
                .filter(g -> g.getId().equals(id))
                .findFirst()
                .orElse(null);
        model.addAttribute("greeting", greeting);
        return "greetingDetail";
    }
}
```

Create another Thymeleaf template for the individual greeting view. Add a file named **greetingDetail.html** in the **src/main/resources/templates** directory:

```html
<!DOCTYPE html>

<html xmlns:th="http://www.thymeleaf.org">

<head>

    <title>Greeting Detail</title>

</head>

<body>

    <h1>Greeting Detail</h1>

    <p th:text="'Greeting ID: ' +
${greeting.id}">Greeting ID</p>

    <p th:text="'Message: ' +
${greeting.message}">Greeting message</p>

    <a href="/mvc/greetings">Back to Greetings List</a>

</body>

</html>
```

In the above sample program, the requests in this Spring MVC application flows as below:

1. A user navigates to **http://localhost:8080/mvc/greetings**. The **DispatcherServlet** intercepts the request.
2. The **DispatcherServlet** consults the handler mappings to determine the appropriate controller method to handle the request. In this case, it maps the request to the **getAllGreetings** method in the **HelloController**.
3. The **getAllGreetings** method is invoked, which populates the model with a list of greetings and returns the logical view name "greetings".
4. The view resolver maps the logical view name "greetings" to the **greetings.html** template in the **src/main/resources/templates** directory.
5. The model data is merged with the view template, and the resulting HTML is returned as the response to the user.

In this organized method, the components of a web application—the dispatcher, controllers, handler mappings, view resolvers, and model objects—collaborate to efficiently handle requests and render responses.

Error Handling in Spring Boot

In Spring Boot, you can handle errors gracefully by using its built-in mechanisms and customizing them to suit your needs in order to ensure that the users receive meaningful error messages and that the application can recover or fail gracefully from unexpected situations.

Built-in Error Handling

Now, the Spring Boot provides a basic error-handling mechanism out of the box. When an error occurs, Spring Boot returns a JSON response containing the error details. For example, if a requested resource is not found, a **`404 Not Found`** status is returned with a JSON body detailing the error.

Scenario: Default Error Response

```
{

  "timestamp": "2023-07-08T10:22:57.722+00:00",

  "status": 404,

  "error": "Not Found",

  "path": "/api/hello/999"

}
```

While this default mechanism is helpful, you often need to customize error responses to provide more specific information or handle different types of errors differently.

Customizing Error Responses

To customize error handling, you can use **`@ControllerAdvice`** and **`@ExceptionHandler`** annotations. **`@ControllerAdvice`** allows you to handle exceptions globally across your application, while **`@ExceptionHandler`** handles specific exceptions within a controller.

Scenario: Global Exception Handling

Create a custom exception class:

```
package com.example.demo.exception;


public class ResourceNotFoundException extends
RuntimeException {

    public ResourceNotFoundException(String message) {

        super(message);

    }

}
```

Create a global exception handler class:

```
package com.example.demo.exception;


import org.springframework.http.HttpStatus;

import org.springframework.http.ResponseEntity;

import
org.springframework.web.bind.annotation.ControllerAdvice;

import
org.springframework.web.bind.annotation.ExceptionHandler;

import
org.springframework.web.bind.annotation.ResponseStatus;


@ControllerAdvice
```

```
public class GlobalExceptionHandler {


    @ExceptionHandler(ResourceNotFoundException.class)
    @ResponseStatus(HttpStatus.NOT_FOUND)
    public ResponseEntity<String>
handleResourceNotFound(ResourceNotFoundException ex) {
        return new ResponseEntity<>(ex.getMessage(),
HttpStatus.NOT_FOUND);
    }


    @ExceptionHandler(Exception.class)
    @ResponseStatus(HttpStatus.INTERNAL_SERVER_ERROR)
    public ResponseEntity<String>
handleGeneralException(Exception ex) {
        return new ResponseEntity<>("An unexpected error
occurred: " + ex.getMessage(),
HttpStatus.INTERNAL_SERVER_ERROR);
    }
}
```

In the above code snippet, the **GlobalExceptionHandler** class handles **ResourceNotFoundException** and general exceptions. When a **ResourceNotFoundException** is thrown, it returns a **404 Not Found** status with a custom message. For other exceptions, it returns a **500 Internal Server Error** status with a generic error message.

Modify the controller to throw the custom exception:

```
package com.example.demo.controller;


import
com.example.demo.exception.ResourceNotFoundException;
import com.example.demo.model.Greeting;
import org.springframework.web.bind.annotation.*;


import java.util.ArrayList;
import java.util.List;
import java.util.stream.Collectors;


@RestController
@RequestMapping("/api")
public class HelloController {


    private List<Greeting> greetings = new ArrayList<>();


    public HelloController() {
        greetings.add(new Greeting(1L, "Hello, GitforGits
Publishing!"));
        greetings.add(new Greeting(2L, "Hello, World!"));
        greetings.add(new Greeting(3L, "Hello, REST!"));
```

```
    }


    @GetMapping("/hello")
    public List<Greeting> getAllGreetings() {
        return greetings;
    }


    @GetMapping("/hello/{id}")
    public Greeting getGreetingById(@PathVariable Long
id) {
        return greetings.stream()
                .filter(greeting ->
greeting.getId().equals(id))
                .findFirst()
                .orElseThrow(() -> new
ResourceNotFoundException("Greeting not found with ID: "
+ id));
    }


    @GetMapping("/hello/search")
    public List<Greeting> searchGreetings(@RequestParam
String message) {
        return greetings.stream()
```

```
                .filter(greeting ->
greeting.getMessage().contains(message))
                .collect(Collectors.toList());
    }

    @PostMapping("/hello")
    public Greeting createGreeting(@RequestBody Greeting
greeting) {
        greeting.setId((long) (greetings.size() + 1));
        greetings.add(greeting);
        return greeting;
    }

    @PutMapping("/hello/{id}")
    public Greeting updateGreeting(@PathVariable Long id,
@RequestBody Greeting newGreeting) {
        Greeting existingGreeting = greetings.stream()
                .filter(greeting ->
greeting.getId().equals(id))
                .findFirst()
                .orElse(null);
        if (existingGreeting != null) {
```

```
existingGreeting.setMessage(newGreeting.getMessage());
            return existingGreeting;
        } else {
            throw new ResourceNotFoundException("Greeting
not found with ID: " + id);
        }
    }


    @DeleteMapping("/hello/{id}")
    public void deleteGreeting(@PathVariable Long id) {
        if (!greetings.removeIf(greeting ->
greeting.getId().equals(id))) {
            throw new ResourceNotFoundException("Greeting
not found with ID: " + id);
        }
    }
}
```

By throwing **ResourceNotFoundException** when a greeting is not found, the global exception handler catches the exception and returns a custom error response.

Handling Validation Errors

Validation errors are common in web applications, especially when processing user input. Spring Boot provides powerful support for validating request data using annotations and the **BindingResult** object.

Scenario: Validating Request Data

Add the necessary validation dependency in your **`pom.xml`**:

```
<dependency>

    <groupId>org.springframework.boot</groupId>

    <artifactId>spring-boot-starter-
validation</artifactId>

</dependency>
```

Update the **`Greeting`** class to include validation annotations:

```
package com.example.demo.model;

import javax.validation.constraints.NotEmpty;


public class Greeting {

    private Long id;


    @NotEmpty(message = "Message cannot be empty")

    private String message;


    public Greeting(Long id, String message) {

        this.id = id;

        this.message = message;

    }
```

```java
    // Getters and setters
    public Long getId() {
        return id;
    }

    public void setId(Long id) {
        this.id = id;
    }

    public String getMessage() {
        return message;
    }

    public void setMessage(String message) {
        this.message = message;
    }
}
```

Update the controller to handle validation errors:

```java
package com.example.demo.controller;

import
com.example.demo.exception.ResourceNotFoundException;
```

```
import com.example.demo.model.Greeting;
import org.springframework.validation.BindingResult;
import org.springframework.web.bind.annotation.*;

import javax.validation.Valid;
import java.util.ArrayList;
import java.util.List;
import java.util.stream.Collectors;

@RestController
@RequestMapping("/api")
public class HelloController {

    private List<Greeting> greetings = new ArrayList<>();

    public HelloController() {
        greetings.add(new Greeting(1L, "Hello, GitforGits
Publishing!"));
        greetings.add(new Greeting(2L, "Hello, World!"));
        greetings.add(new Greeting(3L, "Hello, REST!"));
    }
```

```
    @GetMapping("/hello")
    public List<Greeting> getAllGreetings() {
        return greetings;
    }


    @GetMapping("/hello/{id}")
    public Greeting getGreetingById(@PathVariable Long
id) {
        return greetings.stream()
                .filter(greeting ->
greeting.getId().equals(id))
                .findFirst()
                .orElseThrow(() -> new
ResourceNotFoundException("Greeting not found with ID: "
+ id));
    }


    @GetMapping("/hello/search")
    public List<Greeting> searchGreetings(@RequestParam
String message) {
        return greetings.stream()
                .filter(greeting ->
greeting.getMessage().contains(message))
                .collect(Collectors.toList());
```

```
    }


    @PostMapping("/hello")
    public Greeting createGreeting(@Valid @RequestBody
Greeting greeting, BindingResult result) {
        if (result.hasErrors()) {
            throw new
IllegalArgumentException(result.getFieldError().getDefaul
tMessage());
        }
        greeting.setId((long) (greetings.size() + 1));
        greetings.add(greeting);
        return greeting;
    }


    @PutMapping("/hello/{id}")
    public Greeting updateGreeting(@PathVariable Long id,
@Valid @RequestBody Greeting newGreeting, BindingResult
result) {
        if (result.hasErrors()) {
            throw new
IllegalArgumentException(result.getFieldError().getDefaul
tMessage());
        }
```

```
        Greeting existingGreeting = greetings.stream()
                .filter(greeting ->
greeting.getId().equals(id))
                .findFirst()
                .orElseThrow(() -> new
ResourceNotFoundException("Greeting not found with ID: "
+ id));

existingGreeting.setMessage(newGreeting.getMessage());
        return existingGreeting;
    }

    @DeleteMapping("/hello/{id}")
    public void deleteGreeting(@PathVariable Long id) {
        if (!greetings.removeIf(greeting ->
greeting.getId().equals(id))) {
            throw new ResourceNotFoundException("Greeting
not found with ID: " + id);
        }
    }
}
```

Handle validation errors in the global exception handler:

```
package com.example.demo.exception;
```

```
import org.springframework.http.HttpStatus;

import org.springframework.http.ResponseEntity;

import
org.springframework.web.bind.annotation.ControllerAdvice;

import
org.springframework.web.bind.annotation.ExceptionHandler;

import
org.springframework.web.bind.annotation.ResponseStatus;


@ControllerAdvice

public class GlobalExceptionHandler {


    @ExceptionHandler(ResourceNotFoundException.class)

    @ResponseStatus(HttpStatus.NOT_FOUND)

    public ResponseEntity<String>
handleResourceNotFound(ResourceNotFoundException ex) {

        return new ResponseEntity<>(ex.getMessage(),
HttpStatus.NOT_FOUND);

    }


    @ExceptionHandler(IllegalArgumentException.class)

    @ResponseStatus(HttpStatus.BAD_REQUEST)
```

```
    public ResponseEntity<String>
handleIllegalArgumentException(IllegalArgumentException
ex) {

        return new ResponseEntity<>(ex.getMessage(),
HttpStatus.BAD_REQUEST);

    }



    @ExceptionHandler(Exception.class)

    @ResponseStatus(HttpStatus.INTERNAL_SERVER_ERROR)

    public ResponseEntity<String>
handleGeneralException(Exception ex) {

        return new ResponseEntity<>("An unexpected error
occurred: " + ex.getMessage(),
HttpStatus.INTERNAL_SERVER_ERROR);

    }

}
```

In this above example, validation errors result in an **IllegalArgumentException** being thrown, which is caught by the global exception handler and results in a **400 Bad Request** response.

By following these few outlined strategies, you can build applications that handle errors gracefully, providing a better user experience and ensuring the stability and reliability of your application.

Summary

In this chapter, we focused on building a Spring Boot application, covering various aspects essential for creating a robust RESTful service. We began with creating a basic RESTful service, where we learned to set up a Spring Boot project and define a REST controller using annotations like **@RestController** and **@RequestMapping**. We then explored handling GET and POST requests, implementing endpoints to retrieve all greetings, fetch a specific greeting by ID, and create new greetings. The use of path variables and request parameters was demonstrated, enabling dynamic and flexible API interactions.

Next, we delved into handling PUT and DELETE requests to update and delete resources. This included methods for updating an existing greeting and deleting a greeting by its ID. The importance of message converters in Spring Boot was learned, highlighting how they automatically convert HTTP request and response bodies to and from Java objects. We saw practical examples of JSON conversion using the built-in **`MappingJackson2HttpMessageConverter`**.

The chapter also provided an overview of Spring MVC architecture, explaining the roles of DispatcherServlet, controllers, handler mappings, view resolvers, and ModelAndView objects. We learned how these components interact to handle web requests and render responses. Finally, error handling in Spring Boot was addressed, showing how to use **`@ControllerAdvice`** and **`@ExceptionHandler`** for global and specific exception handling. We also learned about validating request data and handling validation errors.

CHAPTER 3: CONFIGURATION AND PROPERTIES

Chapter Overview

This chapter begins with an overview of Spring Boot configuration, introducing you to the different ways you can set up and manage configurations. You'll learn how to use application properties to define key-value pairs that control your application's behavior. We will explore configuration using YAML files, which offer a more readable and structured way to manage configurations compared to traditional properties files. We will also delve into profiles and environment-specific configurations, enabling you to tailor your application settings for different environments, such as development, testing, and production.

We will then cover externalizing configuration, allowing you to manage configuration outside your application's codebase for greater flexibility and security. You'll learn about the **`@Value`** and **`@ConfigurationProperties`** annotations for injecting configuration values into your Spring components. We will also learn type-safe configuration properties, ensuring that configuration values are properly validated and converted. Furthermore, we will cover how to reload configuration properties at runtime without restarting your application, which is crucial for making dynamic changes. Lastly, we will look into custom configuration properties, allowing you to define and manage custom settings specific to your application's needs.

Spring Boot Configuration Overview

Spring Boot makes configuring your application a seamless and powerful experience, thanks to its robust and flexible configuration capabilities. Configuration in Spring Boot is incredibly versatile. Whether you are building a small project or an enterprise-level application, managing configuration efficiently is crucial. Spring Boot allows you to define configurations in multiple ways, ensuring that your application behaves consistently across different environments. This flexibility comes from a range of options, such as properties files, YAML files, environment variables, and command-line arguments.

Imagine you are working on a complex application that needs to behave differently in development, testing, and production environments. Spring Boot's configuration system lets you define environment-specific settings easily. You can have different configurations for your database, external APIs, or even application-specific features, all managed from a single place.

Application Properties

The most straightforward way to manage configuration in Spring Boot is through the **`application.properties`** file. This file allows you to set key-value pairs that define various aspects of your application's behavior. For instance, you can set the server port, database connection details, logging levels, and more. This centralized approach makes it easy to modify settings without changing your code.

For example, let us take an example of setting the Server Port as below:

```
server.port=8081
```

By changing a single property, you can control the port your application runs on, demonstrating how easy it is to adapt configurations.

YAML for Structured Configuration

While **application.properties** is powerful, YAML files make a more readable and structured way to manage configurations. YAML files support hierarchical data structures, which can make complex configurations more manageable and easier to read. For example, configuring multiple data sources or defining nested properties becomes straightforward with YAML as below:

```
server:

  port: 8081

spring:

  datasource:

    url: jdbc:mysql://localhost:3306/mydb

    username: root

    password: secret
```

YAML's structured format can significantly enhance the clarity of your configurations, especially as your application grows.

Profiles for Environment-Specific Configurations

Spring Boot profiles allow you to define different configurations for different environments. Whether you are deploying to development, testing, or production, profiles help you switch configurations effortlessly. By using profiles, you can ensure that your application uses the correct settings for each environment without manual intervention. Let us take the below example to understand using profiles:

```
# application-dev.properties

spring.datasource.url=jdbc:h2:mem:devdb
```

```
# application-prod.properties

spring.datasource.url=jdbc:mysql://prod-db-server/mydb
```

With simply specifying the active profile, it loads the appropriate configuration, and makes the environment management quite an easy operation.

Externalizing and Securing Configuration

One of the key benefits of Spring Boot's configuration system is the ability to externalize configurations. This means you can manage your application's settings outside the codebase, making it easier to handle sensitive information and modify settings without redeploying the application. Environment variables, command-line arguments, and external configuration files are some of the ways to achieve this.

Consider the below code snippet:

```
java -jar myapp.jar --server.port=8081
```

By passing configuration as command-line arguments or environment variables, you can override settings dynamically.

To summarize, we have learnt how properties files, YAML, profiles, and external configurations can help you manage settings effectively. As we proceed through this chapter, we will explore each of these concepts in greater detail, ensuring you have a solid understanding of how to configure and manage your Spring Boot applications seamlessly.

Using Application Properties

Spring Boot simplifies configuration management with the **application.properties** file, allowing you to centralize and manage your application's settings with ease. This file resides in the **src/main/resources** directory and lets you define key-value pairs that control various aspects of your application's behavior. Let us look into how we can leverage **application.properties** to configure our Spring Boot application.

Basic Configuration

The **application.properties** file is straightforward and intuitive as each property is defined as a key-value pair, making it easy to read and modify. For example, setting the server port is as simple as adding the following line:

```
server.port=8081
```

This line tells Spring Boot to run your application on port 8081 instead of the default port 8080. Similarly, you can configure other properties such as database connection details, logging levels, and more.

Let us take an example of configuring a database connection as below:

```
spring.datasource.url=jdbc:mysql://localhost:3306/mydb

spring.datasource.username=root

spring.datasource.password=secret

spring.datasource.driver-class-
name=com.mysql.cj.jdbc.Driver
```

By setting these properties, you provide the necessary information for Spring Boot to connect to your MySQL database.

Grouping Related Properties

As your application grows, you might find it helpful to group related properties together. This not only keeps your configuration organized but also makes it easier to understand and maintain. For instance, you can group all the data source properties together as shown in the following script:

```
spring.datasource.url=jdbc:mysql://localhost:3306/mydb

spring.datasource.username=root

spring.datasource.password=secret

spring.datasource.driver-class-
name=com.mysql.cj.jdbc.Driver



spring.jpa.hibernate.ddl-auto=update

spring.jpa.show-sql=true

spring.jpa.properties.hibernate.dialect=org.hibernate.dia
```

```
lect.MySQL5Dialect
```

This approach teaches you to see all related settings in one place, thereby making it easier to manage.

Configuring Logging

Spring Boot uses Logback as the default logging framework, but you can configure it using the **application.properties** file. Adjusting logging levels for different packages can help you control the verbosity of logs and focus on the information that matters most. You may configure the logging levels as below:

```
logging.level.org.springframework=INFO

logging.level.com.example.demo=DEBUG

logging.file.name=application.log
```

In the above code snippet, the logging level for Spring-related logs is set to **INFO**, while the logging level for your application's package is set to **DEBUG**. The logs are directed to a file named **application.log**.

Profiles in Application Properties

Spring Boot supports profiles, which allow you to define different configurations for different environments. This is particularly useful for managing separate settings for development, testing, and production environments. Profiles can be defined in separate property files such as **application-dev.properties** and **application-prod.properties**.

Following is a quick demo of defining the Profile-Specific Properties:

```
# application-dev.properties

spring.datasource.url=jdbc:h2:mem:devdb

spring.datasource.username=sa

spring.datasource.password=password



# application-prod.properties
```

```
spring.datasource.url=jdbc:mysql://prod-db-server/mydb

spring.datasource.username=produser

spring.datasource.password=prodsecret
```

To activate a specific profile, you can set the **spring.profiles.active** property. For example, to activate the development profile:

```
spring.profiles.active=dev
```

Spring Boot will automatically load the properties from **application-dev.properties**, overriding the default properties defined in **application.properties**.

External Configuration

Spring Boot also allows you to externalize configuration, making it easy to manage settings outside of your application's codebase. This can be done through environment variables, command-line arguments, or external property files. Check out the below code snippet to witness the overriding properties using environment variables.

```
export
SPRING_DATASOURCE_URL=jdbc:mysql://localhost:3306/mydb

export SPRING_DATASOURCE_USERNAME=root

export SPRING_DATASOURCE_PASSWORD=secret
```

These environment variables will override the corresponding properties defined in your **application.properties** file.

Below is an example of overriding properties with command-line arguments:

```
java -jar myapp.jar --
spring.datasource.url=jdbc:mysql://localhost:3306/mydb --
spring.datasource.username=root --
spring.datasource.password=secret
```

This above command will override the properties at runtime, providing a flexible way to adjust settings without modifying the property files.

Using Application Properties

You can also access the properties defined in **application.properties** within your Spring Boot application using the **@Value** annotation or the **Environment** object as below:

Using '@Value' Annotation

```
import
org.springframework.beans.factory.annotation.Value;

import org.springframework.stereotype.Component;


@Component

public class MyComponent {


    @Value("${spring.datasource.url}")

    private String datasourceUrl;


    public void printDatasourceUrl() {

        System.out.println("Datasource URL: " +
datasourceUrl);

    }

}
```

Using 'Environment' Object

```
import
org.springframework.beans.factory.annotation.Autowired;

import org.springframework.core.env.Environment;
```

```
import org.springframework.stereotype.Component;


@Component
public class MyComponent {


    @Autowired
    private Environment env;


    public void printDatasourceUrl() {
        String datasourceUrl =
env.getProperty("spring.datasource.url");
        System.out.println("Datasource URL: " +
datasourceUrl);
    }
}
```

Both methods allow you to inject configuration properties into your Spring components. The **application.properties** file is a powerful tool for setting up database connections, configuring logging, and defining environment-specific settings.

Configuration with YAML Files

Setting up YAML Configuration

To use YAML for configuration in your Spring Boot application, you can create an **application.yml** file in the **src/main/resources** directory. This file serves the same purpose as the **application.properties** file but provides a more organized structure for your configuration settings as below:

```yaml
server:

  port: 8081


spring:

  datasource:

    url: jdbc:mysql://localhost:3306/mydb

    username: root

    password: secret

    driver-class-name: com.mysql.cj.jdbc.Driver

  jpa:

    hibernate:

      ddl-auto: update

    show-sql: true

    properties:

      hibernate:

        dialect: org.hibernate.dialect.MySQL5Dialect
```

In the above code snippet, the server port and data source configurations are defined in a hierarchical structure, making it clear and easy to manage.

Advantages of YAML

One of the primary advantages of using YAML over properties files is its ability to handle hierarchical data. This is especially beneficial when you have complex configurations with nested properties. YAML's syntax is also more concise and readable, reducing the likelihood of errors and making configurations easier to understand.

Let us consider the following example on nested configuration:

```yaml
app:
  email:
    host: smtp.gitforgits.com
    port: 587
    username: user@gitforgits.com
    password: secret
  security:
    authentication:
      jwt:
        secret: mySecretKey
        expiration: 3600
```

This above nested configuration is easy to read and manage, and provides a clear structure for complex settings.

Profiles with YAML

Just like with properties files, you can define environment-specific configurations using profiles in YAML. This allows you to manage different configurations for development, testing, and production environments seamlessly.

Following is the example on profile-specific YAML files:

```yaml
# application-dev.yml
spring:
  datasource:
    url: jdbc:h2:mem:devdb
    username: sa
```

```
    password: password


# application-prod.yml

spring:

  datasource:

    url: jdbc:mysql://prod-db-server/mydb

    username: produser

    password: prodsecret
```

To activate a specific profile, you can set the **spring.profiles.active** property in your **application.yml** file or as an environment variable as below:

```
spring:

  profiles:

    active: dev
```

This tells Spring Boot to load the **application-dev.yml** file, overriding the default configurations with environment-specific settings.

Accessing YAML Properties

You can access YAML properties in your Spring Boot application using the **@Value** annotation or the **@ConfigurationProperties** annotation. These annotations allow you to inject configuration values directly into your Spring components.

Using @Value Annotation

```
import
org.springframework.beans.factory.annotation.Value;

import org.springframework.stereotype.Component;
```

```
@Component
public class MyComponent {


    @Value("${spring.datasource.url}")
    private String datasourceUrl;


    public void printDatasourceUrl() {
        System.out.println("Datasource URL: " +
datasourceUrl);
    }
}
```

Using @ConfigurationProperties Annotation

- Define a configuration class:

```
import
org.springframework.boot.context.properties.Configuration
Properties;
import org.springframework.stereotype.Component;


@Component
@ConfigurationProperties(prefix = "app.email")
public class EmailConfig {
```

```
private String host;

private int port;

private String username;

private String password;


// Getters and setters

public String getHost() {

    return host;

}


public void setHost(String host) {

    this.host = host;

}


public int getPort() {

    return port;

}


public void setPort(int port) {

    this.port = port;
```

```
    }

    public String getUsername() {
        return username;
    }

    public void setUsername(String username) {
        this.username = username;
    }

    public String getPassword() {
        return password;
    }

    public void setPassword(String password) {
        this.password = password;
    }
}
```

- Enable the configuration properties in your main application class:

```
import org.springframework.boot.SpringApplication;
import
org.springframework.boot.autoconfigure.SpringBootApplicat
```

```
ion;

import
org.springframework.boot.context.properties.EnableConfigu
rationProperties;


@SpringBootApplication

@EnableConfigurationProperties(EmailConfig.class)

public class DemoApplication {

    public static void main(String[] args) {

        SpringApplication.run(DemoApplication.class,
args);

    }

}
```

- And, now use the configuration class in your components:

```
import
org.springframework.beans.factory.annotation.Autowired;

import org.springframework.stereotype.Component;


@Component

public class EmailService {


    private final EmailConfig emailConfig;

```

```
    @Autowired
    public EmailService(EmailConfig emailConfig) {
        this.emailConfig = emailConfig;
    }


    public void printEmailConfig() {
        System.out.println("Email Host: " +
emailConfig.getHost());
        System.out.println("Email Port: " +
emailConfig.getPort());
        System.out.println("Email Username: " +
emailConfig.getUsername());
    }
}
```

With the support for profiles and external configurations, YAML files control your application's behavior across different environments.

Profiles and Environment Specific Configurations

In a real-world application, different environments such as development, testing, and production require different configurations. Managing these configurations can be challenging, but Spring Boot simplifies this process with the concept of profiles. Profiles allow you to define environment-specific configurations that can be activated selectively, ensuring your application behaves correctly in each environment.

Defining Profiles

To define profiles, you can create separate configuration files for each environment. For example, you might have **application-dev.yml** for development, **application-test.yml** for testing, and **application-prod.yml** for production. Each file contains the configuration specific to that environment.

Consider the following example on development profile configuration (application-dev.yml):

```
spring:
  datasource:
    url: jdbc:h2:mem:devdb
    username: sa
    password: password
    driver-class-name: org.h2.Driver
  jpa:
    hibernate:
      ddl-auto: create-drop
    show-sql: true
```

Now, look at the below production profile configuration (application-prod.yml):

```
spring:
  datasource:
    url: jdbc:mysql://prod-db-server/mydb
    username: produser
    password: prodsecret
    driver-class-name: com.mysql.cj.jdbc.Driver
  jpa:
    hibernate:
```

```
      ddl-auto: update

    show-sql: false
```

Activating Profiles

And, to activate a specific profile, you can set the **spring.profiles.active** property in your **application.yml** file, or pass it as a command-line argument or environment variable as shown below:

```
spring:

  profiles:

    active: dev
```

Activating the profile via command-line argument:

```
java -jar myapp.jar --spring.profiles.active=prod
```

You can also activate the profile via environment variable:

```
export SPRING_PROFILES_ACTIVE=prod
```

Using Profile-Specific Beans

In addition to profile-specific configuration files, you can define beans that are only loaded when a specific profile is active. This is done using the **@Profile** annotation as below:

```
import org.springframework.context.annotation.Bean;

import
org.springframework.context.annotation.Configuration;

import org.springframework.context.annotation.Profile;



@Configuration

public class DataSourceConfig {
```

```
    @Bean
    @Profile("dev")
    public DataSource devDataSource() {
        return new H2DataSource("jdbc:h2:mem:devdb",
"sa", "password");
    }

    @Bean
    @Profile("prod")
    public DataSource prodDataSource() {
        return new MysqlDataSource("jdbc:mysql://prod-db-
server/mydb", "produser", "prodsecret");
    }
}
```

In the above code snippet, the **devDataSource** bean is only created when the **dev** profile is active, and the **prodDataSource** bean is only created when the **prod** profile is active.

Combining Profiles

Spring Boot allows you to activate multiple profiles simultaneously. This is useful when you have shared configurations that apply to multiple environments. You can activate multiple profiles by separating them with commas. See the below:

```
java -jar myapp.jar --spring.profiles.active=dev,shared
```

In this example, both the **dev** and **shared** profiles are activated, and Spring Boot will load the configurations from both **application-dev.yml** and **application-shared.yml**.

Profile-Specific Configuration Properties

Spring Boot also supports profile-specific configuration properties within the same file. This is particularly useful when you want to keep all configurations in a single file but still need environment-specific settings.

Consider the following example of Profile-Specific Properties in **`application.yml`**

```yaml
spring:

  profiles:

    active: dev



---

spring:

  profiles: dev

  datasource:

    url: jdbc:h2:mem:devdb

    username: sa

    password: password

    driver-class-name: org.h2.Driver

  jpa:

    hibernate:

      ddl-auto: create-drop

    show-sql: true
```

```
---

spring:

  profiles: prod

  datasource:

    url: jdbc:mysql://prod-db-server/mydb

    username: produser

    password: prodsecret

    driver-class-name: com.mysql.cj.jdbc.Driver

  jpa:

    hibernate:

      ddl-auto: update

    show-sql: false
```

In the above code snippet, the **application.yml** file contains configuration blocks for both **dev** and **prod** profiles. When the **dev** profile is active, Spring Boot loads the configurations under the **spring.profiles: dev** block. Similarly, when the **prod** profile is active, it loads the configurations under the **spring.profiles: prod** block.

Accessing Profile Information

You might need to access the active profiles or check if a specific profile is active within your code. Spring Boot provides several ways to do this as below:

```
import
org.springframework.beans.factory.annotation.Autowired;

import org.springframework.core.env.Environment;

import org.springframework.stereotype.Component;
```

```
@Component
public class ProfileChecker {

    @Autowired
    private Environment env;

    public void checkProfiles() {
        if (env.acceptsProfiles("dev")) {
            System.out.println("Development profile is
active");
        }
        if (env.acceptsProfiles("prod")) {
            System.out.println("Production profile is
active");
        }
    }
}
```

In the above code snippet, the **ProfileChecker** class uses the **Environment** object to check if specific profiles are active and print messages accordingly. Also, when managing profiles and environment-specific configurations, consider the following best practices:

- Keep sensitive information such as passwords and API keys in external configuration files or environment variables to enhance security.
- Use descriptive profile names that clearly indicate their purpose, such as **dev**, **test**, **prod**, **staging**, etc.
- Document the different profiles and their configurations to help team members

understand the setup.

- Test your application with different profiles to ensure that all environment-specific configurations work as expected.

Externalizing Configuration

Externalizing configuration allows you to manage your application settings outside of the codebase. This practice enhances security, flexibility, and maintainability by enabling you to change configurations without modifying the application code or redeploying the application. Externalized configurations can be stored in various sources such as environment variables, command-line arguments, external files, or centralized configuration servers.

Using Environment Variables

Environment variables provide a simple and effective way to externalize configuration. You can set environment variables at the system level, and Spring Boot will automatically pick them up and use them in your application.

Let us do in the below example:

```
export
SPRING_DATASOURCE_URL=jdbc:mysql://localhost:3306/mydb

export SPRING_DATASOURCE_USERNAME=root

export SPRING_DATASOURCE_PASSWORD=secret
```

Spring Boot will automatically map these environment variables to the corresponding properties in your application.

Similarly, let us try to access these environment variables:

```
import
org.springframework.beans.factory.annotation.Value;

import org.springframework.stereotype.Component;



@Component

public class DatabaseConfig {
```

```
    @Value("${spring.datasource.url}")
    private String datasourceUrl;

    @Value("${spring.datasource.username}")
    private String datasourceUsername;

    @Value("${spring.datasource.password}")
    private String datasourcePassword;

    public void printConfig() {
        System.out.println("Datasource URL: " +
datasourceUrl);
        System.out.println("Datasource Username: " +
datasourceUsername);
        System.out.println("Datasource Password: " +
datasourcePassword);
    }
}
```

Centralized Configuration with Spring Cloud Config

For distributed systems and microservices, managing configuration across multiple instances and environments can be challenging. Spring Cloud Config provides a centralized configuration management solution that allows you to store configurations in a Git repository and access them dynamically.

Consider setting up a Spring Cloud config server. To do this,

- Create a new Spring Boot project for the Config Server and add the necessary dependencies:

```
<dependency>

    <groupId>org.springframework.cloud</groupId>

    <artifactId>spring-cloud-config-server</artifactId>

</dependency>
```

- Enable the Config Server in the main application class:

```
import org.springframework.boot.SpringApplication;

import
org.springframework.boot.autoconfigure.SpringBootApplicat
ion;

import
org.springframework.cloud.config.server.EnableConfigServe
r;


@SpringBootApplication

@EnableConfigServer

public class ConfigServerApplication {

    public static void main(String[] args) {

SpringApplication.run(ConfigServerApplication.class,
args);

    }
```

```
}
```

- Configure the Config Server to use a Git repository for storing configurations:

```
spring:
  cloud:
    config:
      server:
        git:
          uri: https://github.com/your-repo/config-repo
          clone-on-start: true
```

When the client application starts, it fetches the configuration from the Config Server, ensuring that all instances of the application use the same configuration.

This is just one way to externalize configuration by using environment variables, command-line arguments, external files, or centralized configuration servers. With this, you can manage your application's settings effectively and adapt it to different environments without touching the codebase.

@Value and @ConfigurationProperties

Configuration annotations like **`@Value`** and **`@ConfigurationProperties`** allow you to inject configuration values directly into your application components. These annotations provide a convenient way to access externalized configuration properties, making your code more flexible and easier to maintain. Now, we will explore these annotations in detail and see how they can be used effectively in your Spring Boot applications.

Using @Value

The **`@Value`** annotation is used to inject values from properties files or environment variables directly into Spring beans. This annotation is simple and effective for injecting individual properties.

Injecting Properties with @Value

- Add properties to your **application.properties** or **application.yml** file:

```
app.name=MyApp

app.version=1.0.0
```

- Use the **@Value** annotation to inject these properties into a Spring bean:

```
import
org.springframework.beans.factory.annotation.Value;

import org.springframework.stereotype.Component;


@Component

public class AppConfig {


    @Value("${app.name}")

    private String appName;


    @Value("${app.version}")

    private String appVersion;


    public void printConfig() {

        System.out.println("App Name: " + appName);

        System.out.println("App Version: " + appVersion);

    }
```

```
}
```

In the above code snippet, the **@Value** annotation injects the **app.name** and **app.version** properties into the **appName** and **appVersion** fields, respectively. The **printConfig** method then prints these values to the console.

Using @ConfigurationProperties

The **@ConfigurationProperties** annotation is a powerful alternative to **@Value** that allows you to bind a group of related properties to a Java object. This approach is especially useful when dealing with complex configurations with multiple related properties.

Defining Configuration Properties with @ConfigurationProperties

- Add properties to your **application.properties** or **application.yml** file:

```
app.datasource.url=jdbc:mysql://localhost:3306/mydb

app.datasource.username=root

app.datasource.password=secret
```

- Define a configuration properties class:

```
import
org.springframework.boot.context.properties.Configuration
Properties;

import org.springframework.stereotype.Component;


@Component

@ConfigurationProperties(prefix = "app.datasource")

public class DataSourceConfig {


    private String url;
```

```
private String username;
private String password;

// Getters and setters
public String getUrl() {
    return url;
}

public void setUrl(String url) {
    this.url = url;
}

public String getUsername() {
    return username;
}

public void setUsername(String username) {
    this.username = username;
}

public String getPassword() {
```

```
        return password;
    }

    public void setPassword(String password) {
        this.password = password;
    }
}
```

In the above code snippet, the **DataSourceConfig** class is annotated with **@ConfigurationProperties(prefix = "app.datasource")**. This tells Spring Boot to bind the properties with the prefix **app.datasource** to the fields in this class. The properties defined in the **application.properties** or **application.yml** file are automatically mapped to the corresponding fields.

- Enable the configuration properties in your main application class:

```
import org.springframework.boot.SpringApplication;
import
org.springframework.boot.autoconfigure.SpringBootApplicat
ion;
import
org.springframework.boot.context.properties.EnableConfigu
rationProperties;


@SpringBootApplication
@EnableConfigurationProperties(DataSourceConfig.class)
public class DemoApplication {
    public static void main(String[] args) {
```

```
        SpringApplication.run(DemoApplication.class,
args);
    }
}
```

- Use the configuration properties class in your components:

```
import
org.springframework.beans.factory.annotation.Autowired;
import org.springframework.stereotype.Component;

@Component
public class DatabaseService {

    private final DataSourceConfig dataSourceConfig;

    @Autowired
    public DatabaseService(DataSourceConfig
dataSourceConfig) {
        this.dataSourceConfig = dataSourceConfig;
    }

    public void printDataSourceConfig() {
        System.out.println("Datasource URL: " +
dataSourceConfig.getUrl());
```

```
        System.out.println("Datasource Username: " +
dataSourceConfig.getUsername());

        System.out.println("Datasource Password: " +
dataSourceConfig.getPassword());

    }

}
```

In the above code snippet, the **DatabaseService** class uses the **DataSourceConfig** bean to access the configuration properties and print them to the console.

Binding Complex Nested Properties

The **@ConfigurationProperties** annotation is particularly useful for binding complex nested properties. You can create hierarchical configurations that map directly to Java objects, making your configuration management more organized and easier to handle. Consider the following example to understand how to bind nested properties.

- First, add nested properties to your **application.properties** or **application.yml** file:

```
app.email.host=smtp.gitforgits.com

app.email.port=587

app.email.username=user@gitforgits.com

app.email.password=secret

app.security.jwt.secret=mySecretKey

app.security.jwt.expiration=3600
```

- Define configuration properties classes for nested properties:

```
import
org.springframework.boot.context.properties.Configuration
Properties;
```

```
import org.springframework.stereotype.Component;

@Component
@ConfigurationProperties(prefix = "app")
public class AppConfig {

    private EmailConfig email = new EmailConfig();
    private SecurityConfig security = new
SecurityConfig();

    // Getters and setters
    public EmailConfig getEmail() {
        return email;
    }

    public void setEmail(EmailConfig email) {
        this.email = email;
    }

    public SecurityConfig getSecurity() {
        return security;
    }
```

```
public void setSecurity(SecurityConfig security) {
    this.security = security;
}

public static class EmailConfig {
    private String host;
    private int port;
    private String username;
    private String password;

    // Getters and setters
    public String getHost() {
        return host;
    }

    public void setHost(String host) {
        this.host = host;
    }

    public int getPort() {
```

```
        return port;
    }

    public void setPort(int port) {
        this.port = port;
    }

    public String getUsername() {
        return username;
    }

    public void setUsername(String username) {
        this.username = username;
    }

    public String getPassword() {
        return password;
    }

    public void setPassword(String password) {
        this.password = password;
```

```
        }
    }

    public static class SecurityConfig {
        private JwtConfig jwt = new JwtConfig();

        // Getters and setters
        public JwtConfig getJwt() {
            return jwt;
        }

        public void setJwt(JwtConfig jwt) {
            this.jwt = jwt;
        }

        public static class JwtConfig {
            private String secret;
            private int expiration;

            // Getters and setters
            public String getSecret() {
```

```
            return secret;
        }

        public void setSecret(String secret) {
            this.secret = secret;
        }

        public int getExpiration() {
            return expiration;
        }

        public void setExpiration(int expiration) {
            this.expiration = expiration;
        }
    }
  }
}
```

- Enable the configuration properties in your main application class:

```
import org.springframework.boot.SpringApplication;
import
org.springframework.boot.autoconfigure.SpringBootApplicat
ion;
```

```
import
org.springframework.boot.context.properties.EnableConfigu
rationProperties;


@SpringBootApplication

@EnableConfigurationProperties(AppConfig.class)

public class DemoApplication {

    public static void main(String[] args) {

        SpringApplication.run(DemoApplication.class,
args);

    }

}
```

- Use the nested configuration properties in your components:

```
import
org.springframework.beans.factory.annotation.Autowired;

import org.springframework.stereotype.Component;


@Component

public class EmailService {



    private final AppConfig appConfig;



    @Autowired
```

```
    public EmailService(AppConfig appConfig) {
        this.appConfig = appConfig;
    }

    public void printEmailConfig() {
        AppConfig.EmailConfig emailConfig =
appConfig.getEmail();
        System.out.println("Email Host: " +
emailConfig.getHost());
        System.out.println("Email Port: " +
emailConfig.getPort());
        System.out.println("Email Username: " +
emailConfig.getUsername());
    }
}
```

In the above code snippet, the **AppConfig** class contains nested classes for email and security configurations. The **EmailService** class uses the **AppConfig** bean to access and print the email configuration properties.

Validation with @ConfigurationProperties

You can also add validation to your configuration properties using JSR-303/JSR-380 annotations. This ensures that your configuration values meet certain constraints before they are used in your application.

Adding Validation to Configuration Properties

- Add the validation dependency to your **pom.xml**:

```
<dependency>
```

```
    <groupId>org.springframework.boot</groupId>

    <artifactId>spring-boot-starter-
validation</artifactId>

</dependency>
```

- Add validation annotations to the configuration properties class:

```
import
org.springframework.boot.context.properties.Configuration
Properties;

import org.springframework.stereotype.Component;


import javax.validation.constraints.NotEmpty;

import javax.validation.constraints.NotNull;


@Component

@ConfigurationProperties(prefix = "app.datasource")

public class DataSourceConfig {


    @NotEmpty

    private String url;


    @NotEmpty

    private String username;
```

```
@NotEmpty
private String password;

// Getters and setters
public String getUrl() {
    return url;
}

public void setUrl(String url) {
    this.url = url;
}

public String getUsername() {
    return username;
}

public void setUsername(String username) {
    this.username = username;
}
```

```
    public String getPassword() {
        return password;
    }

    public void setPassword(String password) {
        this.password = password;
    }
}
```

In the above code snippet, the **DataSourceConfig** class includes validation annotations such as **@NotEmpty** to ensure that the URL, username, and password are not empty.

To summarize, the **@Value** annotation is ideal for injecting individual properties, while the **@ConfigurationProperties** annotation is suited for binding groups of related properties to Java objects. However, both these annotations make your application more flexible, maintainable, and easier to configure.

Type-Safe Configuration Properties

Type-safe configuration is a concept where configuration properties are bound to strongly typed Java objects, ensuring that the properties are validated and converted to the correct types before being used in the application. This approach minimizes errors and makes your configuration more reliable and easier to manage. Spring Boot facilitates type-safe configuration through the **@ConfigurationProperties** annotation, enabling you to create robust and maintainable configurations.

Setting up Type-Safe Configuration Properties

To set up type-safe configuration properties, follow these steps:

- Start by defining your configuration properties in **application.yml** or **application.properties**.

```
app:
```

```
  datasource:
    url: jdbc:mysql://localhost:3306/mydb
    username: root
    password: secret
  email:
    host: smtp.gitforgits.com
    port: 587
    username: user@gitforgits.com
    password: secret
  security:
    jwt:
      secret: mySecretKey
      expiration: 3600
```

- Define a Java class to represent the configuration properties. Use nested classes to represent hierarchical properties, and use JSR-303/JSR-380 annotations for validation.

```
import
org.springframework.boot.context.properties.Configuration
Properties;
import org.springframework.stereotype.Component;


import javax.validation.constraints.NotEmpty;
import javax.validation.constraints.NotNull;
```

```
import javax.validation.constraints.Min;
import javax.validation.constraints.Email;


@Component
@ConfigurationProperties(prefix = "app")
public class AppConfig {


    private final DataSourceConfig datasource = new
DataSourceConfig();
    private final EmailConfig email = new EmailConfig();
    private final SecurityConfig security = new
SecurityConfig();


    public DataSourceConfig getDatasource() {
        return datasource;
    }


    public EmailConfig getEmail() {
        return email;
    }


    public SecurityConfig getSecurity() {
```

```
        return security;
    }

    public static class DataSourceConfig {
        @NotEmpty
        private String url;
        @NotEmpty
        private String username;
        @NotEmpty
        private String password;

        // Getters and setters
        public String getUrl() {
            return url;
        }

        public void setUrl(String url) {
            this.url = url;
        }

        public String getUsername() {
```

```
        return username;
    }

    public void setUsername(String username) {
        this.username = username;
    }

    public String getPassword() {
        return password;
    }

    public void setPassword(String password) {
        this.password = password;
    }
}

public static class EmailConfig {
    @NotEmpty
    @Email
    private String host;
    @NotNull
```

```
@Min(1)
private int port;
@NotEmpty
private String username;
@NotEmpty
private String password;

// Getters and setters
public String getHost() {
    return host;
}

public void setHost(String host) {
    this.host = host;
}

public int getPort() {
    return port;
}

public void setPort(int port) {
```

```
        this.port = port;
    }

    public String getUsername() {
        return username;
    }

    public void setUsername(String username) {
        this.username = username;
    }

    public String getPassword() {
        return password;
    }

    public void setPassword(String password) {
        this.password = password;
    }
}

public static class SecurityConfig {
```

```
private final JwtConfig jwt = new JwtConfig();

public JwtConfig getJwt() {
    return jwt;
}

public static class JwtConfig {
    @NotEmpty
    private String secret;
    @NotNull
    @Min(1)
    private int expiration;

    // Getters and setters
    public String getSecret() {
        return secret;
    }

    public void setSecret(String secret) {
        this.secret = secret;
    }
```

```
                public int getExpiration() {
                    return expiration;
                }

                public void setExpiration(int expiration) {
                    this.expiration = expiration;
                }
            }
        }
    }
```

In this above very long code sample, the **AppConfig** class encapsulates all the configuration properties using nested classes for data source, email, and security configurations. Validation annotations ensure that the properties meet specific constraints.

- Next, in your main application class, to enable the configuration properties use the annotation **@EnableConfigurationProperties**.

```
import org.springframework.boot.SpringApplication;
import
org.springframework.boot.autoconfigure.SpringBootApplicat
ion;
import
org.springframework.boot.context.properties.EnableConfigu
rationProperties;
```

```
@SpringBootApplication

@EnableConfigurationProperties(AppConfig.class)

public class DemoApplication {

    public static void main(String[] args) {

        SpringApplication.run(DemoApplication.class,
args);

    }

}
```

- Inject the configuration properties class into your Spring components to access the configuration values.

```
import
org.springframework.beans.factory.annotation.Autowired;

import org.springframework.stereotype.Component;


@Component

public class EmailService {


    private final AppConfig appConfig;


    @Autowired

    public EmailService(AppConfig appConfig) {

        this.appConfig = appConfig;
```

```
    }

    public void printEmailConfig() {
        AppConfig.EmailConfig emailConfig =
appConfig.getEmail();
        System.out.println("Email Host: " +
emailConfig.getHost());
        System.out.println("Email Port: " +
emailConfig.getPort());
        System.out.println("Email Username: " +
emailConfig.getUsername());
    }
}
```

In the above code snippet, the **EmailService** class uses the **AppConfig** bean to access and print the email configuration properties.

Advanced Type-Safe Configuration

For more advanced use cases, you can combine **@ConfigurationProperties** with custom converters and complex data types. Spring Boot provides flexible options for handling different types of configuration values.

Custom Converter for Complex Data Type

- Define a custom converter:

```
import
org.springframework.core.convert.converter.Converter;

import org.springframework.stereotype.Component;
```

```
@Component

public class StringToDateConverter implements
Converter<String, LocalDate> {


    @Override

    public LocalDate convert(String source) {

        return LocalDate.parse(source);

    }

}
```

- Use the custom converter in your configuration properties:

```
import
org.springframework.boot.context.properties.Configuration
Properties;

import
org.springframework.format.annotation.DateTimeFormat;

import org.springframework.stereotype.Component;


import java.time.LocalDate;



@Component

@ConfigurationProperties(prefix = "app")

public class AppConfig {
```

```
    @DateTimeFormat(iso = DateTimeFormat.ISO.DATE)
    private LocalDate releaseDate;


    // Getters and setters
    public LocalDate getReleaseDate() {
        return releaseDate;
    }


    public void setReleaseDate(LocalDate releaseDate) {
        this.releaseDate = releaseDate;
    }
}
```

In this example, a custom converter is used to parse a date string into a **LocalDate** object, and the **@DateTimeFormat** annotation specifies the date format.

Reloading Configuration Properties at Runtime

In dynamic and rapidly changing environments, it's often necessary to update configuration properties without restarting the application. Spring Boot supports reloading configuration properties at runtime, allowing you to change settings on-the-fly and see the effects immediately. This capability is particularly useful for applications that require high availability and minimal downtime.

Using Spring Cloud Context

Spring Cloud Context provides support for reloading configuration properties at runtime. By integrating Spring Cloud Config with your Spring Boot application, you can manage configuration properties centrally and refresh them without restarting the application.

Add Spring Cloud Dependencies

To enable dynamic reloading of configuration properties, add the necessary dependencies to your **pom.xml**:

```
<dependency>

    <groupId>org.springframework.cloud</groupId>

    <artifactId>spring-cloud-starter-config</artifactId>

</dependency>

<dependency>

    <groupId>org.springframework.cloud</groupId>

    <artifactId>spring-cloud-starter-
bootstrap</artifactId>

</dependency>
```

Enable Configuration Properties Refresh

Annotate your configuration properties class with **@RefreshScope** to enable refreshing at runtime.

```
import
org.springframework.boot.context.properties.Configuration
Properties;

import
org.springframework.cloud.context.config.annotation.Refre
shScope;

import org.springframework.stereotype.Component;


@Component
```

```
@RefreshScope
@ConfigurationProperties(prefix = "app.datasource")
public class DataSourceConfig {

    private String url;
    private String username;
    private String password;

    // Getters and setters
    public String getUrl() {
        return url;
    }

    public void setUrl(String url) {
        this.url = url;
    }

    public String getUsername() {
        return username;
    }
```

```java
    public void setUsername(String username) {
        this.username = username;
    }

    public String getPassword() {
        return password;
    }

    public void setPassword(String password) {
        this.password = password;
    }
}
```

The **@RefreshScope** annotation ensures that the **DataSourceConfig** bean is reloaded when the configuration properties change.

Triggering a Refresh

To trigger a refresh of the configuration properties, you can send a POST request to the **/actuator/refresh** endpoint. Ensure that the Spring Boot Actuator is included in your project to enable this functionality.

```xml
<dependency>
    <groupId>org.springframework.boot</groupId>
    <artifactId>spring-boot-starter-actuator</artifactId>
</dependency>
```

To refresh the configuration properties, send a POST request to

http://localhost:8080/actuator/refresh using Postman.

```
curl -X POST http://localhost:8080/actuator/refresh
```

This triggers a refresh of the configuration properties, allowing the application to pick up the latest values without restarting.

Using Spring Cloud Bus

Spring Cloud Bus extends the refresh capabilities by providing a way to broadcast configuration changes across multiple instances of a distributed system. This is particularly useful for microservices architectures where you need to propagate configuration changes to all running instances.

Add Spring Cloud Bus Dependencies

Add the necessary Spring Cloud Bus dependencies to your **pom.xml**:

```
<dependency>

    <groupId>org.springframework.cloud</groupId>

    <artifactId>spring-cloud-starter-bus-
amqp</artifactId>

</dependency>
```

Configure Spring Cloud Bus

Configure Spring Cloud Bus to use a message broker like RabbitMQ or Kafka for broadcasting configuration changes.

```
spring:

  cloud:

    bus:

      enabled: true

  rabbitmq:

    host: localhost
```

```
    port: 5672
    username: guest
    password: guest
management:
  endpoints:
    web:
      exposure:
        include: bus-refresh
```

Triggering a Global Refresh

To trigger a refresh across all instances, send a POST request to the **/actuator/bus-refresh** endpoint.

```
curl -X POST http://localhost:8080/actuator/bus-refresh
```

This command triggers a refresh event that is propagated to all instances of your application, ensuring that all instances reload the updated configuration properties.

Handling Configuration Reloads

When configuration properties are reloaded, it's important to handle the updates in your code appropriately. For example, if you are updating data source configurations, you might need to reinitialize the data source connections.

```
import
org.springframework.beans.factory.annotation.Autowired;

import
org.springframework.cloud.context.config.annotation.Refre
shScope;

import org.springframework.stereotype.Service;
```

```
import javax.annotation.PostConstruct;


@Service
@RefreshScope
public class DatabaseService {


    private final DataSourceConfig dataSourceConfig;


    @Autowired
    public DatabaseService(DataSourceConfig
dataSourceConfig) {
        this.dataSourceConfig = dataSourceConfig;
    }


    @PostConstruct
    public void init() {
        // Initialize data source with updated
configuration
        System.out.println("Datasource URL: " +
dataSourceConfig.getUrl());
        System.out.println("Datasource Username: " +
dataSourceConfig.getUsername());
```

```
        System.out.println("Datasource Password: " +
dataSourceConfig.getPassword());

    }

}
```

In the above code snippet, the **DatabaseService** class is annotated with **@RefreshScope** and reinitializes the data source configuration when the properties are refreshed.

Monitoring Configuration Changes

Monitoring configuration changes is crucial to ensure that the updates are applied correctly and to identify any issues that may arise. Spring Boot Actuator provides endpoints for monitoring the status and health of your application, including configuration properties.

See the following sample example:

```
management:

  endpoints:

    web:

      exposure:

        include: health, info, env
```

By exposing the **env** endpoint, you can monitor the current configuration properties and verify that the changes have been applied.

```
curl http://localhost:8080/actuator/env
```

This command returns the current environment properties, allowing you to confirm that the latest configuration values are in use.

Overall, reloading configuration properties at runtime allows you to update application settings without restarting the application. Leveraging Spring Cloud Context and Spring Cloud Bus can manage configuration changes dynamically and propagate them across multiple instances in a distributed system.

Summary

Just to recap, the focus was on configuration and properties management in Spring Boot applications. It began with an overview of how Spring Boot simplifies configuration through various methods, such as properties files and YAML files, allowing for clear and structured configurations. The use of application properties was explored, demonstrating how key-value pairs can control application behavior. Configuration with YAML files provided a more readable and hierarchical structure for complex settings. The chapter also covered profiles and environment-specific configurations, enabling different settings for development, testing, and production environments. This included defining profiles in separate configuration files and activating them via properties, command-line arguments, or environment variables.

Externalizing configuration was highlighted as a best practice for managing settings outside the codebase, enhancing security and flexibility. Methods such as environment variables, external files, and centralized configuration with Spring Cloud Config and Vault were learned. The use of the **`@Value`** and **`@ConfigurationProperties`** annotations allowed for injecting configuration values into Spring components, with type-safe configuration ensuring proper validation and conversion of properties.

Reloading configuration properties at runtime was another key topic, demonstrating how to update settings without restarting the application using Spring Cloud Context and Spring Cloud Bus. This included triggering refreshes and handling updates in code. Overall, the chapter provided comprehensive insights into managing configurations effectively, ensuring security, flexibility, and maintainability in Spring Boot applications.

CHAPTER 4: SPRING BOOT PACKAGING AND DEPLOYMENT

Chapter Overview

The sole aim of this chapter is to teach you packaging and deploying your Spring Boot applications efficiently and that too step-wise. You'll first begin by learning the various methods to package a Spring Boot application, including creating executable JAR and WAR files, which are essential for deploying your applications on different platforms. This section will provide a solid foundation for understanding how to bundle your application for smooth deployment.

Next, the chapter will cover deploying Spring Boot applications to popular web servers like Tomcat, Jetty, and Undertow. These deployment methods are fundamental for running your applications in traditional server environments. Following this, you will explore deploying your applications in Docker containers, an increasingly popular method that ensures consistency across different environments.

You will also delve into deploying Spring Boot applications on major cloud platforms primarily AWS. This section will demonstrate how to leverage cloud services to scale and manage your applications effectively. Additionally, running Spring Boot applications in Kubernetes will be explored, highlighting how to manage containerized applications in a cluster. The chapter will teach you how to create Spring Boot Docker images and by the end of this chapter, you are well equipped with various packaging and deployment strategies and to choose the best approach for your specific application.

Packaging a Spring Boot Application

Packaging a Spring Boot application ensures that your application can be deployed and run consistently across different environments. Packaging bundles your application code, its dependencies, and resources into a single unit, simplifying deployment and reducing the risk of missing dependencies or configuration errors. This process is essential for achieving portability, maintainability, and scalability in your software development lifecycle.

Spring Boot offers several packaging options, primarily focusing on creating executable JAR and WAR files. Each format serves different deployment scenarios and provides specific advantages. Understanding these formats and how to create them is crucial for effectively managing your Spring Boot applications.

Understanding Executable JAR Files

Executable JAR (Java ARchive) files are the most common packaging format for Spring Boot applications. An executable JAR file contains all the necessary components to run your application, including compiled code, libraries, and resources. This format simplifies deployment because you only need to distribute a single file, which can be run using the **`java -jar`** command.

The advantages of using executable JAR files include:

- All dependencies are included in a single file, reducing the complexity of managing external libraries.
- The JAR file can be deployed on any platform that supports Java, ensuring consistent behavior across different environments.
- Executable JAR files can be run directly from the command line, simplifying the process for developers and operators.

Understanding Executable WAR Files

While JAR files are suitable for standalone applications, WAR (Web Application Archive) files are often used for deploying applications on traditional web servers like Tomcat, Jetty, or Undertow. A WAR file is a packaged web application that conforms to the Java EE specifications. It includes the application's code, libraries, web components (such as servlets and JSPs), and configuration files (like **`web.xml`**).

The advantages of using WAR files include:

- WAR files are compatible with many enterprise-grade web servers, making them ideal for integrating with existing infrastructure.
- Web servers like Tomcat and Jetty provide robust features for load balancing, session management, and security, which can enhance the scalability of your application.
- WAR files allow you to leverage the full capabilities of Java EE, including advanced web components and enterprise services.

Process of Packaging

The process of packaging a Spring Boot application involves several steps, which ensure that your application and its dependencies are correctly bundled. The primary tool for this task is the build tool, such as Maven or Gradle, which automates the process and handles the complexities of dependency management and file assembly.

Define Dependencies

The first step in packaging your application is defining its dependencies. This is done in your build configuration file (such as **`pom.xml`** for Maven or **`build.gradle`** for Gradle). Dependencies include libraries and frameworks that your application requires to run.

Compile the Code

Once dependencies are defined, the build tool compiles your application's source code into bytecode. This step involves converting your Java source files (**`.java`**) into bytecode files

(**.class**), which are then packaged into a JAR or WAR file.

Package the Application

The packaging step involves bundling the compiled code, dependencies, and resources into a single deployable unit. This unit can be an executable JAR or WAR file, depending on your deployment requirements. The build tool handles this step by including all necessary files and ensuring the correct structure.

Add Metadata

Metadata is essential for the application to run correctly. It includes configuration files such as **application.properties** or **application.yml**, which define runtime settings. For WAR files, metadata also includes the **web.xml** file, which configures the web application.

Create the Executable

For JAR files, the final step is to create an executable JAR. This involves adding a manifest file (**MANIFEST.MF**) that specifies the main class to run when the JAR is executed. The **spring-boot-maven-plugin** or **spring-boot-gradle-plugin** automates this process by creating a JAR file with an embedded web server, making it executable with the **java -jar** command.

Package Verification

After packaging, it is crucial to verify that the resulting JAR or WAR file is correctly assembled and contains all necessary components. This step involves checking the contents of the package and ensuring that all dependencies and resources are included.

Automating Packaging Process

Automation is critically essential and a key part of agile development to ensure speed, consistency and efficiency in the entire packaging process. There are various build tools like Maven and Gradle provide plugins and tasks that automate the steps involved in packaging a Spring Boot application.

Let us take an example of configuring maven as shown below:

```
<build>

    <plugins>

        <plugin>

            <groupId>org.springframework.boot</groupId>
```

```
            <artifactId>spring-boot-maven-
plugin</artifactId>

        </plugin>

    </plugins>

</build>
```

In this Maven configuration, the **spring-boot-maven-plugin** is used to package the application. This plugin provides tasks for compiling the code, creating the executable JAR or WAR file, and including all necessary dependencies and resources.

Take another example about gradle configuration:

```
plugins {

    id 'org.springframework.boot' version '2.5.4'

    id 'io.spring.dependency-management' version
'1.0.11.RELEASE'

    id 'java'

}


dependencies {

    implementation 'org.springframework.boot:spring-boot-
starter'

    implementation 'org.springframework.boot:spring-boot-
starter-web'

}


bootJar {
```

```
    mainClassName = 'com.example.demo.DemoApplication'
}
```

In this Gradle configuration, the **spring-boot-gradle-plugin** is used to package the application. The **bootJar** task is configured to create an executable JAR file, specifying the main class to run.

Automating the packaging process offers several benefits, such as:

- It ensures that the same steps are followed every time, reducing the risk of errors and inconsistencies.
- Automation saves time by eliminating the need for manual steps, allowing developers to focus on coding and testing.
- Automated packaging makes it easy to reproduce builds, ensuring that the same artifacts can be generated across different environments and builds.

Integrating Packaging with CI/CD Pipelines

Continuous Integration (CI) and Continuous Deployment (CD) pipelines automate the entire build, test, and deployment process. Integrating packaging into your CI/CD pipeline ensures that your application is automatically packaged and deployed with every code change, enhancing the development workflow and reducing manual intervention.

For example, see the jenkins pipeline as below:

```
pipeline {
    agent any

    stages {
        stage('Build') {
            steps {
                script {
                    def mvnHome = tool 'M3'
                    sh "${mvnHome}/bin/mvn clean package"
```

```
                }
            }
        }

        stage('Deploy') {
            steps {
                script {
                    sh 'java -jar target/demo-0.0.1-
SNAPSHOT.jar'
                }
            }
        }
    }
}
```

In this Jenkins pipeline, the build stage uses Maven to package the Spring Boot application, and the deploy stage runs the packaged JAR file.

Creating Executable JAR and WAR Files

Creating an Executable JAR File

We will start with the process of creating an executable JAR file using Maven. We will use a simple Spring Boot project as an example. Just ensure you have a basic Spring Boot application set up. Your project should include the necessary dependencies and the **spring-boot-starter-parent** in your **pom.xml**.

```
<parent>
```

```
    <groupId>org.springframework.boot</groupId>

    <artifactId>spring-boot-starter-parent</artifactId>

    <version>2.5.4</version>

</parent>


<dependencies>

    <dependency>

        <groupId>org.springframework.boot</groupId>

        <artifactId>spring-boot-starter-web</artifactId>

    </dependency>

</dependencies>
```

Add the **spring-boot-maven-plugin** to your **pom.xml** to enable building an executable JAR file.

```
<build>

    <plugins>

        <plugin>

            <groupId>org.springframework.boot</groupId>

            <artifactId>spring-boot-maven-
plugin</artifactId>

        </plugin>

    </plugins>

</build>
```

Ensure you have a main application class annotated with **@SpringBootApplication**.

```
package com.example.demo;


import org.springframework.boot.SpringApplication;

import
org.springframework.boot.autoconfigure.SpringBootApplicat
ion;


@SpringBootApplication

public class DemoApplication {

    public static void main(String[] args) {

        SpringApplication.run(DemoApplication.class,
args);

    }

}
```

Run the following Maven command to build your project and create the executable JAR file.

```
mvn clean package
```

This command compiles your application, runs tests, and packages it into a JAR file located in the **target** directory.

Once the JAR file is created, you can run it using the **java -jar** command.

```
java -jar target/demo-0.0.1-SNAPSHOT.jar
```

Your Spring Boot application should now start, using the embedded Tomcat server.

Creating an Executable WAR File

Next, we will create an executable WAR file. This process is similar to creating a JAR file, but with a few additional steps. First, set up or modify the previous project for WAR packaging by modifying the **packaging** element in your **pom.xml**.

```
<packaging>war</packaging>
```

Update your main application class to extend **SpringBootServletInitializer** and override the **configure** method.

```
package com.example.demo;



import org.springframework.boot.SpringApplication;

import
org.springframework.boot.autoconfigure.SpringBootApplicat
ion;

import
org.springframework.boot.builder.SpringApplicationBuilder
;

import
org.springframework.boot.web.servlet.support.SpringBootSe
rvletInitializer;



@SpringBootApplication

public class DemoApplication extends
SpringBootServletInitializer {



    @Override
```

```
    protected SpringApplicationBuilder
configure(SpringApplicationBuilder application) {
        return
application.sources(DemoApplication.class);
    }


    public static void main(String[] args) {
        SpringApplication.run(DemoApplication.class,
args);
    }
}
```

Run the following Maven command to build your project and create the executable WAR file.

```
mvn clean package
```

This command compiles your application, runs tests, and packages it into a WAR file located in the **`target`** directory.

Then, copy the WAR file to the **`webapps`** directory of your Tomcat installation.

```
cp target/demo-0.0.1-SNAPSHOT.war
/path/to/tomcat/webapps/
```

Start your Tomcat server now. The WAR file will be deployed automatically, and your Spring Boot application will be accessible via the configured server URL.

```
/path/to/tomcat/bin/startup.sh
```

To summarize, creating executable JAR and WAR files involves:

1. Setting up your Spring Boot project with the necessary dependencies and plugins.
2. Configuring the project for JAR or WAR packaging.
3. Building the project using Maven commands.

4. Running the packaged application.

Deploying to Tomcat

Now that we have created an executable WAR file, we will move directly to the practical steps for deploying this WAR file to an Apache Tomcat server. Following is the process of deploying the previously created Spring Boot WAR file on a Tomcat server:

Install Tomcat and Copy WAR File

First, ensure that you have Apache Tomcat installed on your system. If you haven't already installed Tomcat, download the latest version from the Tomcat website and follow the installation instructions for your operating system.

Then, locate the WAR file you created in the previous section. It should be in the **target** directory of your Spring Boot project, named something like **demo-0.0.1-SNAPSHOT.war**. Copy this WAR file to the **webapps** directory of your Tomcat installation. This directory is where Tomcat looks for applications to deploy.

```
cp target/demo-0.0.1-SNAPSHOT.war
/path/to/tomcat/webapps/
```

Replace **/path/to/tomcat** with the actual path to your Tomcat installation.

Start the Tomcat Server

Start the Tomcat server by executing the startup script located in the **bin** directory of your Tomcat installation.

```
C:\path\to\tomcat\bin\startup.bat
```

Once Tomcat starts, it automatically deploys the WAR file. Open a web browser and navigate to **http://localhost:8080/demo-0.0.1-SNAPSHOT/** (or the context path defined for your application) to access your Spring Boot application.

You should see your application running as expected, served by the Tomcat server.

Verifying Deployment

To ensure that your application is running correctly, check the Tomcat logs located in the **logs** directory of your Tomcat installation. The **catalina.out** log file contains information about the deployment process and any potential issues.

```
tail -f /path/to/tomcat/logs/catalina.out
```

This command will display the log entries in real-time, allowing you to monitor the deployment process.

Hot Deployment and Redeployment

Tomcat supports hot deployment and redeployment of applications. This means you can update your application without restarting the server. To redeploy an updated WAR file, simply replace the existing WAR file in the **webapps** directory. Tomcat detects the change and redeploys the application automatically.

```
cp target/demo-0.0.1-SNAPSHOT.war
/path/to/tomcat/webapps/
```

After copying the updated WAR file, Tomcat will undeploy the old version and deploy the new version.

Managing Tomcat Deployments

Tomcat provides a Manager application that allows you to manage deployed applications through a web interface. To access the Tomcat Manager, navigate to **http://localhost:8080/manager/html** and log in with the admin credentials configured in the **tomcat-users.xml** file.

In the Manager application, you can:

- **Deploy** a new application by uploading a WAR file.
- **Undeploy** an existing application.
- **Reload** an application to apply changes without redeploying.
- **Start** and **Stop** applications as needed.

To configure the Manager application, add the following user to the **tomcat-users.xml** file located in the **conf** directory of your Tomcat installation:

```
<tomcat-users>

    <role rolename="manager-gui"/>

    <user username="admin" password="admin"
roles="manager-gui"/>
```

```
</tomcat-users>
```

After editing the **tomcat-users.xml** file, restart Tomcat to apply the changes:

```
C:\path\to\tomcat\bin\shutdown.bat

C:\path\to\tomcat\bin\startup.bat
```

Automating Deployment with CI/CD

To automate the deployment process, integrate your WAR file deployment into a CI/CD pipeline. Tools like Jenkins, GitLab CI, and GitHub Actions can automate the build, package, and deploy steps.

See the following example:

```
pipeline {
    agent any

    stages {
        stage('Build') {
            steps {
                script {
                    def mvnHome = tool 'M3'
                    sh "${mvnHome}/bin/mvn clean package"
                }
            }
        }
```

```
        stage('Deploy') {
            steps {
                script {
                    sh 'cp target/demo-0.0.1-SNAPSHOT.war
/path/to/tomcat/webapps/'
                }
            }
        }
    }
}
```

In this Jenkins pipeline, the build stage uses Maven to package the Spring Boot application into a WAR file, and the deploy stage copies the WAR file to the Tomcat **`webapps`** directory.

Deploying to Jetty and Undertow

Jetty is a lightweight, highly scalable web server and servlet container often used in Java applications. It is known for its small footprint, making it an excellent choice for embedded applications and microservices. Jetty's asynchronous processing capabilities enhance its performance and scalability, making it suitable for high-concurrency environments.

Why Jetty?

Jetty is preferred for several reasons:

- Jetty has a small footprint, which reduces resource consumption and startup time.
- Its asynchronous processing model supports high concurrency, making it ideal for handling large numbers of simultaneous connections.
- Jetty can be embedded within applications, providing flexibility and simplifying deployment.
- Jetty's modular architecture allows you to extend its capabilities by adding or removing components based on your requirements.

Jetty Deployment

Now we will see to deploy our previously built Spring Boot WAR file onto Jetty. I have outlined the following steps to configure Jetty and deploy the application.

Configure Jetty for WAR Deployment

Before we begin with, download the latest version of Jetty from the Jetty website and extract the archive to your preferred location.

Jetty comes with a pre-configured **webapps** directory where you can place your WAR files for deployment. By default, Jetty scans this directory for new or updated WAR files and deploys them automatically.

Copy WAR File to Jetty Webapps Directory

Locate the WAR file you created earlier (**demo-0.0.1-SNAPSHOT.war**) and copy it to the **webapps** directory of your Jetty installation.

```
cp target/demo-0.0.1-SNAPSHOT.war /path/to/jetty/webapps/
```

Start the Jetty Server

Start the Jetty server by running the startup script located in the **bin** directory of your Jetty installation.

```
C:\path\to\jetty\bin\jetty.bat start
```

Access the Deployed Application

Open a web browser and navigate to **http://localhost:8080/demo-0.0.1-SNAPSHOT/** to access your Spring Boot application. You should see your application running as expected. And don't forget to check the Jetty logs under the **logs** directory of your Jetty installation for deployment status and potential issues.

```
tail -f /path/to/jetty/logs/jetty.log
```

Undertow Overview

Undertow is a lightweight, high-performance web server and servlet container developed by JBoss. It is designed to handle concurrent connections efficiently and can be used as a standalone server or embedded within applications. Undertow's non-blocking architecture and low memory footprint make it a popular choice for microservices and embedded applications.

Undertow is preferred for several reasons:

- Undertow's non-blocking, asynchronous processing model ensures high performance and scalability.
- With a minimal memory footprint, Undertow is ideal for resource-constrained environments.
- Like Jetty, Undertow can be embedded within applications, providing flexibility and ease of deployment.
- Undertow supports both blocking and non-blocking APIs, allowing developers to choose the appropriate model for their application.

Undertow Deployment

Similar to Jetty, Undertow follows the same steps for configuring and deploying the application.

Install and Configure Undertow

Undertow can be downloaded from the Undertow website or you can use JBoss WildFly, which includes Undertow as its default web server. Download the latest version of WildFly and extract the archive to your preferred location.

WildFly (or standalone Undertow) uses a **deployments** directory to manage application deployments. Place your WAR file in this directory for automatic deployment.

Copy WAR File to Undertow Deployments Directory

Locate the WAR file you created earlier (**demo-0.0.1-SNAPSHOT.war**) and copy it to the **deployments** directory of your WildFly or Undertow installation.

```
cp target/demo-0.0.1-SNAPSHOT.war
/path/to/wildfly/standalone/deployments/
```

Start the Undertow Server

Start the WildFly server (or standalone Undertow) by running the startup script located in the **bin** directory of your installation.

```
C:\path\to\wildfly\bin\standalone.bat
```

Open a web browser and navigate to **http://localhost:8080/demo-0.0.1-SNAPSHOT/** to access your Spring Boot application. You should see your application running as expected.

Verifying Deployment

Check the WildFly (or Undertow) logs located in the **standalone/log** directory of your installation for deployment status and potential issues.

```
tail -f /path/to/wildfly/standalone/log/server.log
```

Undertow also supports hot deployment in order to update your application without restarting the server. Simply replace the existing WAR file in the **deployments** directory, and Undertow will redeploy the application automatically.

```
cp target/demo-0.0.1-SNAPSHOT.war
/path/to/wildfly/standalone/deployments/
```

To summarize, deploying your Spring Boot application to Jetty and Undertow involves the following steps:

1. Ensure you have the latest versions of Jetty and Undertow (or WildFly) installed.
2. Place your WAR file in the appropriate directory (**webapps** for Jetty, **deployments** for Undertow/WildFly).
3. Use the provided startup scripts to start the server.
4. Navigate to the server's URL to access your deployed application.
5. Check server logs for deployment status and troubleshoot any issues.

By following these steps, you can deploy your Spring Boot application to Jetty and Undertow, leveraging their high performance, scalability, and flexibility for running Java applications in various environments.

Deploying to Docker

Docker has become a popular tool among Java developers due to its ability to create consistent and reproducible environments. By containerizing applications, developers can ensure that their code runs identically on different machines, eliminating the "it works on my machine" problem. Docker also simplifies the deployment process by bundling the application and its dependencies into a single container, which can be easily deployed to any environment that supports Docker.

Deploying Spring Boot Application

Let me walk you through the steps to deploy our previously built Spring Boot application to Docker. We will start with creating a Dockerfile, building a Docker image, and then running the

Docker container.

Create a Dockerfile

The Dockerfile is a script that contains instructions on how to build a Docker image for your application.

```
# Use the official Maven image to build the application

FROM maven:3.8.1-openjdk-11 AS build

WORKDIR /app


# Copy the project's pom.xml and source code into the
Docker image

COPY pom.xml .

COPY src ./src


# Build the application

RUN mvn clean package -DskipTests


# Use the official OpenJDK image to run the application

FROM openjdk:11-jre-slim

WORKDIR /app


# Copy the built JAR file from the build stage to the
runtime stage

COPY --from=build /app/target/demo-0.0.1-SNAPSHOT.jar
```

```
app.jar

# Set the entry point to run the JAR file
ENTRYPOINT ["java", "-jar", "app.jar"]
```

This Dockerfile uses a multi-stage build to first build the application using Maven and then copy the resulting JAR file into a minimal OpenJDK runtime image.

Build the Docker Image

Next, build the Docker image using the Dockerfile. Open a terminal, navigate to your project directory, and run the following command:

```
docker build -t spring-boot-demo .
```

This command tells Docker to build the image and tag it as **`spring-boot-demo`**.

Run the Docker Container

After building the Docker image, you can run it as a container. Use the following command to start a container from the image:

```
docker run -d -p 8080:8080 spring-boot-demo
```

This command runs the container in detached mode (**`-d`**) and maps port 8080 of the host to port 8080 of the container (**`-p 8080:8080`**).

Handling Environment Variables

You can pass environment variables to your Docker container to configure your application at runtime. This is useful for managing configurations without modifying the Docker image.

Let us say that you want to pass the environment variables. To do it, first modify your Dockerfile to use environment variables:

```
# Use the official Maven image to build the application
FROM maven:3.8.1-openjdk-11 AS build
WORKDIR /app
```

```
# Copy the project's pom.xml and source code into the
Docker image
COPY pom.xml .
COPY src ./src

# Build the application
RUN mvn clean package -DskipTests

# Use the official OpenJDK image to run the application
FROM openjdk:11-jre-slim
WORKDIR /app

# Copy the built JAR file from the build stage to the
runtime stage
COPY --from=build /app/target/demo-0.0.1-SNAPSHOT.jar
app.jar

# Set the entry point to run the JAR file
ENTRYPOINT ["java", "-jar", "app.jar"]
```

Then, pass the environment variables when running the container:

```
docker run -d -p 8080:8080 -e
SPRING_DATASOURCE_URL=jdbc:mysql://localhost:3306/mydb -e
```

```
SPRING_DATASOURCE_USERNAME=root -e
SPRING_DATASOURCE_PASSWORD=secret spring-boot-demo
```

Here, in this command, the **-e** flag is used to pass environment variables to the container.

For more complex applications that require multiple services (e.g., a database and a web server), Docker Compose can be used to define and run multi-container Docker applications.

Deploying to AWS

Amazon Web Services (AWS) is a widely used cloud platform that provides various services and tools to deploy, manage, and scale applications. Deploying a Spring Boot application to AWS involves several steps, such as creating and configuring infrastructure, deploying the application, and managing the environment. This section will take you through the process of deploying your Spring Boot application to AWS.

Before you begin, ensure you have the following:

- An AWS account
- AWS CLI installed and configured on your local machine
- A Spring Boot application packaged as a JAR or WAR file, which we have already executed.

Setup EC2 Instance

Amazon EC2 (Elastic Compute Cloud) provides scalable computing capacity. We will deploy our Spring Boot application on an EC2 instance.

So first, launch an EC2 instance as below:

- Sign in to the AWS Management Console.
- Navigate to the EC2 Dashboard.
- Click "Launch Instance."
- Choose an Amazon Machine Image (AMI). For this task, select "Amazon Linux 2 AMI."
- Choose an instance type. For basic use, **t2.micro** is suitable.
- Configure instance details, including network and storage settings.
- Add tags if necessary.
- Configure security groups to allow traffic on port 8080 (for your Spring Boot application) and port 22 (for SSH access).

- Review and launch the instance, creating a new key pair or using an existing one.

Then, connect to your EC2 instance by using the key pair to connect to the instance via SSH:

```
ssh -i /path/to/your-key-pair.pem ec2-user@your-ec2-
instance-public-dns
```

Install Java on EC2 Instance

To install java, update the package repository and install Java:

```
sudo yum update -y

sudo amazon-linux-extras install java-openjdk11 -y
```

Verify the Java installation:

```
java -version
```

Transfer Application JAR/WAR File to EC2

Transfer your Spring Boot application JAR or WAR file to the EC2 instance. To do this, use SCP to transfer the file

```
scp -i /path/to/your-key-pair.pem /path/to/your-app.jar
ec2-user@your-ec2-instance-public-dns:/home/ec2-user/
```

Run Application

Navigate to the directory containing your application JAR/WAR file:

```
cd /home/ec2-user
```

Run the Spring Boot application:

```
java -jar your-app.jar
```

Verify the application is running by accessing it via your EC2 instance's public DNS and port 8080:

```
http://your-ec2-instance-public-dns:8080
```

Using AWS Elastic Beanstalk

AWS Elastic Beanstalk is a service that simplifies the deployment and management of applications in the AWS Cloud.

Create an Elastic Beanstalk Environment

- Sign in to the AWS Management Console.
- Navigate to the Elastic Beanstalk Dashboard.
- Click "Create a new environment."
- Choose "Web server environment" and click "Select."
- Configure the environment by selecting the appropriate platform (Java) and uploading your application JAR/WAR file.
- Click "Create environment."

Deploy Application

- Upload the JAR/WAR file directly from your local machine or from an S3 bucket.
- Elastic Beanstalk automatically handles the deployment, including provisioning the necessary infrastructure.

Monitor Environment

- Use the Elastic Beanstalk Dashboard to monitor the health of your application and environment.
- Make any necessary adjustments using the provided tools and logs.

Using AWS Elastic Container Service

If you prefer containerized deployments, AWS ECS provides a way to run Docker containers on AWS infrastructure.

First, authenticate Docker to your ECR registry:

```
aws ecr get-login-password --region your-region | docker
login --username AWS --password-stdin your-ecr-
repository-url
```

Tag your Docker image:

```
docker tag spring-boot-demo:latest your-ecr-repository-
```

```
url/spring-boot-demo:latest
```

Push the Docker image to ECR:

```
docker push your-ecr-repository-url/spring-boot-
demo:latest
```

In the AWS Management Console, navigate to the ECS Dashboard and click "Create Cluster" and follow the prompts to create a new cluster.

Then, create a task definition that specifies your Docker image and the required settings. Run a task using the task definition within your ECS cluster so that ECS manages the deployment and scaling of your containers.

Running Apps in Kubernetes

Kubernetes, often abbreviated as K8s, is an open-source container orchestration platform that automates the deployment, scaling, and management of containerized applications. Developed by Google, Kubernetes has become the de facto standard for container orchestration due to its robust feature set and scalability. It provides mechanisms for deploying, maintaining, and scaling applications in a consistent manner across various environments.

Setting up Kubernetes

Before running a Spring Boot application in Kubernetes, you need to set up a Kubernetes cluster in your development environment. There are several ways to achieve this, including using Minikube, Docker Desktop, or a managed Kubernetes service like Google Kubernetes Engine (GKE), Amazon EKS, or Azure AKS.

For this topic, we will use Minikube, a tool that runs a single-node Kubernetes cluster locally, making it the preferred choice for development and testing purposes.

Installing Minikube

Follow the instructions on the Minikube installation page to install Minikube for your operating system.

Install Kubectl

`kubectl` is the Kubernetes command-line tool used to interact with the cluster. Install **`kubectl`** by following the instructions on the kubectl installation page.

Start Minikube

Once Minikube and **kubectl** are installed, start the Minikube cluster:

```
minikube start
```

This command starts a local Kubernetes cluster, and Minikube configures **kubectl** to use this cluster.

Verify the Installation

Check the status of the Minikube cluster:

```
minikube status
```

Verify that **kubectl** is configured correctly:

```
kubectl cluster-info
```

You should see information about the Kubernetes cluster and the API server.

Deploying Application to Kubernetes

Now that your Kubernetes cluster is up and running, we will deploy the previously built Spring Boot application. We will create a Docker image, push it to a container registry, and then deploy it to the Kubernetes cluster. In case, if you haven't already created a Docker image, follow the steps outlined in the "Deploying to Docker" section to build the image.

Now, push the Docker image to a container registry such as Docker Hub or a private registry. For this example, we will use Docker Hub.

```
docker login

docker tag spring-boot-demo:latest your-dockerhub-
username/spring-boot-demo:latest

docker push your-dockerhub-username/spring-boot-
demo:latest
```

Then, create Kubernetes manifests for deploying the Spring Boot application and exposing it via a service.

```yaml
apiVersion: apps/v1
kind: Deployment
metadata:
  name: spring-boot-demo
spec:
  replicas: 1
  selector:
    matchLabels:
      app: spring-boot-demo
  template:
    metadata:
      labels:
        app: spring-boot-demo
    spec:
      containers:
      - name: spring-boot-demo
        image: your-dockerhub-username/spring-boot-
demo:latest
        ports:
        - containerPort: 8080
```

Then, create a service manifest (service.yaml):

```yaml
apiVersion: v1
```

```
kind: Service
metadata:
  name: spring-boot-demo
spec:
  type: NodePort
  selector:
    app: spring-boot-demo
  ports:
  - port: 8080
    targetPort: 8080
    nodePort: 30000
```

Use **kubectl** to apply the deployment and service manifests to your Kubernetes cluster:

```
kubectl apply -f deployment.yaml
kubectl apply -f service.yaml
```

These commands create the deployment and service, which deploy the Spring Boot application and expose it on port 30000.

Now, check the status of the deployment:

```
kubectl get deployments
```

Verify that the Spring Boot application is running:

```
kubectl get pods
```

Check the status of the service:

```
kubectl get services
```

To access the Spring Boot application, retrieve the Minikube IP address:

```
minikube ip
```

Open a web browser and navigate to **`http://<minikube-ip>:30000`**, replacing **`<minikube-ip>`** with the actual IP address provided by the **`minikube ip`** command. You should see your Spring Boot application running.

To scale the Spring Boot deployment, use the **`kubectl scale`** command:

```
kubectl scale deployment spring-boot-demo --replicas=3
```

Verify that the deployment has been scaled:

```
kubectl get deployments

kubectl get pods
```

Kubernetes will automatically balance the load and ensure high availability by distributing traffic across the pods. The process guarantees that your applications are resilient, highly available, and prepared to handle production workloads.

Creating Spring Boot Docker Images

Workflow for Docker Images

Creating Docker images for your Spring Boot application involves a series of steps that ensure your application and its dependencies are packaged into a consistent, portable container. The typical workflow includes:

- **`Writing a Dockerfile`**: This file contains instructions for building the Docker image.
- **`Building the Docker Image`**: Use Docker commands to build the image from the Dockerfile.
- **`Tagging the Docker Image`**: Assign a meaningful tag to the image for easy identification.
- **`Pushing the Image to a Registry`**: Store the image in a container registry like Docker Hub or a private registry.
- **`Running the Docker Container`**: Deploy and run the containerized application

using the created image.

Sample Program: Creation of Docker Images

We will go through the practical steps to create Docker images for our Spring Boot application.

Write a Dockerfile

Create a **Dockerfile** in the root of your Spring Boot project. This file will define the steps to build the Docker image. Following is the example**:**

```
# Use the official Maven image to build the application

FROM maven:3.8.1-openjdk-11 AS build

WORKDIR /app



# Copy the project's pom.xml and source code into the
Docker image

COPY pom.xml .

COPY src ./src



# Build the application

RUN mvn clean package -DskipTests



# Use the official OpenJDK image to run the application

FROM openjdk:11-jre-slim

WORKDIR /app



# Copy the built JAR file from the build stage to the
```

```
runtime stage

COPY --from=build /app/target/demo-0.0.1-SNAPSHOT.jar
app.jar



# Set the entry point to run the JAR file

ENTRYPOINT ["java", "-jar", "app.jar"]
```

Build the Docker Image

Navigate to your project directory, and run the following command to build the Docker image:

```
docker build -t spring-boot-demo .
```

This command tells Docker to build the image using the instructions in the Dockerfile and tag it as **spring-boot-demo**.

Tag the Docker Image

Tagging the Docker image is optional but useful for identifying different versions of your image.

```
docker tag spring-boot-demo:latest your-dockerhub-
username/spring-boot-demo:latest
```

Push the Docker Image to a Registry

Push the Docker image to a container registry such as Docker Hub.

```
docker login

docker push your-dockerhub-username/spring-boot-
demo:latest
```

Use the Docker image to run a container and verify that your application is working correctly.

```
docker run -d -p 8080:8080 spring-boot-demo
```

This command runs the container in detached mode (**-d**) and maps port 8080 of the host to port

8080 of the container (**-p 8080:8080**).

These steps will lead you through the method of creating Docker images for your Spring Boot application, storing them in a registry, and then consistently deploying them across different environments.

Summary

To summarize, the focus of this chapter was on packaging and deploying Spring Boot applications. The chapter began with the importance of packaging, emphasizing how bundling the application and its dependencies into a JAR or WAR file ensures consistent deployment across different environments. The process of creating executable JAR and WAR files was explained, including configuring the project with Maven and building the application.

Deploying the application to various servers was covered next. For Tomcat, instructions included downloading Tomcat, copying the WAR file to the webapps directory, and starting the server to access the application. Similarly, deploying to Jetty involved installing Jetty, copying the WAR file to the webapps directory, and running the server. For Undertow, the steps included using JBoss WildFly, copying the WAR file to the deployments directory, and starting the server.

Deploying to Docker was also detailed, with an explanation of why Java developers prefer Docker for its consistent environment and ease of deployment. The practical steps included writing a Dockerfile, building the Docker image, tagging it, pushing it to Docker Hub, and running the Docker container. Handling environment variables in Docker was explored, explaining how to set, manage, and monitor these variables using Docker commands, Docker Compose, and **.env** files. Securing environment variables with Docker secrets was also covered, highlighting the importance of keeping sensitive data secure.

Finally, deploying to AWS was explained, including setting up an EC2 instance, installing Java, transferring the application, and running it. The use of AWS Elastic Beanstalk for simplified deployment and AWS ECS for containerized deployments was also explored. The chapter provided a comprehensive teaching to packaging and deploying Spring Boot applications in various environments, ensuring scalability, flexibility, and security.

CHAPTER 5: SPRING BOOT AUTO-CONFIGURATION

Chapter Overview

This chapter will teach how auto-configuration works to harness its capabilities for your Spring Boot applications. The topics will start with an understanding of the core concept of auto-configuration, exploring how Spring Boot automatically configures beans and settings based on the dependencies present in the classpath. You will then move on to customizing auto-configuration to suit specific application needs, allowing you to tweak and optimize the default settings provided by Spring Boot. This section will also cover how to disable specific auto-configurations when necessary, giving you greater control over your application's configuration. Conditional beans, a key feature of Spring Boot, will be explained to show how beans can be created based on certain conditions, enhancing flexibility and modularity in your configurations.

Additionally, you will learn to write custom auto-configuration, enabling you to create reusable configurations that can be shared across multiple applications. The chapter will also explore Spring Boot Starter POMs, which simplify dependency management by providing a curated set of dependencies. You will understand how auto-configuration interacts with Spring factories, and how to troubleshoot common auto-configuration issues that may arise. Later, the chapter will cover advanced auto-configuration techniques, equipping you with the knowledge to handle complex configuration scenarios. By the end of this chapter, you will have a comprehensive understanding of Spring Boot auto-configuration, enabling you to build and maintain applications with greater efficiency and flexibility.

Understanding Auto-configuration

Auto-configuration Overview

Spring Boot's auto-configuration feature simplifies application development by automatically configuring Spring applications based on the dependencies and classes available in the classpath. The idea is to eliminate the need for boilerplate configuration, allowing developers to focus on writing business logic. This feature leverages the power of Spring Framework's **`@Conditional`** annotations to activate configurations only when specific conditions are met.

Auto-configuration works by scanning the classpath at runtime to detect the presence of certain libraries and then configuring beans accordingly. For instance, if a database driver is detected, Spring Boot will automatically configure a **`DataSource`** bean. This mechanism relies on a series of conditions defined in the **`META-INF/spring.factories`** file, which lists all the auto-configuration classes to be loaded by Spring Boot.

Key Components of Auto-configuration

- **`@EnableAutoConfiguration:`** This annotation is used in the main application class to enable Spring Boot's auto-configuration feature. It tells Spring Boot to start auto-configuring the application context based on the dependencies present.

- **@Conditional:** These annotations are used within auto-configuration classes to apply conditions under which specific beans should be created. Common conditional annotations include **@ConditionalOnClass**, **@ConditionalOnMissingBean**, and **@ConditionalOnProperty**.
- **META-INF/spring.factories:** This file contains the list of auto-configuration classes that Spring Boot should load. It maps the **EnableAutoConfiguration** entry to a list of configuration classes.
- **Auto-configuration Classes:** These classes contain the actual configuration logic, which typically includes bean definitions and other configuration settings. They are annotated with **@Configuration** and various **@Conditional** annotations.

Sample Program: Auto-configuration using JPA and H2

Let us checkout the demonstration of auto-configuration with a simple example using Spring Data JPA and H2 database.

Entity Class

Create an entity class **User** with some basic fields and annotate it with **@Entity**.

```
package com.example.demo;


import javax.persistence.Entity;

import javax.persistence.GeneratedValue;

import javax.persistence.GenerationType;

import javax.persistence.Id;


@Entity

public class User {

    @Id
```

```java
    @GeneratedValue(strategy = GenerationType.IDENTITY)
    private Long id;
    private String name;
    private String email;

    // Getters and setters
}
```

Repository Interface

Create a repository interface **UserRepository** that extends **JpaRepository**.

```java
package com.example.demo;

import
org.springframework.data.jpa.repository.JpaRepository;

public interface UserRepository extends
JpaRepository<User, Long> {
}
```

CommandLineRunner to Preload Data

Use a **CommandLineRunner** to preload some data into the database.

```java
package com.example.demo;

import org.springframework.boot.CommandLineRunner;
```

```
import org.springframework.boot.SpringApplication;

import
org.springframework.boot.autoconfigure.SpringBootApplicat
ion;

import org.springframework.context.annotation.Bean;


@SpringBootApplication

public class DemoApplication {

    public static void main(String[] args) {

        SpringApplication.run(DemoApplication.class,
args);

    }


    @Bean

    public CommandLineRunner loadData(UserRepository
repository) {

        return args -> {

            repository.save(new User("John Doe",
"john@gitforgits.com"));

            repository.save(new User("Jane Doe",
"jane@gitforgits.com"));

        };

    }
```

```
}
```

Application Properties

Configure the H2 database in **application.properties**.

```
spring.datasource.url=jdbc:h2:mem:testdb

spring.datasource.driverClassName=org.h2.Driver

spring.datasource.username=sa

spring.datasource.password=password

spring.jpa.database-
platform=org.hibernate.dialect.H2Dialect

spring.h2.console.enabled=true
```

Once done as shown above, start the application. The auto-configuration mechanism will automatically configure the H2 database, the JPA entity manager, and the transaction manager. You can verify the data by accessing the H2 console at **http://localhost:8080/h2-console**.

Accessing Data via a REST Controller

Create a simple REST controller to expose the **User** data.

```
package com.example.demo;



import
org.springframework.beans.factory.annotation.Autowired;

import
org.springframework.web.bind.annotation.GetMapping;

import
org.springframework.web.bind.annotation.RestController;
```

```java
import java.util.List;


@RestController
public class UserController {


    @Autowired
    private UserRepository userRepository;


    @GetMapping("/users")
    public List<User> getAllUsers() {
        return userRepository.findAll();
    }
}
```

With the above setup, you can access the list of users by navigating to **http://localhost:8080/users**.

Customizing Auto-configuration

While Spring Boot's auto-configuration provides a convenient way to set up applications, there are scenarios where you may need to customize or override the default configurations to better suit your specific requirements. The customization of auto-configuration allows you to tweak the behavior of your application by providing custom beans, settings, or even replacing the default beans that Spring Boot configures.

Overriding Default Beans

One of the primary ways to customize auto-configuration is by overriding the default beans provided by Spring Boot. If you define a bean of the same type and name as the auto-configured bean, Spring Boot will use your custom bean instead of the default one.

Define a Custom DataSource Bean

Suppose you want to customize the **DataSource** bean to use a different configuration. You can define your own **DataSource** bean in a **@Configuration** class.

```
package com.example.demo;



import org.springframework.context.annotation.Bean;

import
org.springframework.context.annotation.Configuration;

import
org.springframework.beans.factory.annotation.Value;

import org.apache.commons.dbcp2.BasicDataSource;



import javax.sql.DataSource;



@Configuration

public class CustomDataSourceConfig {



    @Value("${custom.datasource.url}")

    private String url;
```

```
    @Value("${custom.datasource.username}")
    private String username;

    @Value("${custom.datasource.password}")
    private String password;

    @Bean
    public DataSource dataSource() {
        BasicDataSource dataSource = new
BasicDataSource();
        dataSource.setUrl(url);
        dataSource.setUsername(username);
        dataSource.setPassword(password);
        return dataSource;
    }
}
```

Configure Properties

Update your **application.properties** to include the custom data source properties.

```
custom.datasource.url=jdbc:mysql://localhost:3306/mydb
custom.datasource.username=root
custom.datasource.password=secret
```

By defining your own **DataSource** bean, Spring Boot will use it instead of the default auto-configured **DataSource**.

Conditional Beans and Customization

Spring Boot uses conditional annotations extensively to configure beans based on specific conditions. You can leverage the following annotations to customize the configuration further.

@ConditionalOnMissingBean

Use this annotation to provide a default bean only if a bean of the same type does not already exist.

```
package com.example.demo;



import
org.springframework.boot.autoconfigure.condition.Conditio
nalOnMissingBean;

import org.springframework.context.annotation.Bean;

import
org.springframework.context.annotation.Configuration;

import org.springframework.orm.jpa.JpaTransactionManager;

import
org.springframework.orm.jpa.LocalContainerEntityManagerFa
ctoryBean;

import
org.springframework.transaction.PlatformTransactionManage
r;



import javax.persistence.EntityManagerFactory;
```

```
@Configuration
public class CustomJpaConfig {

    @Bean
    @ConditionalOnMissingBean
    public LocalContainerEntityManagerFactoryBean
entityManagerFactory() {
        LocalContainerEntityManagerFactoryBean
factoryBean = new
LocalContainerEntityManagerFactoryBean();
        // Custom configuration here
        return factoryBean;
    }

    @Bean
    @ConditionalOnMissingBean
    public PlatformTransactionManager
transactionManager(EntityManagerFactory
entityManagerFactory) {
        return new
JpaTransactionManager(entityManagerFactory);
    }
}
```

In the above code snippet, **LocalContainerEntityManagerFactoryBean** and **PlatformTransactionManager** beans are provided only if they are not already defined in the application context.

@ConditionalOnProperty

Use this annotation to conditionally configure beans based on the value of a Spring environment property.

```
package com.example.demo;


import
org.springframework.boot.autoconfigure.condition.Conditio
nalOnProperty;

import
org.springframework.cache.annotation.EnableCaching;

import org.springframework.context.annotation.Bean;

import
org.springframework.context.annotation.Configuration;

import
org.springframework.cache.concurrent.ConcurrentMapCacheMa
nager;


@Configuration

@EnableCaching

public class CacheConfig {


    @Bean
```

```
    @ConditionalOnProperty(name = "cache.enabled",
havingValue = "true")

    public ConcurrentMapCacheManager cacheManager() {

        return new ConcurrentMapCacheManager("entities");

    }

}
```

In the above code snippet, the **ConcurrentMapCacheManager** bean is only created if the **cache.enabled** property is set to **true**.

Customizing Configuration with @ConfigurationProperties

Boot's **@ConfigurationProperties** annotation allows you to bind externalized properties to strongly-typed Java beans, making it easier to manage complex configurations.

Define a Configuration Properties Class

Create a class annotated with **@ConfigurationProperties** to map properties from **application.properties** or **application.yml**.

```
package com.example.demo;



import
org.springframework.boot.context.properties.Configuration
Properties;

import org.springframework.stereotype.Component;



@Component

@ConfigurationProperties(prefix = "app")

public class AppProperties {
```

```
    private String name;
    private String description;

    // Getters and setters

    public String getName() {
        return name;
    }

    public void setName(String name) {
        this.name = name;
    }

    public String getDescription() {
        return description;
    }

    public void setDescription(String description) {
        this.description = description;
    }
}
```

Configure Properties

Define the properties in **application.properties** or **application.yml**.

```
app.name=MyApplication

app.description=This is a sample Spring Boot application.
```

Use the Configuration Properties Bean

Inject the **AppProperties** bean into any Spring-managed component to access the configured properties.

```
package com.example.demo;


import
org.springframework.beans.factory.annotation.Autowired;

import org.springframework.stereotype.Service;


@Service

public class SomeService {


    private final AppProperties appProperties;


    @Autowired

    public SomeService(AppProperties appProperties) {

        this.appProperties = appProperties;

    }
```

```
    public void printAppProperties() {

        System.out.println("App Name: " +
appProperties.getName());

        System.out.println("App Description: " +
appProperties.getDescription());

    }

}
```

Customizing Auto-configuration with Custom Annotations

You can create custom annotations to combine multiple configuration aspects into a single annotation, simplifying the configuration process.

Define a Custom Annotation

Create a custom annotation that combines multiple Spring annotations.

```
package com.example.demo;



import
org.springframework.context.annotation.Configuration;

import org.springframework.context.annotation.Import;



import java.lang.annotation.ElementType;

import java.lang.annotation.Retention;

import java.lang.annotation.RetentionPolicy;

import java.lang.annotation.Target;
```

```
@Target(ElementType.TYPE)
@Retention(RetentionPolicy.RUNTIME)
@Import(FeatureConfig.class)
@Configuration
public @interface EnableFeature {
}
```

Create the Configuration Class

Define the configuration class that will be imported by the custom annotation.

```
package com.example.demo;


import org.springframework.context.annotation.Bean;
import
org.springframework.context.annotation.Configuration;


@Configuration
public class FeatureConfig {


    @Bean
    public SomeFeatureService someFeatureService() {
        return new SomeFeatureService();
    }
```

```
}
```

Use the Custom Annotation

Use the custom annotation in your main application class or any configuration class.

```
package com.example.demo;


import org.springframework.boot.SpringApplication;

import
org.springframework.boot.autoconfigure.SpringBootApplicat
ion;


@SpringBootApplication

@EnableFeature

public class DemoApplication {

    public static void main(String[] args) {

        SpringApplication.run(DemoApplication.class,
args);

    }

}
```

Your Spring Boot application configuration can be made easier and more modular with the help of custom annotations.

Exploring Spring Boot Starter POMs

Spring Boot Starter POMs provide a curated set of dependencies for different use cases, such as web applications, JPA, or security. These POMs simplify dependency management by grouping related dependencies into a single starter by simplifying adding the desired starter POM to your

pom.xml as shown below:

```
<dependencies>

    <dependency>

        <groupId>org.springframework.boot</groupId>

        <artifactId>spring-boot-starter-web</artifactId>

    </dependency>

    <dependency>

        <groupId>org.springframework.boot</groupId>

        <artifactId>spring-boot-starter-data-
jpa</artifactId>

    </dependency>

    <dependency>

        <groupId>org.springframework.boot</groupId>

        <artifactId>spring-boot-starter-
security</artifactId>

    </dependency>

</dependencies>
```

Using starter POMs reduces the complexity of managing individual dependencies and ensures compatibility among them. This ability to customize auto-configuration provides flexibility and control over how your Spring Boot application is configured and managed.

Using Conditional Beans

Conditional beans allow defining beans that are only created when certain conditions are met. This capability is useful for creating modular and flexible configurations that adapt based on the application's environment or the presence of specific classes, properties, or beans. Conditional beans are defined using various **@Conditional** annotations provided by Spring Framework.

Common Conditional Annotations

Spring Boot provides several conditional annotations to control bean creation:

- **@ConditionalOnClass**: Creates a bean only if a specific class is present on the classpath.
- **@ConditionalOnMissingBean**: Creates a bean only if a specific bean is not already defined in the application context.
- **@ConditionalOnProperty**: Creates a bean based on the value of a Spring environment property.
- **@ConditionalOnBean**: Creates a bean only if a specific bean is already defined in the application context.
- **@ConditionalOnMissingClass**: Creates a bean only if a specific class is not present on the classpath.

Sample Program: Using Conditional Annotations

Let us dive into how to use the above learned conditional annotations with a quick demonstration.

Using @ConditionalOnClass

This annotation checks for the presence of a specific class on the classpath before creating a bean. It's useful for enabling or disabling features based on the availability of third-party libraries. Let us take a simple example of conditional logging configuration.

```
package com.example.demo;


import org.springframework.context.annotation.Bean;

import
org.springframework.context.annotation.Configuration;

import
org.springframework.boot.autoconfigure.condition.Conditio
nalOnClass;

import ch.qos.logback.classic.Logger;
```

```
@Configuration
public class LoggingConfig {

    @Bean
    @ConditionalOnClass(Logger.class)
    public MyLoggingService loggingService() {
        return new MyLoggingService();
    }
}

public class MyLoggingService {
    // Logging service implementation
}
```

In the above code snippet, **MyLoggingService** is only created if the **Logger** class from Logback is present on the classpath.

Using @ConditionalOnMissingBean

This annotation creates a bean only if a specific bean is not already defined in the application context. See the following example on default service implementation.

```
package com.example.demo;

import org.springframework.context.annotation.Bean;
```

```
import
org.springframework.context.annotation.Configuration;
import
org.springframework.boot.autoconfigure.condition.Conditio
nalOnMissingBean;

@Configuration
public class DefaultServiceConfig {

    @Bean
    @ConditionalOnMissingBean
    public MyService myService() {
        return new DefaultMyService();
    }
}

public interface MyService {
    // Service methods
}

public class DefaultMyService implements MyService {
    // Default implementation
```

```
}
```

In the above code snippet, **DefaultMyService** is only created if no other **MyService** bean is defined.

Using @ConditionalOnProperty

This annotation creates a bean based on the value of a Spring environment property. Check out the following example on conditional cache manager.

```
package com.example.demo;


import org.springframework.context.annotation.Bean;

import
org.springframework.context.annotation.Configuration;

import
org.springframework.boot.autoconfigure.condition.Conditio
nalOnProperty;

import
org.springframework.cache.concurrent.ConcurrentMapCacheMa
nager;


@Configuration

public class CacheConfig {


    @Bean

    @ConditionalOnProperty(name = "cache.enabled",
havingValue = "true")

    public ConcurrentMapCacheManager cacheManager() {
```

```
        return new ConcurrentMapCacheManager("entities");
    }
}
```

```
cache.enabled=true
```

In this example, the **ConcurrentMapCacheManager** bean is only created if the **cache.enabled** property is set to **true**.

Using @ConditionalOnBean

This annotation creates a bean only if a specific bean is already defined in the application context. See the following example on the conditional audit service.

```
package com.example.demo;


import org.springframework.context.annotation.Bean;

import
org.springframework.context.annotation.Configuration;

import
org.springframework.boot.autoconfigure.condition.Conditio
nalOnBean;


@Configuration

public class AuditConfig {


    @Bean

    @ConditionalOnBean(name = "dataSource")
```

```
    public AuditService auditService() {
        return new AuditService();
    }
}

public class AuditService {
    // Audit service implementation
}
```

In this example, **`AuditService`** is only created if a **`dataSource`** bean is already defined in the application context.

Using @ConditionalOnMissingClass

This annotation creates a bean only if a specific class is not present on the classpath. Let us look into the example of implementing fallback service as below:

```
package com.example.demo;


import org.springframework.context.annotation.Bean;
import
org.springframework.context.annotation.Configuration;
import
org.springframework.boot.autoconfigure.condition.Conditio
nalOnMissingClass;


@Configuration
public class FallbackServiceConfig {
```

```
    @Bean
@ConditionalOnMissingClass("com.example.external.External
Service")
    public MyService fallbackService() {
        return new FallbackMyService();
    }
}

public class FallbackMyService implements MyService {
    // Fallback implementation
}
```

In the above code snippet, **`FallbackMyService`** is created only if **`com.example.external.ExternalService`** is not present on the classpath.

It is very evident from the above that the use of conditional beans provides a powerful mechanism to create flexible and modular applications. Leveraging these annotations helps to define beans that adapt to the application's environment and configuration dynamically.

Writing Custom Auto-configuration

Custom Auto-configuration Workflow

The creation of custom auto-configuration requires a series of steps to ensure your custom configurations are applied only when certain conditions are met. The typical workflow includes following 5 steps:

1. Define a class annotated with **`@Configuration`** to hold your custom configuration.
2. Apply conditional annotations to control when your custom configuration should be

applied.

3. If your configuration requires externalized properties, use **@ConfigurationProperties** to map them.
4. Register your custom configuration class in the **META-INF/spring.factories** file to enable auto-detection by Spring Boot.
5. Verify that your custom auto-configuration works as expected by creating test cases or running the application.

Sample Program: Writing Custom Auto-configuration

Now, we will create a custom auto-configuration for a hypothetical feature in our Spring Boot application wherein we assume that we need a custom auto-configuration for a logging service that should only be configured if a specific property is enabled.

Create the Configuration Properties Class

First, define a properties class to hold the configuration properties.

```
package com.example.demo;


import
org.springframework.boot.context.properties.Configuration
Properties;

import org.springframework.stereotype.Component;


@Component

@ConfigurationProperties(prefix = "custom.logging")

public class LoggingProperties {

    private boolean enabled;

    private String level;
```

```
    // Getters and setters

    public boolean isEnabled() {
        return enabled;
    }

    public void setEnabled(boolean enabled) {
        this.enabled = enabled;
    }

    public String getLevel() {
        return level;
    }

    public void setLevel(String level) {
        this.level = level;
    }
}
```

Create the Custom Configuration Class

Define a configuration class annotated with **`@Configuration`** and use conditional annotations to control when this configuration should be applied.

```
package com.example.demo;
```

```
import
org.springframework.boot.autoconfigure.condition.Conditio
nalOnProperty;

import org.springframework.context.annotation.Bean;

import
org.springframework.context.annotation.Configuration;


@Configuration

@ConditionalOnProperty(prefix = "custom.logging", name =
"enabled", havingValue = "true")

public class LoggingAutoConfiguration {


    private final LoggingProperties loggingProperties;


    public LoggingAutoConfiguration(LoggingProperties
loggingProperties) {

        this.loggingProperties = loggingProperties;

    }


    @Bean

    public LoggingService loggingService() {

        return new
LoggingService(loggingProperties.getLevel());
```

```
    }
}

public class LoggingService {
    private final String level;

    public LoggingService(String level) {
        this.level = level;
    }

    public void log(String message) {
        // Log the message at the specified level
        System.out.println("[" + level + "] " + message);
    }
}
```

In the above code snippet, **LoggingAutoConfiguration** is only applied if the **custom.logging.enabled** property is set to **true**.

Register the Configuration in spring.factories

Create a **META-INF/spring.factories** file if it doesn't exist, and register the custom auto-configuration class.

```
org.springframework.boot.autoconfigure.EnableAutoConfiguration=\
  com.example.demo.LoggingAutoConfiguration
```

Configure Properties

Add the necessary properties to **application.properties** or **application.yml**.

```
custom.logging.enabled=true

custom.logging.level=DEBUG
```

Test the Configuration

Create a test or run the application to verify that the custom auto-configuration is applied correctly.

```
package com.example.demo;



import org.springframework.boot.CommandLineRunner;

import org.springframework.boot.SpringApplication;

import
org.springframework.boot.autoconfigure.SpringBootApplicat
ion;

import org.springframework.context.annotation.Bean;



@SpringBootApplication

public class DemoApplication {

    public static void main(String[] args) {

        SpringApplication.run(DemoApplication.class,
args);

    }
```

```
    @Bean

    public CommandLineRunner
commandLineRunner(LoggingService loggingService) {

        return args -> {

            loggingService.log("This is a custom logging
message.");

        };

    }

}
```

When you run the application, the custom logging service should log messages at the specified level if the **`custom.logging.enabled`** property is set to **`true`**.

Exploring Starter POMs

Spring Boot Starter POMs (Project Object Models) are a set of curated dependency descriptors provided by Spring Boot to simplify the configuration of common libraries and frameworks. Starters are a set of convenient dependency descriptors that you can include in your application. They bring in a set of transitive dependencies that work well together, reducing the complexity of managing dependencies individually. This approach helps you get started quickly with a Spring Boot application.

Common Spring Boot Starter POMs

- **`spring-boot-starter`**: The core starter, including auto-configuration support, logging, and YAML configuration.
- **`spring-boot-starter-web`**: Starter for building web, including RESTful, applications using Spring MVC. It uses Tomcat as the default embedded container.
- **`spring-boot-starter-data-jpa`**: Starter for using Spring Data JPA with Hibernate.
- **`spring-boot-starter-security`**: Starter for using Spring Security.
- **`spring-boot-starter-test`**: Starter for testing Spring Boot applications with libraries such as JUnit, Hamcrest, and Mockito.

Sample Program: Using Starter POMs

We will explore some common Spring Boot Starter POMs with practical examples.

Using spring-boot-starter-web

The **spring-boot-starter-web** starter includes all the necessary dependencies to create a web application using Spring MVC, along with an embedded Tomcat server.

```
package com.example.demo;


import org.springframework.boot.SpringApplication;

import
org.springframework.boot.autoconfigure.SpringBootApplicat
ion;

import
org.springframework.web.bind.annotation.GetMapping;

import
org.springframework.web.bind.annotation.RestController;


@SpringBootApplication

public class DemoApplication {

    public static void main(String[] args) {

        SpringApplication.run(DemoApplication.class,
args);

    }

}
```

```
@RestController
class HelloController {
    @GetMapping("/hello")
    public String sayHello() {
        return "Hello, World!";
    }
}
```

Running this application will start an embedded Tomcat server and expose a REST endpoint at **`http://localhost:8080/hello`**.

Using spring-boot-starter-data-jpa

The **`spring-boot-starter-data-jpa`** starter includes dependencies for Spring Data JPA and Hibernate, making it easy to create applications that interact with relational databases.

```
package com.example.demo;


import javax.persistence.Entity;
import javax.persistence.GeneratedValue;
import javax.persistence.GenerationType;
import javax.persistence.Id;


@Entity
public class User {
    @Id
```

```
    @GeneratedValue(strategy = GenerationType.IDENTITY)
    private Long id;
    private String name;
    private String email;

    // Getters and setters
}
package com.example.demo;

import
org.springframework.data.jpa.repository.JpaRepository;

public interface UserRepository extends
JpaRepository<User, Long> {
}

package com.example.demo;

import org.springframework.boot.CommandLineRunner;
import org.springframework.boot.SpringApplication;
import
org.springframework.boot.autoconfigure.SpringBootApplicat
ion;
```

```
import org.springframework.context.annotation.Bean;


@SpringBootApplication
public class DemoApplication {
    public static void main(String[] args) {
        SpringApplication.run(DemoApplication.class,
args);
    }


    @Bean
    public CommandLineRunner loadData(UserRepository
repository) {
        return args -> {
            repository.save(new User("John Doe",
"john@gitforgits.com"));
            repository.save(new User("Jane Doe",
"jane@gitforgits.com"));
        };
    }
}
```

This configuration sets up a simple JPA repository and loads some initial data into an H2 in-memory database.

Using spring-boot-starter-security

The **`spring-boot-starter-security`** starter includes dependencies for Spring Security, allowing you to secure your application with minimal configuration.

```
package com.example.demo;



import org.springframework.context.annotation.Bean;

import
org.springframework.context.annotation.Configuration;

import
org.springframework.security.config.annotation.web.builde
rs.HttpSecurity;

import
org.springframework.security.config.annotation.web.config
uration.EnableWebSecurity;

import
org.springframework.security.config.annotation.web.config
uration.WebSecurityConfigurerAdapter;

import
org.springframework.security.core.userdetails.User;

import
org.springframework.security.core.userdetails.UserDetails
Service;

import
org.springframework.security.provisioning.InMemoryUserDet
ailsManager;
```

```
@Configuration
@EnableWebSecurity
public class SecurityConfig extends
WebSecurityConfigurerAdapter {

    @Override
    protected void configure(HttpSecurity http) throws
Exception {
        http
            .authorizeRequests()
                .antMatchers("/public").permitAll()
                .anyRequest().authenticated()
                .and()
            .formLogin()
                .and()
            .httpBasic();
    }

    @Bean
    @Override
    public UserDetailsService userDetailsService() {
        InMemoryUserDetailsManager manager = new
```

```
InMemoryUserDetailsManager();


manager.createUser(User.withDefaultPasswordEncoder().user
name("user").password("password").roles("USER").build());

        return manager;

    }

}


package com.example.demo;


import org.springframework.boot.SpringApplication;

import
org.springframework.boot.autoconfigure.SpringBootApplicat
ion;

import
org.springframework.web.bind.annotation.GetMapping;

import
org.springframework.web.bind.annotation.RestController;


@SpringBootApplication

public class DemoApplication {

    public static void main(String[] args) {

        SpringApplication.run(DemoApplication.class,
args);
```

```
    }
}

@RestController
class HelloController {
    @GetMapping("/public")
    public String publicEndpoint() {
        return "This is a public endpoint";
    }

    @GetMapping("/private")
    public String privateEndpoint() {
        return "This is a private endpoint";
    }
}
```

This configuration sets up basic security with form login and basic authentication. The public endpoint is accessible without authentication, while the private endpoint requires authentication.

Using spring-boot-starter-test

The **spring-boot-starter-test** starter includes testing libraries like JUnit, Hamcrest, and Mockito, making it easier to write unit and integration tests.

```
package com.example.demo;
```

```
import org.junit.jupiter.api.Test;

import
org.springframework.boot.test.context.SpringBootTest;


@SpringBootTest

public class DemoApplicationTests {


    @Test

    public void contextLoads() {

    }

}
```

This configuration sets up a basic test class to ensure that the application context loads correctly.

Using all these starters, one can quickly configure your application with the necessary libraries and frameworks, and can reduce boilerplate code, and maintain compatibility among dependencies.

Summary

Overall, the prime focus of this chapter was on customizing Spring Boot's auto-configuration. It began by explaining the working mechanism of auto-configuration, which uses the presence of certain classes and beans to automatically configure the application context. The chapter demonstrated how to customize auto-configuration by overriding default beans and using conditional annotations such as **`@ConditionalOnClass`**, **`@ConditionalOnMissingBean`**, and **`@ConditionalOnProperty`** to control bean creation based on specific conditions.

The process of writing custom auto-configuration was detailed, showing how to create a configuration class, use **`@ConfigurationProperties`** for externalized properties, and register the custom configuration in the **`spring.factories`** file. An example was provided to illustrate creating a custom logging service configuration that activates only when a specific property is enabled.

And, the last topic of this chapter explored Spring Boot Starter POMs wherein it highlighted the benefits of using starter dependencies to simplify and streamline project setup. Examples included are **spring-boot-starter-web**, **spring-boot-starter-data-jpa**, **spring-boot-starter-security**, and **spring-boot-starter-test** to quickly configure applications for web development, data access, security, and testing, respectively.

CHAPTER 6: DATA ACCESS WITH SPRING DATA JPA

Chapter Overview

This chapter drives us through the powerful capabilities of Spring Data JPA for managing and accessing data in Spring Boot applications. This chapter begins with an introduction to Spring Data JPA, explaining its role in simplifying database operations by providing a repository-based abstraction. You will learn how to configure a data source, setting up the necessary connections between your application and the database, ensuring efficient data handling. The chapter progresses to cover JPA entities and relationships, detailing how to map Java objects to database tables and define relationships such as one-to-one, one-to-many, and many-to-many. This understanding is crucial for modeling complex data structures. We will then explore query methods and custom queries, demonstrating how to use Spring Data JPA's repository methods to perform CRUD operations and create custom queries for more specific data retrieval needs.

Further, we will delve into the JPA Criteria API, a powerful tool for building type-safe queries programmatically. Paging and sorting will also be addressed, showing how to manage large datasets efficiently by retrieving data in manageable chunks and ordering it as required. The chapter will also cover handling transactions in Spring Boot, ensuring data integrity and consistency through transactional management. Finally, we will integrate Liquibase and Flyway for database migrations, providing you with tools to manage and version your database schema changes effectively. By the end of this chapter, you will have a solid understanding of using Spring Data JPA to manage data access in your Spring Boot applications, ensuring robust and maintainable data management practices.

Introduction to Spring Data JPA

Spring Data JPA is part of the larger Spring Data family, a collection of projects aimed at simplifying data access and providing a consistent programming model. Spring Data JPA specifically focuses on integrating the Java Persistence API (JPA) with the Spring Framework, offering a repository-based approach to managing and accessing relational data. It abstracts the complexity of data access layers, allowing developers to perform CRUD operations, create queries, and handle transactions with minimal boilerplate code.

Key Features of Spring Data JPA

- Spring Data JPA provides a repository abstraction over the JPA entities, enabling developers to perform CRUD operations without writing implementation code. The repository interfaces automatically generate the necessary queries based on method names and parameters.
- Methods in repository interfaces can be named following specific conventions, and Spring Data JPA will automatically generate the corresponding queries. For example, **`findByLastName(String lastName)`** generates a query to find entities by the

lastName field.

- In addition to derived queries, Spring Data JPA supports custom queries defined using the **@Query** annotation or through the JPA Criteria API.
- Built-in support for pagination and sorting allows developers to handle large datasets efficiently by retrieving data in chunks and ordering it according to specified criteria.
- Automatic auditing capabilities to track changes in entities, such as creation and modification timestamps.
- Seamless integration with other Spring projects like Spring Boot, Spring Security, and Spring MVC, providing a cohesive and comprehensive development experience.

Up and Running with Spring Data JPA

To get started with Spring Data JPA, you need to add the necessary dependencies to your project and configure your data source or you may simply follow the below given step-by-step procedure:

Add Dependencies

Ensure your **pom.xml** includes the Spring Data JPA and database driver dependencies as below:

```
<dependencies>

    <dependency>

        <groupId>org.springframework.boot</groupId>

        <artifactId>spring-boot-starter-data-
jpa</artifactId>

    </dependency>

    <dependency>

        <groupId>com.h2database</groupId>

        <artifactId>h2</artifactId>

        <scope>runtime</scope>

    </dependency>
```

```
</dependencies>
```

Configure Data Source

Define the data source properties in **application.properties**.

```
spring.datasource.url=jdbc:h2:mem:testdb

spring.datasource.username=sa

spring.datasource.password=password

spring.datasource.driver-class-name=org.h2.Driver

spring.jpa.database-
platform=org.hibernate.dialect.H2Dialect
```

Define JPA Entities

Create entity classes that represent the database tables. Annotate these classes with **@Entity** and define fields with **@Id** and other JPA annotations.

```
package com.example.demo;


import javax.persistence.Entity;

import javax.persistence.GeneratedValue;

import javax.persistence.GenerationType;

import javax.persistence.Id;


@Entity

public class User {

    @Id
```

```java
    @GeneratedValue(strategy = GenerationType.IDENTITY)
    private Long id;
    private String firstName;
    private String lastName;
    private String email;

    // Getters and setters
}
```

Create Repository Interfaces

Define repository interfaces that extend **`JpaRepository`**. These interfaces provide CRUD operations and can be extended with custom query methods.

```java
package com.example.demo;

import
org.springframework.data.jpa.repository.JpaRepository;

public interface UserRepository extends
JpaRepository<User, Long> {
    User findByLastName(String lastName);
}
```

Implement Service Layer

Create a service class to encapsulate the business logic and interact with the repository.

```
package com.example.demo;


import
org.springframework.beans.factory.annotation.Autowired;
import org.springframework.stereotype.Service;


import java.util.List;


@Service
public class UserService {


    @Autowired
    private UserRepository userRepository;


    public List<User> findAllUsers() {
        return userRepository.findAll();
    }


    public User findUserByLastName(String lastName) {
        return userRepository.findByLastName(lastName);
    }
```

```
    public void saveUser(User user) {
        userRepository.save(user);
    }
}
```

Create Controller Layer

Implement a controller to expose endpoints for accessing and managing user data.

```
package com.example.demo;


import
org.springframework.beans.factory.annotation.Autowired;
import org.springframework.web.bind.annotation.*;


import java.util.List;


@RestController
@RequestMapping("/users")
public class UserController {


    @Autowired
    private UserService userService;


    @GetMapping
```

```
    public List<User> getAllUsers() {
        return userService.findAllUsers();
    }

    @GetMapping("/{lastName}")
    public User getUserByLastName(@PathVariable String
lastName) {
        return userService.findUserByLastName(lastName);
    }

    @PostMapping
    public void saveUser(@RequestBody User user) {
        userService.saveUser(user);
    }
}
```

This introduction lays the foundation for the following topics in the chapter, where we will delve deeper into configuring data sources, managing JPA entities and relationships, using the JPA Criteria API, handling transactions, and integrating with Liquibase and Flyway for database migrations.

Configuring Data Source

Information like the database's URL, login credentials, and other connection properties are part of the data source configuration. With these settings in place, your app will be able to establish a connection to the database, execute CRUD commands, and process transactions. Next, we will go over the specifics of configuring the H2 in-memory database as a data source for our Spring Boot application using Spring Data JPA.

Adding Dependencies

To begin, you need to ensure that your project has the necessary dependencies for Spring Data JPA and the H2 database. These dependencies are added in the **pom.xml** file.

```
<dependencies>

    <dependency>

        <groupId>org.springframework.boot</groupId>

        <artifactId>spring-boot-starter-data-
jpa</artifactId>

    </dependency>

    <dependency>

        <groupId>com.h2database</groupId>

        <artifactId>h2</artifactId>

        <scope>runtime</scope>

    </dependency>

</dependencies>
```

In the above example code,

- **spring-boot-starter-data-jpa** provides the necessary libraries for Spring Data JPA, including Hibernate.
- **h2** dependency includes the H2 database driver, allowing our application to connect to an H2 in-memory database.

Defining Data Source Properties

Next, you need to configure the data source properties in the **application.properties** file. This configuration includes the JDBC URL, username, password, driver class, and additional JPA settings as shown below:

```
spring.datasource.url=jdbc:h2:mem:testdb
```

```
spring.datasource.username=sa

spring.datasource.password=password

spring.datasource.driver-class-name=org.h2.Driver

spring.jpa.database-
platform=org.hibernate.dialect.H2Dialect

spring.jpa.show-sql=true

spring.h2.console.enabled=true
```

In the above snippet,

- **spring.datasource.url**: The JDBC URL for the H2 database. **mem:testdb** indicates an in-memory database named **testdb**.
- **spring.datasource.username** and **spring.datasource.password**: Credentials for accessing the database.
- **spring.datasource.driver-class-name**: Specifies the driver class for H2.
- **spring.jpa.database-platform**: The Hibernate dialect for H2, ensuring Hibernate generates the appropriate SQL for H2.
- **spring.jpa.show-sql**: Enables logging of SQL statements.
- **spring.h2.console.enabled**: Enables the H2 web console for interactive database management.

Creating JPA Entities

Define JPA entities to map Java objects to database tables. Annotate these classes with **@Entity** and define fields with **@Id** and other relevant JPA annotations.

```
package com.example.demo;



import javax.persistence.Entity;

import javax.persistence.GeneratedValue;
```

```java
import javax.persistence.GenerationType;
import javax.persistence.Id;

@Entity
public class User {
    @Id
    @GeneratedValue(strategy = GenerationType.IDENTITY)
    private Long id;
    private String firstName;
    private String lastName;
    private String email;

    // Getters and setters

    public Long getId() {
        return id;
    }

    public void setId(Long id) {
        this.id = id;
    }
```

```
public String getFirstName() {
    return firstName;
}

public void setFirstName(String firstName) {
    this.firstName = firstName;
}

public String getLastName() {
    return lastName;
}

public void setLastName(String lastName) {
    this.lastName = lastName;
}

public String getEmail() {
    return email;
}
```

```
    public void setEmail(String email) {
        this.email = email;
    }
}
```

In this above example,

- **@Entity** marks this class as a JPA entity.
- **@Id** and **@GeneratedValue** indicate that the **id** field is the primary key and its value is generated automatically.

Creating Repository Interfaces

Define repository interfaces that extend **JpaRepository** to provide CRUD operations for the entities.

```
package com.example.demo;


import
org.springframework.data.jpa.repository.JpaRepository;


public interface UserRepository extends
JpaRepository<User, Long> {
    User findByLastName(String lastName);
}
```

In the above snippet,

- **JpaRepository<User, Long>** provides CRUD operations for the **User** entity.
- **findByLastName(String lastName)** method will generate a query to find a user by their last name.

Implementing Service Layer

First, create a service class to encapsulate business logic and interact with the repository.

```
package com.example.demo;


import
org.springframework.beans.factory.annotation.Autowired;

import org.springframework.stereotype.Service;


import java.util.List;


@Service

public class UserService {


    @Autowired

    private UserRepository userRepository;


    public List<User> findAllUsers() {

        return userRepository.findAll();

    }


    public User findUserByLastName(String lastName) {

        return userRepository.findByLastName(lastName);
```

```
    }


    public void saveUser(User user) {
        userRepository.save(user);
    }
}
```

Here in the above code,

- **@Service** marks this class as a service component.
- **UserService** provides methods to find all users, find a user by last name, and save a user.

Creating Controller Layer

Now, implement a controller to expose REST endpoints for accessing and managing user data.

```
package com.example.demo;


import
org.springframework.beans.factory.annotation.Autowired;
import org.springframework.web.bind.annotation.*;


import java.util.List;


@RestController
@RequestMapping("/users")
public class UserController {
```

```
    @Autowired
    private UserService userService;


    @GetMapping
    public List<User> getAllUsers() {
        return userService.findAllUsers();
    }


    @GetMapping("/{lastName}")
    public User getUserByLastName(@PathVariable String
lastName) {
        return userService.findUserByLastName(lastName);
    }


    @PostMapping
    public void saveUser(@RequestBody User user) {
        userService.saveUser(user);
    }
}
```

The above code snippet implements,

- **`@RestController`** marks this class as a REST controller.

- **@RequestMapping("/users")** specifies the base URL for the endpoints.
- Methods annotated with **@GetMapping** and **@PostMapping** handle HTTP GET and POST requests, respectively.

Following this above method will get us configured the data source for your Spring Boot application, ensuring a seamless connection to the H2 database. This setup enables efficient data management and access, forming the foundation for more advanced data access and manipulation tasks covered in subsequent sections.

JPA Entities and Relationships

JPA (Java Persistence API) provides a way to map Java objects to relational database tables. In Spring Data JPA, entities are Java classes that are annotated to define the relationship between the class and the database table. This section will explore how to define JPA entities and various types of relationships, such as one-to-one, one-to-many, many-to-one, and many-to-many, in the context of our project.

Defining JPA Entities

A JPA entity is a lightweight, persistent domain object. To define an entity, annotate the class with **@Entity** and specify the table name using **@Table** (optional). Each entity must have an **@Id** field that represents the primary key.

```
package com.example.demo;


import javax.persistence.Entity;

import javax.persistence.GeneratedValue;

import javax.persistence.GenerationType;

import javax.persistence.Id;


@Entity

public class User {

    @Id
```

```
    @GeneratedValue(strategy = GenerationType.IDENTITY)
    private Long id;
    private String firstName;
    private String lastName;
    private String email;

    // Getters and setters
}
```

One-to-One Relationship

A one-to-one relationship is where one entity is associated with exactly one instance of another entity. This can be represented using **@OneToOne**.

```
package com.example.demo;

import javax.persistence.*;

@Entity
public class UserProfile {
    @Id
    @GeneratedValue(strategy = GenerationType.IDENTITY)
    private Long id;
    private String address;
    private String phoneNumber;
```

```
    @OneToOne

    @JoinColumn(name = "user_id")

    private User user;



    // Getters and setters

}
```

In this example:

- **@OneToOne** specifies a one-to-one relationship.
- **@JoinColumn(name = "user_id")** defines the foreign key column in **UserProfile** that references the **User** entity.

One-to-Many and Many-to-One Relationships

A one-to-many relationship is where one entity is associated with multiple instances of another entity. The inverse of this is a many-to-one relationship.

```
package com.example.demo;



import javax.persistence.*;

import java.util.Date;



@Entity

public class Order {

    @Id

    @GeneratedValue(strategy = GenerationType.IDENTITY)
```

```
    private Long id;
    private Date orderDate;
    private Double amount;

    @ManyToOne
    @JoinColumn(name = "user_id")
    private User user;

    // Getters and setters
}
```

Following is the User.java (updated):

```
package com.example.demo;

import javax.persistence.*;
import java.util.List;

@Entity
public class User {
    @Id
    @GeneratedValue(strategy = GenerationType.IDENTITY)
    private Long id;
```

```
    private String firstName;

    private String lastName;

    private String email;


    @OneToMany(mappedBy = "user")

    private List<Order> orders;


    // Getters and setters

}
```

In these examples:

- **`@ManyToOne`** in **`Order`** specifies a many-to-one relationship to **`User`**.
- **`@JoinColumn(name = "user_id")`** defines the foreign key column in **`Order`** that references the **`User`** entity.
- **`@OneToMany(mappedBy = "user")`** in **`User`** specifies the one-to-many relationship and references the **`user`** field in **`Order`**.

Many-to-Many Relationship

A many-to-many relationship is where multiple instances of one entity are associated with multiple instances of another entity. This is typically represented using a join table.

```
package com.example.demo;


import javax.persistence.*;

import java.util.List;
```

```
@Entity
public class Role {
    @Id
    @GeneratedValue(strategy = GenerationType.IDENTITY)
    private Long id;
    private String name;

    @ManyToMany(mappedBy = "roles")
    private List<User> users;

    // Getters and setters
}

package com.example.demo;

import javax.persistence.*;
import java.util.List;

@Entity
public class User {
    @Id
```

```
    @GeneratedValue(strategy = GenerationType.IDENTITY)
    private Long id;
    private String firstName;
    private String lastName;
    private String email;

    @OneToMany(mappedBy = "user")
    private List<Order> orders;

    @ManyToMany
    @JoinTable(
        name = "user_role",
        joinColumns = @JoinColumn(name = "user_id"),
        inverseJoinColumns = @JoinColumn(name =
"role_id")
    )
    private List<Role> roles;

    // Getters and setters
}
```

In the above code snippet:

- **`@ManyToMany`** in **`Role`** specifies a many-to-many relationship to **`User`**.

- **@ManyToMany** in **User** specifies the many-to-many relationship to **Role**.
- **@JoinTable** defines the join table **user_role** with join columns **user_id** and **role_id**.

You have successfully defined JPA entities and numerous relationships in your Spring Boot application by following these detailed steps. In this configuration, you can efficiently manage and access relational data, which paves the way for more complex data manipulation tasks.

Query Methods and Custom Queries

Spring Data JPA simplifies the data access layer by providing a repository abstraction and powerful query capabilities. Query methods are defined in repository interfaces and allow you to perform CRUD operations and more complex queries using method names. Custom queries, on the other hand, are explicitly defined using the **@Query** annotation or the JPA Criteria API. This section will explore how to define query methods and write custom queries using our ongoing example project.

Defining Query Methods

Spring Data JPA allows you to define query methods directly in your repository interfaces. These methods are automatically translated into queries based on their names. We will explore how to define these methods.

```
package com.example.demo;



import
org.springframework.data.jpa.repository.JpaRepository;

import java.util.List;



public interface UserRepository extends
JpaRepository<User, Long> {

    User findByLastName(String lastName);

    List<User> findByFirstName(String firstName);
```

```
    List<User> findByFirstNameAndLastName(String
firstName, String lastName);

    List<User> findByEmailContaining(String email);

}
```

In this example:

- **findByLastName(String lastName)** generates a query to find a user by their last name.
- **findByFirstName(String firstName)** finds users with the specified first name.
- **findByFirstNameAndLastName(String firstName, String lastName)** finds users matching both first and last names.
- **findByEmailContaining(String email)** finds users whose email contains the specified string.

Now, by using query methods:

```
package com.example.demo;


import
org.springframework.beans.factory.annotation.Autowired;

import org.springframework.web.bind.annotation.*;

import java.util.List;


@RestController

@RequestMapping("/users")

public class UserController {
```

```
    @Autowired
    private UserService userService;


    @GetMapping
    public List<User> getAllUsers() {
        return userService.findAllUsers();
    }


    @GetMapping("/lastname/{lastName}")
    public User getUserByLastName(@PathVariable String
lastName) {
        return userService.findUserByLastName(lastName);
    }


    @GetMapping("/firstname/{firstName}")
    public List<User> getUsersByFirstName(@PathVariable
String firstName) {
        return
userService.findUsersByFirstName(firstName);
    }


    @GetMapping("/fullname")
```

```
    public List<User>
getUsersByFirstAndLastName(@RequestParam String
firstName, @RequestParam String lastName) {

        return
userService.findUsersByFirstAndLastName(firstName,
lastName);

    }



    @GetMapping("/email/{email}")

    public List<User>
getUsersByEmailContaining(@PathVariable String email) {

        return
userService.findUsersByEmailContaining(email);

    }



    @PostMapping

    public void saveUser(@RequestBody User user) {

        userService.saveUser(user);

    }

}
```

With these additions, you can now perform various queries through HTTP endpoints.

Writing Custom Queries with @Query

Sometimes, the derived query methods are not sufficient for complex queries. In such cases, you can use the **`@Query`** annotation to define custom queries.

```
package com.example.demo;

import
org.springframework.data.jpa.repository.JpaRepository;
import org.springframework.data.jpa.repository.Query;
import org.springframework.data.repository.query.Param;
import java.util.List;

public interface UserRepository extends
JpaRepository<User, Long> {

    User findByLastName(String lastName);

    List<User> findByFirstName(String firstName);

    List<User> findByFirstNameAndLastName(String
firstName, String lastName);

    List<User> findByEmailContaining(String email);

    @Query("SELECT u FROM User u WHERE u.email = :email")
    User findUserByEmail(@Param("email") String email);
```

```
    @Query("SELECT u FROM User u WHERE u.firstName LIKE
%:name% OR u.lastName LIKE %:name%")

    List<User> findUsersByNameContaining(@Param("name")
String name);

}
```

In this example:

- **findUserByEmail(@Param("email") String email)** uses the **@Query** annotation to define a custom JPQL query to find a user by email.
- **findUsersByNameContaining(@Param("name") String name)** defines a custom query to find users whose first or last name contains the specified string.

And by using custom queries,

```
package com.example.demo;


import
org.springframework.beans.factory.annotation.Autowired;

import org.springframework.web.bind.annotation.*;

import java.util.List;


@RestController

@RequestMapping("/users")

public class UserController {


    @Autowired
```

```
    private UserService userService;


    @GetMapping
    public List<User> getAllUsers() {
        return userService.findAllUsers();
    }


    @GetMapping("/lastname/{lastName}")
    public User getUserByLastName(@PathVariable String
lastName) {
        return userService.findUserByLastName(lastName);
    }


    @GetMapping("/firstname/{firstName}")
    public List<User> getUsersByFirstName(@PathVariable
String firstName) {
        return
userService.findUsersByFirstName(firstName);
    }


    @GetMapping("/fullname")
    public List<User>
getUsersByFirstAndLastName(@RequestParam String
```

```
firstName, @RequestParam String lastName) {
        return
userService.findUsersByFirstAndLastName(firstName,
lastName);
    }

    @GetMapping("/email/{email}")
    public List<User>
getUsersByEmailContaining(@PathVariable String email) {
        return
userService.findUsersByEmailContaining(email);
    }

    @GetMapping("/email")
    public User getUserByEmail(@RequestParam String
email) {
        return userService.findUserByEmail(email);
    }

    @GetMapping("/name/{name}")
    public List<User>
getUsersByNameContaining(@PathVariable String name) {
        return
userService.findUsersByNameContaining(name);
```

```
    }


    @PostMapping
    public void saveUser(@RequestBody User user) {
        userService.saveUser(user);
    }
}
```

Using JPA Criteria API

The JPA Criteria API provides a type-safe way to create dynamic queries in Java. Unlike JPQL (Java Persistence Query Language), which uses string-based queries, the Criteria API allows you to build queries programmatically using Java objects. This is particularly useful when building complex queries dynamically, as it avoids syntax errors and provides compile-time safety.

Why Criteria API?

1. The Criteria API leverages the type system of Java to ensure that queries are type-safe, reducing runtime errors and improving code reliability.
2. It enables the creation of dynamic queries that can be constructed programmatically based on various conditions at runtime.
3. Criteria queries are easier to refactor and maintain compared to string-based JPQL queries, as they are constructed using Java code.
4. It is suitable for building complex queries with multiple predicates and conditions that would be cumbersome to write in JPQL.

Sample Program: Using JPA Criteria API

We will explore how to use the Criteria API with our ongoing example project. First, the Criteria API is part of the JPA specification, so no additional dependencies are needed beyond the existing JPA setup.

Creating a Custom Repository Interface

Define a custom repository interface for methods that will use the Criteria API.

```
package com.example.demo;


import java.util.List;


public interface UserRepositoryCustom {

    List<User> findUsersByCriteria(String email, String
firstName, String lastName);

}
```

Implementing Custom Repository

Implement the custom repository interface using the Criteria API to build dynamic queries.

```
package com.example.demo;


import
org.springframework.beans.factory.annotation.Autowired;

import javax.persistence.EntityManager;

import javax.persistence.criteria.CriteriaBuilder;

import javax.persistence.criteria.CriteriaQuery;

import javax.persistence.criteria.Predicate;

import javax.persistence.criteria.Root;

import java.util.ArrayList;
```

```
import java.util.List;

public class UserRepositoryCustomImpl implements
UserRepositoryCustom {

    @Autowired
    private EntityManager entityManager;

    @Override
    public List<User> findUsersByCriteria(String email,
String firstName, String lastName) {
        CriteriaBuilder cb =
entityManager.getCriteriaBuilder();
        CriteriaQuery<User> query =
cb.createQuery(User.class);
        Root<User> user = query.from(User.class);

        List<Predicate> predicates = new ArrayList<>();

        if (email != null && !email.isEmpty()) {
            predicates.add(cb.equal(user.get("email"),
email));
        }
```

```
        if (firstName != null && !firstName.isEmpty()) {
            predicates.add(cb.like(user.get("firstName"),
"%" + firstName + "%"));
        }
        if (lastName != null && !lastName.isEmpty()) {
            predicates.add(cb.like(user.get("lastName"),
"%" + lastName + "%"));
        }

        query.where(predicates.toArray(new
Predicate[0]));

        return
entityManager.createQuery(query).getResultList();
    }
}
```

In this implementation:

- **CriteriaBuilder** is used to construct the query.
- **CriteriaQuery** represents the query.
- **Root** defines the query's source (the **User** entity).
- **Predicate** objects represent the conditions in the query.

Extending Main Repository Interface

Extend the main repository interface to include the custom repository.

```
package com.example.demo;
```

```
import
org.springframework.data.jpa.repository.JpaRepository;


public interface UserRepository extends
JpaRepository<User, Long>, UserRepositoryCustom {
}
```

Criteria API in Service Layer

Add a method in the service layer to use the new Criteria API query.

```
package com.example.demo;


import
org.springframework.beans.factory.annotation.Autowired;
import org.springframework.stereotype.Service;
import java.util.List;


@Service
public class UserService {


    @Autowired
    private UserRepository userRepository;
```

```
    public List<User> findAllUsers() {
        return userRepository.findAll();
    }


    public User findUserByLastName(String lastName) {
        return userRepository.findByLastName(lastName);
    }


    public List<User> findUsersByFirstName(String
firstName) {
        return userRepository.findByFirstName(firstName);
    }


    public List<User> findUsersByFirstAndLastName(String
firstName, String lastName) {
        return
userRepository.findByFirstNameAndLastName(firstName,
lastName);
    }


    public List<User> findUsersByEmailContaining(String
email) {
        return
```

```
userRepository.findByEmailContaining(email);

    }


    public User findUserByEmail(String email) {

        return userRepository.findUserByEmail(email);

    }


    public List<User> findUsersByNameContaining(String
name) {

        return
userRepository.findUsersByNameContaining(name);

    }


    public List<User> findUsersByCriteria(String email,
String firstName, String lastName) {

        return userRepository.findUsersByCriteria(email,
firstName, lastName);

    }


    public void saveUser(User user) {

        userRepository.save(user);

    }

}
```

Exposing Criteria API Query in Controller Layer

Add an endpoint in the controller layer to use the Criteria API query.

```
package com.example.demo;


import
org.springframework.beans.factory.annotation.Autowired;

import org.springframework.web.bind.annotation.*;

import java.util.List;


@RestController

@RequestMapping("/users")

public class UserController {


    @Autowired

    private UserService userService;


    @GetMapping

    public List<User> getAllUsers() {

        return userService.findAllUsers();

    }


    @GetMapping("/lastname/{lastName}")
```

```
    public User getUserByLastName(@PathVariable String
lastName) {

        return userService.findUserByLastName(lastName);

    }


    @GetMapping("/firstname/{firstName}")

    public List<User> getUsersByFirstName(@PathVariable
String firstName) {

        return
userService.findUsersByFirstName(firstName);

    }


    @GetMapping("/fullname")

    public List<User>
getUsersByFirstAndLastName(@RequestParam String
firstName, @RequestParam String lastName) {

        return
userService.findUsersByFirstAndLastName(firstName,
lastName);

    }


    @GetMapping("/email/{email}")

    public List<User>
getUsersByEmailContaining(@PathVariable String email) {
```

```
        return
userService.findUsersByEmailContaining(email);

    }


    @GetMapping("/email")

    public User getUserByEmail(@RequestParam String
email) {

        return userService.findUserByEmail(email);

    }


    @GetMapping("/name/{name}")

    public List<User>
getUsersByNameContaining(@PathVariable String name) {

        return
userService.findUsersByNameContaining(name);

    }


    @GetMapping("/criteria")

    public List<User>
getUsersByCriteria(@RequestParam(required = false) String
email,


@RequestParam(required = false) String firstName,
```

```
@RequestParam(required = false) String lastName) {
        return userService.findUsersByCriteria(email,
firstName, lastName);
    }


    @PostMapping
    public void saveUser(@RequestBody User user) {
        userService.saveUser(user);
    }
}
```

This endpoint allows clients to perform searches using dynamic criteria provided as request parameters.

Following these steps will teach you how to use the JPA Criteria API to create dynamic, type-safe queries in a Spring Boot application. Your application will be able to retrieve and manage data efficiently with this approach's flexibility and power for handling complex query scenarios.

Paging and Sorting with Spring Data JPA

Brief Overview

Paging and sorting are of importance when dealing with large datasets in an application. They help manage and display data efficiently by dividing it into manageable chunks and ordering it based on specified criteria. Spring Data JPA provides built-in support for paging and sorting, simplifying these tasks with minimal configuration.

Setting up Paging and Sorting

Spring Data JPA's repository interfaces extend **`PagingAndSortingRepository`**, which adds methods to handle pagination and sorting. In this section, we will explore how to use these features in our ongoing example project.

Extend Repository Interface

Ensure that your repository interface extends **PagingAndSortingRepository** or **JpaRepository**, as both provide paging and sorting capabilities.

```
package com.example.demo;



import
org.springframework.data.jpa.repository.JpaRepository;

import
org.springframework.data.repository.PagingAndSortingRepos
itory;



public interface UserRepository extends
JpaRepository<User, Long>, UserRepositoryCustom {

}
```

In this case, **JpaRepository** already extends **PagingAndSortingRepository**, so it includes methods for paging and sorting.

Using Paging and Sorting in the Service Layer

Add methods in the service layer to handle paging and sorting.

```
package com.example.demo;



import
org.springframework.beans.factory.annotation.Autowired;

import org.springframework.data.domain.Page;

import org.springframework.data.domain.PageRequest;
```

```
import org.springframework.data.domain.Pageable;

import org.springframework.data.domain.Sort;

import org.springframework.stereotype.Service;


import java.util.List;


@Service

public class UserService {


    @Autowired

    private UserRepository userRepository;


    public List<User> findAllUsers() {

        return userRepository.findAll();

    }


    public User findUserByLastName(String lastName) {

        return userRepository.findByLastName(lastName);

    }


    public List<User> findUsersByFirstName(String
firstName) {
```

```
        return userRepository.findByFirstName(firstName);

    }


    public List<User> findUsersByFirstAndLastName(String
firstName, String lastName) {

        return
userRepository.findByFirstNameAndLastName(firstName,
lastName);

    }


    public List<User> findUsersByEmailContaining(String
email) {

        return
userRepository.findByEmailContaining(email);

    }


    public User findUserByEmail(String email) {

        return userRepository.findUserByEmail(email);

    }


    public List<User> findUsersByNameContaining(String
name) {

        return
userRepository.findUsersByNameContaining(name);
```

```
    }


    public List<User> findUsersByCriteria(String email,
String firstName, String lastName) {
        return userRepository.findUsersByCriteria(email,
firstName, lastName);
    }


    public void saveUser(User user) {
        userRepository.save(user);
    }


    public Page<User> findPaginatedUsers(int page, int
size) {
        Pageable pageable = PageRequest.of(page, size);
        return userRepository.findAll(pageable);
    }


    public Page<User> findSortedUsers(int page, int size,
String sortBy) {
        Pageable pageable = PageRequest.of(page, size,
Sort.by(sortBy));
        return userRepository.findAll(pageable);
```

```
    }
}
```

In this example:

- **findPaginatedUsers(int page, int size)** retrieves users in a paginated manner.
- **findSortedUsers(int page, int size, String sortBy)** retrieves users with pagination and sorting.

Exposing Paging and Sorting Endpoints in the Controller Layer

Add endpoints in the controller layer to access paginated and sorted data.

```
package com.example.demo;


import
org.springframework.beans.factory.annotation.Autowired;
import org.springframework.data.domain.Page;
import org.springframework.web.bind.annotation.*;


import java.util.List;


@RestController
@RequestMapping("/users")
public class UserController {


    @Autowired
```

```
    private UserService userService;


    @GetMapping
    public List<User> getAllUsers() {
        return userService.findAllUsers();
    }


    @GetMapping("/lastname/{lastName}")
    public User getUserByLastName(@PathVariable String
lastName) {
        return userService.findUserByLastName(lastName);
    }


    @GetMapping("/firstname/{firstName}")
    public List<User> getUsersByFirstName(@PathVariable
String firstName) {
        return
userService.findUsersByFirstName(firstName);
    }


    @GetMapping("/fullname")
    public List<User>
getUsersByFirstAndLastName(@RequestParam String
```

```
firstName, @RequestParam String lastName) {

        return
userService.findUsersByFirstAndLastName(firstName,
lastName);

    }


    @GetMapping("/email/{email}")

    public List<User>
getUsersByEmailContaining(@PathVariable String email) {

        return
userService.findUsersByEmailContaining(email);

    }


    @GetMapping("/email")

    public User getUserByEmail(@RequestParam String
email) {

        return userService.findUserByEmail(email);

    }


    @GetMapping("/name/{name}")

    public List<User>
getUsersByNameContaining(@PathVariable String name) {

        return
userService.findUsersByNameContaining(name);
```

```
    }


    @GetMapping("/criteria")

    public List<User>
getUsersByCriteria(@RequestParam(required = false) String
email,

@RequestParam(required = false) String firstName,

@RequestParam(required = false) String lastName) {

        return userService.findUsersByCriteria(email,
firstName, lastName);

    }


    @PostMapping

    public void saveUser(@RequestBody User user) {

        userService.saveUser(user);

    }


    @GetMapping("/paginated")

    public Page<User> getPaginatedUsers(@RequestParam int
page, @RequestParam int size) {

        return userService.findPaginatedUsers(page,
size);
```

```
    }


    @GetMapping("/sorted")
    public Page<User> getSortedUsers(@RequestParam int
page, @RequestParam int size, @RequestParam String
sortBy) {
        return userService.findSortedUsers(page, size,
sortBy);
    }
}
```

These endpoints allow clients to request paginated and sorted data.

Following these steps, you learn to implement paging and sorting using Spring Data JPA in your Spring Boot application. These features help manage and display large datasets efficiently, enhancing the performance and user experience of your application.

Handling Transactions in Spring Boot

Transactions ensure the integrity and consistency of data in your application. They allow multiple operations to be executed as a single unit of work, ensuring that either all operations succeed or none do. Spring Boot simplifies transaction management using annotations, making it easy to ensure data integrity and consistency across multiple operations.

Enabling Transaction Management

To use transactions in Spring Boot, you need to enable transaction management by annotating a configuration class with **@EnableTransactionManagement**.

```
package com.example.demo;


import
org.springframework.context.annotation.Configuration;
```

```
import
org.springframework.transaction.annotation.EnableTransact
ionManagement;


@Configuration

@EnableTransactionManagement

public class ApplicationConfig {

}
```

Using @Transactional Annotation

The **@Transactional** annotation is used to define the scope of a transaction at the method level. When a method annotated with **@Transactional** is called, a transaction is started, and it commits when the method completes successfully. If an exception occurs, the transaction is rolled back. Let us take an example to explore this annotation in detail with following steps:

Defining the Service

We will update the **UserService** to include a method that performs multiple database operations within a transaction.

```
package com.example.demo;


import
org.springframework.beans.factory.annotation.Autowired;

import org.springframework.stereotype.Service;

import
org.springframework.transaction.annotation.Transactional;


import java.util.List;
```

```
@Service
public class UserService {

    @Autowired
    private UserRepository userRepository;

    @Autowired
    private OrderRepository orderRepository;

    public List<User> findAllUsers() {
        return userRepository.findAll();
    }

    public User findUserByLastName(String lastName) {
        return userRepository.findByLastName(lastName);
    }

    public List<User> findUsersByFirstName(String
firstName) {
        return userRepository.findByFirstName(firstName);
    }
```

```
    public List<User> findUsersByFirstAndLastName(String
firstName, String lastName) {

        return
userRepository.findByFirstNameAndLastName(firstName,
lastName);

    }


    public List<User> findUsersByEmailContaining(String
email) {

        return
userRepository.findByEmailContaining(email);

    }


    public User findUserByEmail(String email) {

        return userRepository.findUserByEmail(email);

    }


    public List<User> findUsersByNameContaining(String
name) {

        return
userRepository.findUsersByNameContaining(name);

    }
```

```
    public List<User> findUsersByCriteria(String email,
String firstName, String lastName) {

        return userRepository.findUsersByCriteria(email,
firstName, lastName);

    }


    public void saveUser(User user) {

        userRepository.save(user);

    }


    @Transactional

    public void createUserWithOrder(User user, Order
order) {

        userRepository.save(user);

        order.setUser(user);

        orderRepository.save(order);

    }

}
```

In the above code snippet, the **createUserWithOrder** method is annotated with **@Transactional**, meaning that both the user and order creation operations will be executed within a single transaction. If either operation fails, both will be rolled back.

Testing the Transaction

We will create a controller method to test our transactional method.

```
package com.example.demo;

import
org.springframework.beans.factory.annotation.Autowired;
import org.springframework.web.bind.annotation.*;

import java.util.List;

@RestController
@RequestMapping("/users")
public class UserController {

    @Autowired
    private UserService userService;

    @GetMapping
    public List<User> getAllUsers() {
        return userService.findAllUsers();
    }

    @GetMapping("/lastname/{lastName}")
    public User getUserByLastName(@PathVariable String
```

```
lastName) {
        return userService.findUserByLastName(lastName);
    }

    @GetMapping("/firstname/{firstName}")
    public List<User> getUsersByFirstName(@PathVariable
String firstName) {
        return
userService.findUsersByFirstName(firstName);
    }

    @GetMapping("/fullname")
    public List<User>
getUsersByFirstAndLastName(@RequestParam String
firstName, @RequestParam String lastName) {
        return
userService.findUsersByFirstAndLastName(firstName,
lastName);
    }

    @GetMapping("/email/{email}")
    public List<User>
getUsersByEmailContaining(@PathVariable String email) {
        return
```

```
userService.findUsersByEmailContaining(email);
    }

    @GetMapping("/email")
    public User getUserByEmail(@RequestParam String
email) {
        return userService.findUserByEmail(email);
    }

    @GetMapping("/name/{name}")
    public List<User>
getUsersByNameContaining(@PathVariable String name) {
        return
userService.findUsersByNameContaining(name);
    }

    @GetMapping("/criteria")
    public List<User>
getUsersByCriteria(@RequestParam(required = false) String
email,

@RequestParam(required = false) String firstName,

@RequestParam(required = false) String lastName) {
```

```
        return userService.findUsersByCriteria(email,
firstName, lastName);

    }


    @PostMapping

    public void saveUser(@RequestBody User user) {

        userService.saveUser(user);

    }


    @PostMapping("/createUserWithOrder")

    public void createUserWithOrder(@RequestBody
CreateUserWithOrderRequest request) {


userService.createUserWithOrder(request.getUser(),
request.getOrder());

    }

}


class CreateUserWithOrderRequest {

    private User user;

    private Order order;


    public User getUser() {
```

```
        return user;
    }

    public void setUser(User user) {
        this.user = user;
    }

    public Order getOrder() {
        return order;
    }

    public void setOrder(Order order) {
        this.order = order;
    }
}
```

This controller method allows us to test the transactional **createUserWithOrder** method via an HTTP POST request.

Transaction Scenarios

Successful Transaction

Both User and Order entities are saved successfully within a single transaction.

```
POST http://localhost:8080/users/createUserWithOrder
Content-Type: application/json
```

```
{
    "user": {
        "firstName": "John",
        "lastName": "Doe",
        "email": "john.doe@gitforgits.com"
    },
    "order": {
        "orderDate": "2023-07-20",
        "amount": 100.0
    }
}
```

If this request is successful, both the user and order are saved to the database.

Transaction Rollback

We will simulate an error to see how the transaction is rolled back. Assume we add a validation constraint on the **`Order`** amount.

```
package com.example.demo;


import javax.persistence.*;
import javax.validation.constraints.Min;
import java.util.Date;
```

```java
@Entity
public class Order {
    @Id
    @GeneratedValue(strategy = GenerationType.IDENTITY)
    private Long id;
    private Date orderDate;

    @Min(0)
    private Double amount;

    @ManyToOne
    @JoinColumn(name = "user_id")
    private User user;

    // Getters and setters
}
```

Now, if we try to create an order with a negative amount, the transaction should fail and roll back.

```
POST http://localhost:8080/users/createUserWithOrder
Content-Type: application/json

{
```

```
    "user": {
        "firstName": "Jane",
        "lastName": "Doe",
        "email": "jane.doe@gitforgits.com"
    },
    "order": {
        "orderDate": "2023-07-20",
        "amount": -100.0
    }
}
```

In this case, the **createUserWithOrder** method will throw a validation exception due to the negative amount, and both the user and order will not be saved.

Additional Transaction Management

Propagation and Isolation Levels

The @Transactional annotation provides options to control transaction propagation and isolation levels. For example, you can specify that a method should always run within a new transaction or should never be part of an existing transaction.

```
package com.example.demo;


import
org.springframework.beans.factory.annotation.Autowired;
import org.springframework.stereotype.Service;
import
```

```
org.springframework.transaction.annotation.Propagation;
import
org.springframework.transaction.annotation.Transactional;

import java.util.List;

@Service
public class UserService {

    @Autowired
    private UserRepository userRepository;

    @Autowired
    private OrderRepository orderRepository;

    public List<User> findAllUsers() {
        return userRepository.findAll();
    }

    @Transactional(propagation =
Propagation.REQUIRES_NEW)
    public void createUserWithNewTransaction(User user) {
```

```
        userRepository.save(user);

    }


    @Transactional(isolation = Isolation.SERIALIZABLE)

    public void
createOrderWithSerializableIsolation(Order order) {

        orderRepository.save(order);

    }

}
```

In this example:

- **`createUserWithNewTransaction`** will always run in a new transaction, independent of any existing transactions.
- **`createOrderWithSerializableIsolation`** will run with a serializable isolation level, ensuring complete isolation from other transactions.

By adhering to these procedures, you have acquired the knowledge of managing transactions in a Spring Boot application.

Integrating with Liquibase and Flyway for Database Migrations

Database migrations are crucial for maintaining the integrity and consistency of your database schema across different environments. Spring Boot provides seamless integration with Liquibase and Flyway, two popular tools for managing and versioning database schema changes. This section will instruct configuring both Liquibase and Flyway and using them to perform database migrations.

Configuring Liquibase

Liquibase is an open-source database schema change management tool that allows you to define database changes in XML, YAML, JSON, or SQL formats.

Add Dependencies

Add the Liquibase dependency to your **pom.xml** file.

```
<dependencies>

    <dependency>

        <groupId>org.springframework.boot</groupId>

        <artifactId>spring-boot-starter-data-
jpa</artifactId>

    </dependency>

    <dependency>

        <groupId>com.h2database</groupId>

        <artifactId>h2</artifactId>

        <scope>runtime</scope>

    </dependency>

    <dependency>

        <groupId>org.liquibase</groupId>

        <artifactId>liquibase-core</artifactId>

    </dependency>

</dependencies>
```

Create Liquibase ChangeLog

Define your database changes in a changelog file. This file can be in XML, YAML, JSON, or SQL format.

For this example, we will use XML.

```
<?xml version="1.0" encoding="UTF-8" standalone="no"?>
```

```
<databaseChangeLog

    xmlns="http://www.liquibase.org/xml/ns/dbchangelog"

    xmlns:xsi="http://www.w3.org/2001/XMLSchema-instance"

xsi:schemaLocation="http://www.liquibase.org/xml/ns/dbcha
ngelog

http://www.liquibase.org/xml/ns/dbchangelog/dbchangelog-
3.8.xsd">


    <changeSet id="1" author="author">

        <createTable tableName="user">

            <column name="id" type="BIGINT"
autoIncrement="true">

                <constraints primaryKey="true"/>

            </column>

            <column name="first_name"
type="VARCHAR(255)"/>

            <column name="last_name"
type="VARCHAR(255)"/>

            <column name="email" type="VARCHAR(255)"/>

        </createTable>

    </changeSet>
```

```
    <changeSet id="2" author="author">
        <createTable tableName="orders">
            <column name="id" type="BIGINT"
autoIncrement="true">
                <constraints primaryKey="true"/>
            </column>
            <column name="order_date" type="TIMESTAMP"/>
            <column name="amount" type="DOUBLE"/>
            <column name="user_id" type="BIGINT">
                <constraints nullable="false"
foreignKeyName="fk_order_user"
                                references="user(id)"/>
            </column>
        </createTable>
    </changeSet>
</databaseChangeLog>
```

Configure Liquibase in application.properties

Set the location of the changelog file in your **application.properties** file.

```
spring.datasource.url=jdbc:h2:mem:testdb
spring.datasource.username=sa
spring.datasource.password=password
spring.datasource.driver-class-name=org.h2.Driver
```

```
spring.jpa.database-
platform=org.hibernate.dialect.H2Dialect

spring.jpa.show-sql=true

spring.h2.console.enabled=true



spring.liquibase.change-
log=classpath:db/changelog/db.changelog-master.xml
```

Now, start your Spring Boot application and Liquibase will automatically apply the changes defined in the changelog file to the database.

Configuring Flyway

Flyway is another popular database migration tool that allows you to manage and version your database schema using SQL scripts.

Add Dependencies

Add the Flyway dependency to your **pom.xml** file.

```
<dependencies>

    <dependency>

        <groupId>org.springframework.boot</groupId>

        <artifactId>spring-boot-starter-data-
jpa</artifactId>

    </dependency>

    <dependency>

        <groupId>com.h2database</groupId>

        <artifactId>h2</artifactId>

        <scope>runtime</scope>
```

```
    </dependency>

    <dependency>

        <groupId>org.flywaydb</groupId>

        <artifactId>flyway-core</artifactId>

    </dependency>

</dependencies>
```

Create Flyway Migration Scripts

Flyway uses a specific naming convention for migration scripts: **`V<VERSION>__<DESCRIPTION>.sql`**. Place your migration scripts in the **`db/migration`** directory.

```
CREATE TABLE user (

    id BIGINT AUTO_INCREMENT PRIMARY KEY,

    first_name VARCHAR(255),

    last_name VARCHAR(255),

    email VARCHAR(255)

);

CREATE TABLE orders (

    id BIGINT AUTO_INCREMENT PRIMARY KEY,

    order_date TIMESTAMP,

    amount DOUBLE,

    user_id BIGINT,

    CONSTRAINT fk_order_user FOREIGN KEY (user_id)
REFERENCES user (id)
```

```
);
```

Configure Flyway in application.properties

Set the location of the migration scripts in your **application.properties** file. By default, Flyway looks for SQL scripts in **classpath:db/migration**.

```
spring.datasource.url=jdbc:h2:mem:testdb

spring.datasource.username=sa

spring.datasource.password=password

spring.datasource.driver-class-name=org.h2.Driver

spring.jpa.database-platform=org.hibernate.dialect.H2Dialect

spring.jpa.show-sql=true

spring.h2.console.enabled=true


spring.flyway.locations=classpath:db/migration
```

Once you start the Spring Boot application, Flyway will automatically detect the migration scripts and apply the changes to the database.

Performing Database Migrations

Once both Liquibase and Flyway are configured, you can perform database migrations by simply starting your Spring Boot application. Both tools will automatically apply the changes defined in their respective changelog files or migration scripts.

The Liquibase will apply the changes defined in **db/changelog/db.changelog-master.xml** to create the **user** and **orders** tables.

And, the Flyway will apply the changes defined in **db/migration/V1__Create_user_table.sql** and **db/migration/V2__Create_order_table.sql** to create the **user** and **orders** tables.

Sample Program: Combining Liquibase and Flyway

There are situations where you might want to use both Liquibase and Flyway in the same application. While it is generally recommended to stick with one tool for consistency, following is how you can configure both together.

Configure Both Tools in application.properties

```
spring.datasource.url=jdbc:h2:mem:testdb

spring.datasource.username=sa

spring.datasource.password=password

spring.datasource.driver-class-name=org.h2.Driver

spring.jpa.database-
platform=org.hibernate.dialect.H2Dialect

spring.jpa.show-sql=true

spring.h2.console.enabled=true



spring.liquibase.change-
log=classpath:db/changelog/db.changelog-master.xml

spring.flyway.locations=classpath:db/migration
```

Prioritize One Tool Over the Other

By default, Flyway will run before Liquibase. If you need Liquibase to run first, you can adjust the **application.properties** to control the execution order.

```
spring.flyway.enabled=false

spring.liquibase.enabled=true
```

```
spring.liquibase.change-
log=classpath:db/changelog/db.changelog-master.xml
```

Then, after Liquibase has run, you can enable Flyway.

```
spring.flyway.enabled=true

spring.liquibase.enabled=false


spring.flyway.locations=classpath:db/migration
```

Now, run the application twice, first with Liquibase enabled and Flyway disabled, then with Flyway enabled and Liquibase disabled. This ensures that Liquibase changes are applied first, followed by Flyway migrations. Both these tools provide robust solutions for maintaining database schema changes for consistency and version control across different environments.

Summary

Simply said, this chapter covered the basics of using Spring Data JPA for data access management. The chapter began with an overview of Spring Data JPA, elucidating its repository abstraction and its ability to streamline data access by minimizing redundant code. The process of configuring the data source has been shown by utilizing an H2 in-memory database, accompanied by comprehensive guidelines for establishing the required dependencies and properties. The chapter then delved into JPA entities and relationships, demonstrating the process of mapping Java objects to database tables and defining different types of relationships, including one-to-one, one-to-many, many-to-one, and many-to-many.

The next topic covered was query methods and custom queries. This section focused on explaining how to define query methods in repository interfaces and utilize the @Query annotation for more intricate queries. The JPA Criteria API was implemented to provide a type-safe approach for constructing dynamic queries programmatically, accompanied by concrete examples of its usage. The concept of paging and sorting was subsequently elucidated, showcasing the efficient management of large datasets by retrieving data in segments and arranging it according to specified criteria.

Another important subject covered was the management of transactions in Spring Boot. The @Transactional annotation was employed to establish transactional boundaries, guaranteeing the integrity and consistency of data across multiple operations. Illustrative instances encompassed the process of generating a user and an order simultaneously within a singular transaction, as well as reverting transactions in the event of errors.

Ultimately, the chapter explored the process of incorporating Liquibase and Flyway for the purpose of executing database migrations. Creating changelogs and migration scripts, as well as automating the application of database changes, were all described with detailed instructions. This chapter provided you with extensive knowledge and practical skills for effectively managing data access and database migrations in Spring Boot applications.

CHAPTER 7: BUILDING WEB APPLICATIONS

Chapter Overview

This chapter aims to create dynamic, responsive web applications using Spring Boot and Spring MVC. The chapter begins with an introduction to Spring MVC, explaining its role in the Model-View-Controller architecture and how it facilitates the development of web applications. We will learn to create controllers and views, allowing us to handle web requests and display responses to users. The chapter then explores using Thymeleaf templates to build interactive and dynamic web pages. Handling form submissions and validating user input will also be covered, ensuring that data entered by users is correctly processed and validated before being used in the application. Additionally, we will explore using WebSockets in Spring Boot to enable real-time communication between the server and clients.

Handling file uploads and downloads is another crucial aspect covered in this chapter, demonstrating how to manage file data efficiently. Exception handling in web applications will teach us how to manage errors gracefully, providing a better user experience. Finally, we will look at integrating front-end frameworks like Angular and React with Spring Boot, enabling the creation of modern, single-page applications with a robust back-end. By the end of this chapter, you will have a comprehensive understanding of building web applications with Spring Boot, from creating dynamic web pages and handling user input to managing files and integrating front-end technologies.

Introduction to Spring MVC

Spring MVC (Model-View-Controller) is a framework within the Spring Framework designed to build web applications. It follows the MVC design pattern, which separates the application logic into three interconnected components: Model, View, and Controller. This separation allows for more manageable, scalable, and testable code. In this section, we will explore each component of Spring MVC in detail, understanding how they interact and work together to create dynamic web applications.

Model-View-Controller Architecture

The MVC architecture divides an application into three main components:

- *Model: Represents the application's data and business logic.*
- *View: Represents the presentation layer, displaying data to the user.*
- *Controller: Handles user input, processes it, and returns the appropriate response.*

Spring MVC Components

DispatcherServlet

The **DispatcherServlet** is the central component of Spring MVC. It acts as a front controller, intercepting all incoming HTTP requests and dispatching them to the appropriate handler (controller). It is responsible for managing the entire request-processing workflow, from receiving the request to rendering the response.

For a better understanding, here is an example configuration of the **DispatcherServlet**:

```
<servlet>

    <servlet-name>dispatcher</servlet-name>

    <servlet-class>org.springframework.web.servlet.DispatcherServlet</servlet-class>

    <load-on-startup>1</load-on-startup>

</servlet>

<servlet-mapping>

    <servlet-name>dispatcher</servlet-name>

    <url-pattern>/</url-pattern>

</servlet-mapping>
```

The **DispatcherServlet** is automatically configured, so you don't need to add this configuration manually.

HandlerMapping

HandlerMapping is responsible for mapping incoming requests to the appropriate handler (controller) based on the URL pattern. It maintains a registry of mappings between URL patterns and handlers, determining which controller should handle a given request.

Consider the following example of configuring the **HandlerMapping**:

```
@Bean

public HandlerMapping handlerMapping() {

    SimpleUrlHandlerMapping mapping = new
SimpleUrlHandlerMapping();

    mapping.setOrder(0);

    mapping.setMappings(properties);

    return mapping;

}
```

In Spring Boot, this is automatically configured through annotations on controller methods.

Controller

A **Controller** in Spring MVC handles user input and interacts with the model to process the request and return a response. Controllers are typically annotated with **@Controller** and contain methods annotated with **@RequestMapping** (or other request mapping annotations) to handle specific HTTP requests.

To see how this works in practice, here is an example configuration for the **UserController.java**:

```
package com.example.demo;



import org.springframework.stereotype.Controller;

import org.springframework.ui.Model;
```

```
import
org.springframework.web.bind.annotation.GetMapping;

import
org.springframework.web.bind.annotation.PostMapping;

import
org.springframework.web.bind.annotation.RequestParam;


@Controller

public class UserController {


    @GetMapping("/users")

    public String getUsers(Model model) {

        // Fetch users from the model

        List<User> users = userService.findAllUsers();

        model.addAttribute("users", users);

        return "userList";

    }


    @PostMapping("/users")

    public String addUser(@RequestParam String firstName,
@RequestParam String lastName, @RequestParam String
email, Model model) {

        // Add a new user to the model
```

```
        User user = new User(firstName, lastName, email);
        userService.saveUser(user);
        return "redirect:/users";
    }
}
```

ModelAndView

ModelAndView is a container for both the model and the view in a Spring MVC application. It holds the model data that needs to be rendered and the name of the view that will render it. This allows the controller to return a single object encapsulating both the data and the view information.

The following example demonstrates the configuration for **ModelAndView** Usage:

```
@GetMapping("/userDetails")
public ModelAndView getUserDetails(@RequestParam Long id)
{
    User user = userService.findUserById(id);
    ModelAndView mav = new ModelAndView("userDetails");
    mav.addObject("user", user);
    return mav;
}
```

ViewResolver

ViewResolver is responsible for resolving the view names returned by controllers into actual view implementations. It looks up the view name and maps it to a specific view technology, such as JSP, Thymeleaf, or FreeMarker.

We will take a look at the example configuration for the **ViewResolver**:

```
@Bean

public InternalResourceViewResolver viewResolver() {

    InternalResourceViewResolver resolver = new
InternalResourceViewResolver();

    resolver.setPrefix("/WEB-INF/views/");

    resolver.setSuffix(".jsp");

    return resolver;

}
```

Very commonly, Thymeleaf is often used as the default view resolver, and it is automatically configured.

View

The **View** component is responsible for rendering the model data to the user. Views are typically implemented using templates (such as Thymeleaf or JSP) that generate the HTML content sent to the client.

Consider the following example of Thymeleaf Template (**userList.html**):

```
<!DOCTYPE html>

<html xmlns:th="http://www.thymeleaf.org">

<head>

    <title>User List</title>

</head>

<body>

    <h1>User List</h1>

    <table>
```

```
        <tr>
            <th>First Name</th>
            <th>Last Name</th>
            <th>Email</th>
        </tr>
        <tr th:each="user : ${users}">
            <td th:text="${user.firstName}"></td>
            <td th:text="${user.lastName}"></td>
            <td th:text="${user.email}"></td>
        </tr>
    </table>
</body>
</html>
```

In the above example,

- The client sends an HTTP request to the server.
- The **DispatcherServlet** receives the request and consults **HandlerMapping** to determine the appropriate controller.
- The controller processes the request, interacts with the model, and returns a **ModelAndView** or view name.
- The **ModelAndView** contains both the model data and the view information.
- The **ViewResolver** resolves the view name to a specific view implementation.
- The view renders the model data to generate the HTML response.
- The server sends the HTML response back to the client.

Sample Program: Creating a User Management System using Spring MVC

We will create a simple user management system to demonstrate Spring MVC components in action.

Controller

Consider the following example of configuring the **UserController.java**:

```
package com.example.demo;


import
org.springframework.beans.factory.annotation.Autowired;

import org.springframework.stereotype.Controller;

import org.springframework.ui.Model;

import org.springframework.web.bind.annotation.*;


import java.util.List;


@Controller

public class UserController {


    @Autowired

    private UserService userService;


    @GetMapping("/users")
```

```
    public String getUsers(Model model) {
        List<User> users = userService.findAllUsers();
        model.addAttribute("users", users);
        return "userList";
    }

    @GetMapping("/users/new")
    public String showUserForm(Model model) {
        model.addAttribute("user", new User());
        return "userForm";
    }

    @PostMapping("/users")
    public String addUser(@ModelAttribute User user) {
        userService.saveUser(user);
        return "redirect:/users";
    }

    @GetMapping("/users/{id}")
    public String getUserDetails(@PathVariable Long id,
Model model) {
        User user = userService.findUserById(id);
```

```
        model.addAttribute("user", user);
        return "userDetails";
    }
}
```

Service

Below is an example configuration of **UserService.java**:

```
package com.example.demo;


import
org.springframework.beans.factory.annotation.Autowired;
import org.springframework.stereotype.Service;


import java.util.List;


@Service
public class UserService {


    @Autowired
    private UserRepository userRepository;


    public List<User> findAllUsers() {
        return userRepository.findAll();
```

```
    }


    public User findUserById(Long id) {
        return userRepository.findById(id).orElse(null);
    }


    public void saveUser(User user) {
        userRepository.save(user);
    }
}
```

Repository

Below is an example configuration of **UserRepository.java**:

```
package com.example.demo;


import
org.springframework.data.jpa.repository.JpaRepository;


public interface UserRepository extends
JpaRepository<User, Long> {
}
```

Entity

Below is an example configuration of **User.java**:

```java
package com.example.demo;

import javax.persistence.*;

@Entity
public class User {

    @Id
    @GeneratedValue(strategy = GenerationType.IDENTITY)
    private Long id;
    private String firstName;
    private String lastName;
    private String email;

    // Getters and setters

    public Long getId() {
        return id;
    }

    public void setId(Long id) {
```

```
        this.id = id;
    }

    public String getFirstName() {
        return firstName;
    }

    public void setFirstName(String firstName) {
        this.firstName = firstName;
    }

    public String getLastName() {
        return lastName;
    }

    public void setLastName(String lastName) {
        this.lastName = lastName;
    }

    public String getEmail() {
        return email;
```

```
    }

    public void setEmail(String email) {
        this.email = email;
    }
}
```

Thymeleaf Templates

Below is an example configuration of **userList.html**:

```
<!DOCTYPE html>
<html xmlns:th="http://www.thymeleaf.org">
<head>
    <title>User List</title>
</head>
<body>
    <h1>User List</h1>
    <table>
        <tr>
            <th>First Name</th>
            <th>Last Name</th>
            <th>Email</th>
        </tr>
```

```
        <tr th:each="user : ${users}">
            <td th:text="${user.firstName}"></td>
            <td th:text="${user.lastName}"></td>
            <td th:text="${user.email}"></td>
        </tr>
    </table>
    <a href="/users/new">Add New User</a>
</body>
</html>
```

Below is an example configuration of **userForm.html**:

```
<!DOCTYPE html>
<html xmlns:th="http://www.thymeleaf.org">
<head>
    <title>Add User</title>
</head>
<body>
    <h1>Add User</h1>
    <form th:action="@{/users}" th:object="${user}"
method="post">
        <label>First Name:</label>
        <input type="text" th:field="*{firstName}" />
```

```
        <br/>
        <label>Last Name:</label>
        <input type="text" th:field="*{lastName}" />
        <br/>
        <label>Email:</label>
        <input type="text" th:field="*{email}" />
        <br/>
        <button type="submit">Save</button>
    </form>
</body>
</html>
```

Below is an example configuration of **userDetails.html**:

```
<!DOCTYPE html>
<html xmlns:th="http://www.thymeleaf.org">
<head>
    <title>User Details</title>
</head>
<body>
    <h1>User Details</h1>
    <p>First Name: <span
th:text="${user.firstName}"></span></p>
```

```
    <p>Last Name: <span
th:text="${user.lastName}"></span></p>

    <p>Email: <span th:text="${user.email}"></span></p>

    <a href="/users">Back to User List</a>

</body>

</html>
```

We now have a fully operational Spring MVC application for user management with these components installed. All the pieces of the Spring MVC framework come together in this application to process data, handle requests, and render responses to the client.

Creating Controllers and Views

Building upon the foundational understanding of Spring MVC, we will now focus on creating controllers and views for our user management system. Controllers handle user requests and responses, while views display data to the user. In this section, we will create practical examples of controllers and views, by utilizing the knowledge from the previous topic.

Creating Controllers

Controllers together make it as a backbone of a Spring MVC application, managing the flow of data and user interaction. Controllers are annotated with **@Controller** and contain methods mapped to specific URLs using annotations like **@RequestMapping**, **@GetMapping**, and **@PostMapping**.

UserController

We will create a **UserController** to manage user-related actions such as listing users, adding new users, and viewing user details.

```
package com.example.demo;


import
org.springframework.beans.factory.annotation.Autowired;
```

```java
import org.springframework.stereotype.Controller;
import org.springframework.ui.Model;
import org.springframework.web.bind.annotation.*;

import java.util.List;

@Controller
public class UserController {

    @Autowired
    private UserService userService;

    @GetMapping("/users")
    public String getUsers(Model model) {
        List<User> users = userService.findAllUsers();
        model.addAttribute("users", users);
        return "userList";
    }

    @GetMapping("/users/new")
    public String showUserForm(Model model) {
```

```
        model.addAttribute("user", new User());
        return "userForm";
    }

    @PostMapping("/users")
    public String addUser(@ModelAttribute User user) {
        userService.saveUser(user);
        return "redirect:/users";
    }

    @GetMapping("/users/{id}")
    public String getUserDetails(@PathVariable Long id,
Model model) {
        User user = userService.findUserById(id);
        model.addAttribute("user", user);
        return "userDetails";
    }
}
```

In the above example,

- **`@GetMapping("/users")`** maps to the **`/users`** URL and handles HTTP GET requests to list all users.
- **`@GetMapping("/users/new")`** maps to **`/users/new`** and displays a form for creating a new user.

- **@PostMapping("/users")** handles form submissions for adding a new user.
- **@GetMapping("/users/{id}")** maps to **/users/{id}** and displays the details of a specific user.

Creating Views

Views are responsible for rendering the model data to the user. We will use Thymeleaf, a popular templating engine, to create our views. Thymeleaf templates are HTML files with embedded expressions to display dynamic data.

User List View

This view will display a list of users. The following example demonstrates **userList.html**:

```
<!DOCTYPE html>

<html xmlns:th="http://www.thymeleaf.org">

<head>

    <title>User List</title>

</head>

<body>

    <h1>User List</h1>

    <table>

        <tr>

            <th>First Name</th>

            <th>Last Name</th>

            <th>Email</th>

            <th>Actions</th>

        </tr>
```

```
        <tr th:each="user : ${users}">
            <td th:text="${user.firstName}"></td>
            <td th:text="${user.lastName}"></td>
            <td th:text="${user.email}"></td>
            <td><a
th:href="@{/users/{id}(id=${user.id})}">View</a></td>
        </tr>
    </table>
    <a href="/users/new">Add New User</a>
</body>
</html>
```

In the above snippet,

- The **th:each** attribute iterates over the **users** model attribute and renders a table row for each user.
- The **th:text** attribute binds the table cell content to the corresponding user properties.
- The **th:href** attribute generates a URL to view the details of a specific user.

User Form View

This view will display a form for creating a new user. Let's take a look at **userForm.html**:

```
<!DOCTYPE html>
<html xmlns:th="http://www.thymeleaf.org">
<head>
    <title>Add User</title>
</head>
```

```
<body>

    <h1>Add User</h1>

    <form th:action="@{/users}" th:object="${user}"
method="post">

        <label>First Name:</label>

        <input type="text" th:field="*{firstName}" />

        <br/>

        <label>Last Name:</label>

        <input type="text" th:field="*{lastName}" />

        <br/>

        <label>Email:</label>

        <input type="text" th:field="*{email}" />

        <br/>

        <button type="submit">Save</button>

    </form>

</body>

</html>
```

In the above example,

- The **th:action** attribute sets the form's action URL to **/users**.
- The **th:object** attribute binds the form to the **user** model attribute.
- The **th:field** attribute binds input fields to the corresponding user properties.

User Details View

This view will display the details of a specific user. Below is an example of userDetails.html:

```
<!DOCTYPE html>

<html xmlns:th="http://www.thymeleaf.org">

<head>

    <title>User Details</title>

</head>

<body>

    <h1>User Details</h1>

    <p>First Name: <span
th:text="${user.firstName}"></span></p>

    <p>Last Name: <span
th:text="${user.lastName}"></span></p>

    <p>Email: <span th:text="${user.email}"></span></p>

    <a href="/users">Back to User List</a>

</body>

</html>
```

Here, the **`th:text`** attribute displays the user property values within the HTML elements. With this, we have successfully created controllers and views for our user management system, leveraging the knowledge from the previous topic. We configured a **`UserController`** to handle various user-related actions and created Thymeleaf templates to display user data. These steps build a functional Spring MVC application that manages users, and provides flexibility of Spring MVC in building web applications.

Using Thymeleaf Templates

Setting up Thymeleaf

Building on our previous sections, where we introduced Thymeleaf templates and integrated them with Spring MVC controllers, we will now aim to utilize Thymeleaf for our user management system. As said previously, Thymeleaf is a modern server-side Java template engine for web and standalone environments, capable of processing HTML, XML, JavaScript, CSS, and plain text.

Thymeleaf is already configured in our Spring Boot application through dependencies in the **pom.xml** file. So now, we will focus on enhancing our templates and adding more functionalities to our project.

Basic Syntax and Expressions

Thymeleaf expressions are used to dynamically render data in HTML templates. The main types of expressions are variable expressions (**${...}**), selection expressions (***{...}**), and message expressions (**#{...}**).

```
<p th:text="${user.firstName}">First Name</p>
```

We will add more details and formatting to the user list view to make it more informative and visually appealing. For a better understanding, here is an example of the **userList.html**:

```
<!DOCTYPE html>

<html xmlns:th="http://www.thymeleaf.org">

<head>

    <title>User List</title>

    <link rel="stylesheet" type="text/css"
href="/css/styles.css">

</head>

<body>

    <h1>User List</h1>

    <table>
```

```
        <thead>
            <tr>
                <th>First Name</th>
                <th>Last Name</th>
                <th>Email</th>
                <th>Actions</th>
            </tr>
        </thead>
        <tbody>
            <tr th:each="user : ${users}">
                <td th:text="${user.firstName}"></td>
                <td th:text="${user.lastName}"></td>
                <td th:text="${user.email}"></td>
                <td>
                    <a
th:href="@{/users/{id}(id=${user.id})}">View</a>
                    <a
th:href="@{/users/edit/{id}(id=${user.id})}">Edit</a>
                    <a
th:href="@{/users/delete/{id}(id=${user.id})}">Delete</a>
                </td>
            </tr>
```

```
        </tbody>
    </table>
    <a href="/users/new">Add New User</a>
</body>
</html>
```

In the above example,

- Added a **thead** element for table headers.
- Included more action links for viewing, editing, and deleting users.
- Linked a stylesheet for better visual presentation.

Creating a User Form with Validation

To handle form submissions with validation, we will enhance our user form view. Thymeleaf provides support for form validation error messages.

Take the example of **userForm.html**:

```
<!DOCTYPE html>
<html xmlns:th="http://www.thymeleaf.org">
<head>
    <title>Add User</title>
    <link rel="stylesheet" type="text/css"
href="/css/styles.css">
</head>
<body>
    <h1>Add User</h1>
    <form th:action="@{/users}" th:object="${user}"
```

```
method="post">

        <div>

            <label>First Name:</label>

            <input type="text" th:field="*{firstName}" />

            <span
th:if="${#fields.hasErrors('firstName')}"
th:errors="*{firstName}">First Name Error</span>

        </div>

        <div>

            <label>Last Name:</label>

            <input type="text" th:field="*{lastName}" />

            <span
th:if="${#fields.hasErrors('lastName')}"
th:errors="*{lastName}">Last Name Error</span>

        </div>

        <div>

            <label>Email:</label>

            <input type="text" th:field="*{email}" />

            <span th:if="${#fields.hasErrors('email')}"
th:errors="*{email}">Email Error</span>

        </div>

        <button type="submit">Save</button>

    </form>
```

```
    <a href="/users">Back to User List</a>

</body>

</html>
```

In the above code,

- Added **th:if** and **th:errors** attributes to display validation error messages.
- Enhanced form styling with linked CSS.

Implementing User Details View

The user details view will now include a more detailed and formatted display. Consider the following example of **userDetails.html**:

```
<!DOCTYPE html>

<html xmlns:th="http://www.thymeleaf.org">

<head>

    <title>User Details</title>

    <link rel="stylesheet" type="text/css"
href="/css/styles.css">

</head>

<body>

    <h1>User Details</h1>

    <div>

        <label>First Name:</label>

        <span th:text="${user.firstName}"></span>

    </div>

    <div>
```

```
        <label>Last Name:</label>
        <span th:text="${user.lastName}"></span>
    </div>
    <div>
        <label>Email:</label>
        <span th:text="${user.email}"></span>
    </div>
    <a href="/users">Back to User List</a>
</body>
</html>
```

The above example enhances the display with better layout and styling.

Adding a CSS File for Styling

Create a CSS file to improve the appearance of the views. Below is an example of **`styles.css`**:

```
body {
    font-family: Arial, sans-serif;
    margin: 20px;
}
table {
    width: 100%;
    border-collapse: collapse;
}
```

```
th, td {
    padding: 10px;
    border: 1px solid #ddd;
}
th {
    background-color: #f4f4f4;
}
h1 {
    color: #333;
}
form div {
    margin-bottom: 10px;
}
form label {
    display: inline-block;
    width: 100px;
}
form input {
    padding: 5px;
    width: 200px;
}
```

```
form span {
    color: red;
}
a {
    color: #007bff;
    text-decoration: none;
}
a:hover {
    text-decoration: underline;
}
```

Here, this CSS file enhances the visual appearance of our HTML templates, providing a consistent and clean look across all views.

Updating the Application to Serve Static Content

Ensure Spring Boot is configured to serve static content like CSS files from the **`src/main/resources/static`** directory. Following is the directory structure:

```
src
└── main
    └── resources
        └── static
            └── css
                └── styles.css
```

Using these procedures, we were able to improve the views of our user management system by utilizing Thymeleaf templates. The application is now more polished and user-friendly thanks to the improved templates, which offer better structure, styling, and validation.

Handling Form Submissions

In the previous sections, we created Thymeleaf templates for displaying user data and forms. Now, we will focus on managing form submissions, including processing user input, validating data, and updating the model. This section builds upon our existing user management system, ensuring a seamless transition from form display to data processing.

Form Binding with Thymeleaf

Thymeleaf provides robust support for form handling. It binds HTML form fields to the properties of a model object, allowing seamless data transfer between the client and server. We've previously created a user form view. Let's revisit and enhance it to handle form submissions effectively.

We will take a look at the example for **userForm.html**:

```
<!DOCTYPE html>

<html xmlns:th="http://www.thymeleaf.org">

<head>

    <title>Add User</title>

    <link rel="stylesheet" type="text/css"
href="/css/styles.css">

</head>

<body>

    <h1>Add User</h1>

    <form th:action="@{/users}" th:object="${user}"
method="post">

        <div>
```

```
            <label>First Name:</label>

            <input type="text" th:field="*{firstName}" />

            <span
th:if="${#fields.hasErrors('firstName')}"
th:errors="*{firstName}">First Name Error</span>

        </div>

        <div>

            <label>Last Name:</label>

            <input type="text" th:field="*{lastName}" />

            <span
th:if="${#fields.hasErrors('lastName')}"
th:errors="*{lastName}">Last Name Error</span>

        </div>

        <div>

            <label>Email:</label>

            <input type="text" th:field="*{email}" />

            <span th:if="${#fields.hasErrors('email')}"
th:errors="*{email}">Email Error</span>

        </div>

        <button type="submit">Save</button>

    </form>

    <a href="/users">Back to User List</a>

</body>
```

```
</html>
```

Here in this example,

- **th:field** binds the form input fields to the corresponding properties of the **user** object.
- **th:if** and **th:errors** display validation error messages.

Controller Method for Handling Form Submissions

We need to ensure our **UserController** can process the form data sent by the user and handle any validation errors. We will update the **UserController** to include validation logic and handle form submissions.

The following example demonstrates the **UserController.java**:

```
package com.example.demo;


import
org.springframework.beans.factory.annotation.Autowired;

import org.springframework.stereotype.Controller;

import org.springframework.ui.Model;

import org.springframework.validation.BindingResult;

import org.springframework.web.bind.annotation.*;


import javax.validation.Valid;

import java.util.List;


@Controller

public class UserController {
```

```
    @Autowired
    private UserService userService;

    @GetMapping("/users")
    public String getUsers(Model model) {
        List<User> users = userService.findAllUsers();
        model.addAttribute("users", users);
        return "userList";
    }

    @GetMapping("/users/new")
    public String showUserForm(Model model) {
        model.addAttribute("user", new User());
        return "userForm";
    }

    @PostMapping("/users")
    public String addUser(@Valid @ModelAttribute User
user, BindingResult result, Model model) {
        if (result.hasErrors()) {
            return "userForm";
```

```
        }

        userService.saveUser(user);

        return "redirect:/users";

    }


    @GetMapping("/users/{id}")

    public String getUserDetails(@PathVariable Long id,
Model model) {

        User user = userService.findUserById(id);

        model.addAttribute("user", user);

        return "userDetails";

    }

}
```

In this example,

- **@Valid** ensures that the **user** object is validated against the constraints defined in the **User** class.
- **BindingResult** captures validation errors, allowing the controller to handle them appropriately.
- If validation errors are present, the form is re-displayed with error messages. Otherwise, the user is saved, and the browser is redirected to the user list.

Adding Validation Constraints

For validation to work, we need to add constraints to our **User** entity. To see how this works in practice, here is an updated example of **User.java**:

```
package com.example.demo;
```

```
import javax.persistence.Entity;
import javax.persistence.GeneratedValue;
import javax.persistence.GenerationType;
import javax.persistence.Id;
import javax.validation.constraints.Email;
import javax.validation.constraints.NotBlank;

@Entity
public class User {

    @Id
    @GeneratedValue(strategy = GenerationType.IDENTITY)
    private Long id;

    @NotBlank(message = "First name is mandatory")
    private String firstName;

    @NotBlank(message = "Last name is mandatory")
    private String lastName;
```

```
@Email(message = "Email should be valid")
@NotBlank(message = "Email is mandatory")
private String email;

// Getters and setters

public Long getId() {
    return id;
}

public void setId(Long id) {
    this.id = id;
}

public String getFirstName() {
    return firstName;
}

public void setFirstName(String firstName) {
    this.firstName = firstName;
}
```

```
    public String getLastName() {
        return lastName;
    }

    public void setLastName(String lastName) {
        this.lastName = lastName;
    }

    public String getEmail() {
        return email;
    }

    public void setEmail(String email) {
        this.email = email;
    }
}
```

Here,

- **`@NotBlank`** ensures that the field is not null and not empty.
- **`@Email`** ensures that the email field contains a valid email address.

Handling Form Submission and Validation Errors

With the above configurations, we have set up a complete flow for handling form submissions and validation errors. For example,

Display Form

- Navigate to **`http://localhost:8080/users/new`**.
- The form for adding a new user is displayed.

Submit Form with Errors

- Leave the **`firstName`** and **`lastName`** fields empty and submit the form.
- Validation errors are displayed: "First name is mandatory" and "Last name is mandatory."

Submit Form Successfully

- Fill in all fields correctly and submit the form.
- The user is saved, and you are redirected to the user list at **`http://localhost:8080/users`**.

With this, we have integrated form submissions with our user management system, allowing users to add new users via a form. By utilizing Thymeleaf for form binding and Spring MVC for handling form submissions and validation, we have created a robust and user-friendly system. This flow ensures that user input is processed correctly, validation errors are managed, and data integrity is maintained.

Validating User Input

Building on the previous section where we set up form submissions, we will now focus on validating user input in detail. Validating user input ensures data integrity and helps prevent errors and security vulnerabilities. We will explore how to enforce validation rules on form data, display validation errors to users, and manage these errors in our Spring Boot application.

Adding Validation Constraints to the Entity

To validate user input, we use JSR-380 (Bean Validation 2.0) annotations in our entity classes. These annotations specify the validation rules that the input data must adhere to. Consider the following example of **`User.java`**:

```
package com.example.demo;


import javax.persistence.Entity;
```

```
import javax.persistence.GeneratedValue;

import javax.persistence.GenerationType;

import javax.persistence.Id;

import javax.validation.constraints.Email;

import javax.validation.constraints.NotBlank;

import javax.validation.constraints.Size;


@Entity

public class User {


    @Id

    @GeneratedValue(strategy = GenerationType.IDENTITY)

    private Long id;


    @NotBlank(message = "First name is mandatory")

    @Size(min = 2, max = 30, message = "First name must
be between 2 and 30 characters")

    private String firstName;


    @NotBlank(message = "Last name is mandatory")

    @Size(min = 2, max = 30, message = "Last name must be
between 2 and 30 characters")
```

```
private String lastName;

@Email(message = "Email should be valid")
@NotBlank(message = "Email is mandatory")
private String email;

// Getters and setters

public Long getId() {
    return id;
}

public void setId(Long id) {
    this.id = id;
}

public String getFirstName() {
    return firstName;
}

public void setFirstName(String firstName) {
```

```
        this.firstName = firstName;
    }

    public String getLastName() {
        return lastName;
    }

    public void setLastName(String lastName) {
        this.lastName = lastName;
    }

    public String getEmail() {
        return email;
    }

    public void setEmail(String email) {
        this.email = email;
    }
}
```

In the above example,

- **`@NotBlank`**: Ensures the field is not null and not empty.
- **`@Size`**: Ensures the string length is within specified bounds.

- **`@Email`**: Ensures the field contains a valid email address.

Updating Controller to Handle Validation

The controller method that handles form submissions should be updated to include validation logic. We will use **`@Valid`** to trigger validation and **`BindingResult`** to capture any validation errors in the following example of **`UserController.java`**:

```
package com.example.demo;


import
org.springframework.beans.factory.annotation.Autowired;

import org.springframework.stereotype.Controller;

import org.springframework.ui.Model;

import org.springframework.validation.BindingResult;

import org.springframework.web.bind.annotation.*;


import javax.validation.Valid;

import java.util.List;


@Controller

public class UserController {


    @Autowired

    private UserService userService;
```

```
    @GetMapping("/users")
    public String getUsers(Model model) {
        List<User> users = userService.findAllUsers();
        model.addAttribute("users", users);
        return "userList";
    }

    @GetMapping("/users/new")
    public String showUserForm(Model model) {
        model.addAttribute("user", new User());
        return "userForm";
    }

    @PostMapping("/users")
    public String addUser(@Valid @ModelAttribute User
user, BindingResult result, Model model) {
        if (result.hasErrors()) {
            return "userForm";
        }
        userService.saveUser(user);
        return "redirect:/users";
    }
```

```
    @GetMapping("/users/{id}")
    public String getUserDetails(@PathVariable Long id,
Model model) {
        User user = userService.findUserById(id);
        model.addAttribute("user", user);
        return "userDetails";
    }
}
```

Here,

- **@Valid**: Triggers the validation process.
- **BindingResult**: Captures any validation errors. If errors are present, the form is re-displayed with error messages.

Updating Form to Display Validation Errors

The Thymeleaf form should be updated to display validation error messages next to the corresponding fields. Consider the following example of **userForm.html**:

```
<!DOCTYPE html>
<html xmlns:th="http://www.thymeleaf.org">
<head>
    <title>Add User</title>
    <link rel="stylesheet" type="text/css"
href="/css/styles.css">
</head>
```

```
<body>

    <h1>Add User</h1>

    <form th:action="@{/users}" th:object="${user}"
method="post">

        <div>

            <label>First Name:</label>

            <input type="text" th:field="*{firstName}" />

            <span
th:if="${#fields.hasErrors('firstName')}"
th:errors="*{firstName}">First Name Error</span>

        </div>

        <div>

            <label>Last Name:</label>

            <input type="text" th:field="*{lastName}" />

            <span
th:if="${#fields.hasErrors('lastName')}"
th:errors="*{lastName}">Last Name Error</span>

        </div>

        <div>

            <label>Email:</label>

            <input type="text" th:field="*{email}" />

            <span th:if="${#fields.hasErrors('email')}"
th:errors="*{email}">Email Error</span>
```

```
        </div>

        <button type="submit">Save</button>

    </form>

    <a href="/users">Back to User List</a>

</body>

</html>
```

Here,

- **th:if**: Checks if there are any validation errors for the field.
- **th:errors**: Displays the error messages for the field.

With everything in place, we can test the validation flow by submitting the form with various inputs.

Utilizing WebSockets

Brief Overview

WebSockets provide a full-duplex communication channel over a single, long-lived connection. This technology is ideal for applications that require real-time updates, such as chat applications, live notifications, or collaborative editing. In this section, we will configure WebSockets in a Spring Boot application and establish bidirectional communication. We will integrate WebSockets with the user management system to notify all connected clients whenever a new user is added.

Configuring WebSockets

Add Dependencies

Add the necessary WebSocket dependencies to your pom.xml.

```
<dependencies>

    <!-- Other dependencies -->

    <dependency>
```

```
        <groupId>org.springframework.boot</groupId>

        <artifactId>spring-boot-starter-
websocket</artifactId>

    </dependency>

</dependencies>
```

WebSocket Configuration

Create a configuration class to enable WebSocket support. The following example demonstrates the configuration for **WebSocketConfig.java**:

```
package com.example.demo;


import
org.springframework.context.annotation.Configuration;

import
org.springframework.messaging.simp.config.MessageBrokerRe
gistry;

import
org.springframework.web.socket.config.annotation.EnableWe
bSocketMessageBroker;

import
org.springframework.web.socket.config.annotation.StompEnd
pointRegistry;

import
org.springframework.web.socket.config.annotation.WebSocke
tMessageBrokerConfigurer;
```

```
@Configuration

@EnableWebSocketMessageBroker

public class WebSocketConfig implements
WebSocketMessageBrokerConfigurer {


    @Override

    public void
configureMessageBroker(MessageBrokerRegistry config) {

        config.enableSimpleBroker("/topic");

        config.setApplicationDestinationPrefixes("/app");

    }


    @Override

    public void
registerStompEndpoints(StompEndpointRegistry registry) {

        registry.addEndpoint("/ws").withSockJS();

    }

}
```

In the above example,

- **`@EnableWebSocketMessageBroker`** enables WebSocket message handling, backed by a message broker.
- **`configureMessageBroker`** sets up a message broker that broadcasts messages to connected clients on destinations prefixed with **`/topic`**.
- **`registerStompEndpoints`** registers the WebSocket endpoint that clients will use

to connect to the server.

Create a WebSocket Controller

Create a controller to handle WebSocket messages. For example, Consider the following **WebSocketController.java**:

```
package com.example.demo;


import
org.springframework.messaging.handler.annotation.MessageM
apping;

import
org.springframework.messaging.handler.annotation.SendTo;

import org.springframework.stereotype.Controller;


@Controller

public class WebSocketController {


    @MessageMapping("/hello")

    @SendTo("/topic/greetings")

    public GreetingMessage greet(HelloMessage message)
throws Exception {

        Thread.sleep(1000); // simulated delay

        return new GreetingMessage("Hello, " +
message.getName() + "!");

    }
```

```
}

class HelloMessage {
    private String name;

    public String getName() {
        return name;
    }

    public void setName(String name) {
        this.name = name;
    }
}

class GreetingMessage {
    private String content;

    public GreetingMessage(String content) {
        this.content = content;
    }
```

```
    public String getContent() {

        return content;

    }

}
```

Here,

- **@MessageMapping** maps messages to the **/hello** destination.
- **@SendTo** broadcasts the return value to all subscribers of the **/topic/greetings** destination.

Creating HTML for WebSocket Communication

Create an HTML page to connect to the WebSocket server and send/receive messages. Given below is an example of **index.html**:

```
<!DOCTYPE html>

<html>

<head>

    <title>WebSocket Demo</title>

    <script src="https://cdn.jsdelivr.net/npm/sockjs-
client@1.4.0/dist/sockjs.min.js"></script>

    <script src="https://cdn.jsdelivr.net/npm/stomp-
websocket@2.3.3/lib/stomp.min.js"></script>

    <script src="https://code.jquery.com/jquery-
3.5.1.min.js"></script>

    <script type="text/javascript">

        var stompClient = null;
```

```
        function connect() {
            var socket = new SockJS('/ws');
            stompClient = Stomp.over(socket);
            stompClient.connect({}, function (frame) {
                setConnected(true);
                console.log('Connected: ' + frame);
                stompClient.subscribe('/topic/greetings',
function (greeting) {

showGreeting(JSON.parse(greeting.body).content);
                });
            });
        }

        function disconnect() {
            if (stompClient !== null) {
                stompClient.disconnect();
            }
            setConnected(false);
            console.log("Disconnected");
        }
```

```
        function sendName() {
            stompClient.send("/app/hello", {},
JSON.stringify({'name': $("#name").val()}));
        }

        function setConnected(connected) {
            $("#connect").prop("disabled", connected);
            $("#disconnect").prop("disabled",
!connected);
            if (connected) {
                $("#conversation").show();
            }
            else {
                $("#conversation").hide();
            }
            $("#greetings").html("");
        }

        function showGreeting(message) {
            $("#greetings").append("<tr><td>" + message +
"</td></tr>");
        }
```

```
        $(function () {
            $("form").on('submit', function (e) {
                e.preventDefault();
            });
            $( "#connect" ).click(function() { connect();
});
            $( "#disconnect" ).click(function() {
disconnect(); });
            $( "#send" ).click(function() { sendName();
});
        });
    </script>
</head>
<body>
    <div>
        <button id="connect">Connect</button>
        <button id="disconnect"
disabled="disabled">Disconnect</button>
        <form>
            <input type="text" id="name"
placeholder="Enter your name"/>
            <button id="send">Send</button>
```

```
        </form>

        <div id="conversation" style="display:none;">

            <table id="greetings">

                <tr><th>Greetings</th></tr>

            </table>

        </div>

    </div>

</body>

</html>
```

In the above example,

- **SockJS** and **Stomp** are used to create a WebSocket connection and communicate with the server.
- The page includes buttons to connect/disconnect and a form to send messages.

Integrating WebSockets with User Management System

We will notify all connected clients when a new user is added. For a better understanding, here is an example of **UserController.java**:

```
package com.example.demo;



import
org.springframework.beans.factory.annotation.Autowired;

import
org.springframework.messaging.simp.SimpMessagingTemplate;

import org.springframework.stereotype.Controller;

import org.springframework.ui.Model;
```

```java
import org.springframework.validation.BindingResult;
import org.springframework.web.bind.annotation.*;

import javax.validation.Valid;
import java.util.List;

@Controller
public class UserController {

    @Autowired
    private UserService userService;

    @Autowired
    private SimpMessagingTemplate template;

    @GetMapping("/users")
    public String getUsers(Model model) {
        List<User> users = userService.findAllUsers();
        model.addAttribute("users", users);
        return "userList";
    }
```

```
    @GetMapping("/users/new")
    public String showUserForm(Model model) {
        model.addAttribute("user", new User());
        return "userForm";
    }

    @PostMapping("/users")
    public String addUser(@Valid @ModelAttribute User
user, BindingResult result, Model model) {
        if (result.hasErrors()) {
            return "userForm";
        }
        userService.saveUser(user);
        template.convertAndSend("/topic/userUpdates",
"New user added: " + user.getFirstName() + " " +
user.getLastName());
        return "redirect:/users";
    }

    @GetMapping("/users/{id}")
    public String getUserDetails(@PathVariable Long id,
Model model) {
```

```
        User user = userService.findUserById(id);

        model.addAttribute("user", user);

        return "userDetails";

    }

}
```

Here, **SimpMessagingTemplate** is used to send WebSocket messages to the **/topic/userUpdates** destination.

Updating HTML for User Notifications

Add functionality to display user notifications on the HTML page by updating **index.html**:

```
<!DOCTYPE html>

<html>

<head>

    <title>WebSocket Demo</title>

    <script src="https://cdn.jsdelivr.net/npm/sockjs-
client@1.4.0/dist/sockjs.min.js"></script>

    <script src="https://cdn.jsdelivr.net/npm/stomp-
websocket@2.3.3/lib/stomp.min.js"></script>

    <script src="https://code.jquery.com/jquery-
3.5.1.min.js"></script>

    <script type="text/javascript">

        var stompClient = null;


        function connect() {
```

```
            var socket = new SockJS('/ws');
            stompClient = Stomp.over(socket);
            stompClient.connect({}, function (frame) {
                setConnected(true);
                console.log('Connected: ' + frame);

stompClient.subscribe('/topic/userUpdates', function
(message) {

showMessage(JSON.parse(message.body).content);
                });
            });
        }

        function disconnect() {
            if (stompClient !== null) {
                stompClient.disconnect();
            }
            setConnected(false);
            console.log("Disconnected");
        }
```

```
        function sendName() {
            stompClient.send("/app/hello", {},
JSON.stringify({'name': $("#name").val()}));
        }

        function setConnected(connected) {
            $("#connect").prop("disabled", connected);
            $("#disconnect").prop("disabled",
!connected);
            if (connected) {
                $("#conversation").show();
            }
            else {
                $("#conversation").hide();
            }
            $("#greetings").html("");
        }

        function showMessage(message) {
            $("#greetings").append("<tr><td>" + message +
"</td></tr>");
        }
```

```
        $(function () {
            $("form").on('submit', function (e) {
                e.preventDefault();
            });
            $("#connect").click(function() { connect();
});
            $("#disconnect").click(function() {
disconnect(); });
            $("#send").click(function() { sendName(); });
        });
    </script>
</head>
<body>
    <div>
        <button id="connect">Connect</button>
        <button id="disconnect"
disabled="disabled">Disconnect</button>
        <form>
            <input type="text" id="name"
placeholder="Enter your name"/>
            <button id="send">Send</button>
        </form>
```

```
        <div id="conversation" style="display:none;">
            <table id="greetings">
                <tr><th>Messages</th></tr>
            </table>
        </div>
    </div>
</body>
</html>
```

By doing so, we added functionality to display messages received from the **/topic/userUpdates** destination.

By following these steps, you have successfully integrated WebSockets into your Spring Boot application, thereby having successful real-time notifications to all connected clients whenever a new user is added.

File Upload and Download Handling

It is necessary for many web applications to manage file uploads and downloads. Spring Boot streamlines the procedure by offering strong support for uploading files in multiple parts. Here we will take a look at the user management system's capabilities for uploading and downloading various file types (photos, documents, etc.).

Configuring File Uploads

Add Dependencies

Ensure that the spring-boot-starter-web dependency is included in your pom.xml, as it provides the necessary components for handling file uploads.

```
<dependencies>
    <!-- Other dependencies -->
    <dependency>
```

```
        <groupId>org.springframework.boot</groupId>
        <artifactId>spring-boot-starter-web</artifactId>
    </dependency>
</dependencies>
```

Configure Multipart File Uploads

Spring Boot automatically configures multipart file uploads with default settings. You can customize these settings in your **application.properties** file if needed as below:

```
spring.servlet.multipart.max-file-size=2MB
spring.servlet.multipart.max-request-size=2MB
```

Creating a File Upload Controller

File Upload Controller

Create a controller to handle file uploads. For example, create a file called FileUploadController.java:

```
package com.example.demo;


import
org.springframework.beans.factory.annotation.Value;
import org.springframework.stereotype.Controller;
import org.springframework.ui.Model;
import
org.springframework.web.bind.annotation.GetMapping;
import
org.springframework.web.bind.annotation.PostMapping;
```

```
import
org.springframework.web.bind.annotation.RequestParam;

import org.springframework.web.multipart.MultipartFile;


import java.io.File;

import java.io.IOException;


@Controller

public class FileUploadController {


    @Value("${upload.path}")

    private String uploadPath;


    @GetMapping("/upload")

    public String showUploadForm(Model model) {

        return "uploadForm";

    }


    @PostMapping("/upload")

    public String handleFileUpload(@RequestParam("file")
MultipartFile file, Model model) {

        if (!file.isEmpty()) {
```

```
            try {
                String filePath = uploadPath +
File.separator + file.getOriginalFilename();
                file.transferTo(new File(filePath));
                model.addAttribute("message", "File
uploaded successfully: " + file.getOriginalFilename());
            } catch (IOException e) {
                model.addAttribute("message", "Failed to
upload file: " + e.getMessage());
            }
        } else {
            model.addAttribute("message", "Please select
a file to upload");
        }
        return "uploadStatus";
    }
}
```

Here,

- **`@Value("${upload.path}")`**: Reads the file upload directory path from the application properties.
- **`handleFileUpload`**: Handles the file upload logic.

Create the Upload Form View

Create an HTML form to allow users to upload files. Consider the following example **`uploadForm.html`**:

```
<!DOCTYPE html>

<html xmlns:th="http://www.thymeleaf.org">

<head>

    <title>File Upload</title>

    <link rel="stylesheet" type="text/css"
href="/css/styles.css">

</head>

<body>

    <h1>Upload File</h1>

    <form method="post" enctype="multipart/form-data"
th:action="@{/upload}">

        <div>

            <label>Select file:</label>

            <input type="file" name="file"/>

        </div>

        <button type="submit">Upload</button>

    </form>

</body>

</html>
```

In this, **enctype="multipart/form-data"** specifies that the form will handle file uploads.

Create the Upload Status View

Create an HTML page to display the status of the file upload. The file can be

uploadStatus.html as below:

```
<!DOCTYPE html>

<html xmlns:th="http://www.thymeleaf.org">

<head>

    <title>Upload Status</title>

    <link rel="stylesheet" type="text/css"
href="/css/styles.css">

</head>

<body>

    <h1>Upload Status</h1>

    <p th:text="${message}"></p>

    <a href="/upload">Back to Upload Form</a>

</body>

</html>
```

The above code displays the upload status message.

Handling File Downloads

File Download Controller

Create a controller to handle file downloads. The controlled can be named as FileDownloadController.java:

```
package com.example.demo;



import
org.springframework.beans.factory.annotation.Value;
```

```
import org.springframework.core.io.FileSystemResource;

import org.springframework.core.io.Resource;

import org.springframework.http.HttpHeaders;

import org.springframework.http.HttpStatus;

import org.springframework.http.ResponseEntity;

import org.springframework.stereotype.Controller;

import
org.springframework.web.bind.annotation.GetMapping;

import
org.springframework.web.bind.annotation.PathVariable;


import java.io.File;


@Controller

public class FileDownloadController {


    @Value("${upload.path}")

    private String uploadPath;


    @GetMapping("/download/{filename}")

    public ResponseEntity<Resource>
downloadFile(@PathVariable String filename) {
```

```
        File file = new File(uploadPath + File.separator
+ filename);

        if (file.exists()) {

            Resource resource = new
FileSystemResource(file);

            return ResponseEntity.ok()

.header(HttpHeaders.CONTENT_DISPOSITION, "attachment;
filename=\"" + file.getName() + "\"")

                    .body(resource);

        } else {

            return
ResponseEntity.status(HttpStatus.NOT_FOUND)

.header(HttpHeaders.CONTENT_DISPOSITION, "attachment;
filename=\"" + filename + "\"")

                    .body(null);

        }

    }

}
```

Here, **downloadFile** handles the file download logic by returning a **ResponseEntity** with the file resource.

Create a View to List Downloadable Files

Create an HTML page "**fileList.html**" to list files available for download.

```
<!DOCTYPE html>

<html xmlns:th="http://www.thymeleaf.org">

<head>

    <title>File List</title>

    <link rel="stylesheet" type="text/css"
href="/css/styles.css">

</head>

<body>

    <h1>Files Available for Download</h1>

    <table>

        <thead>

            <tr>

                <th>File Name</th>

                <th>Actions</th>

            </tr>

        </thead>

        <tbody>

            <tr th:each="file : ${files}">

                <td th:text="${file}"></td>

                <td>

                    <a
th:href="@{/download/{filename}(filename=${file})}">Downl
```

```
oad</a>
                    </td>
                </tr>
            </tbody>
        </table>
</body>
</html>
```

It will now list files available in the upload directory with download links.

Then, update the FileUploadController to provide the list of uploaded files to the view as below:

```
package com.example.demo;


import
org.springframework.beans.factory.annotation.Value;
import org.springframework.stereotype.Controller;
import org.springframework.ui.Model;
import
org.springframework.web.bind.annotation.GetMapping;
import
org.springframework.web.bind.annotation.PostMapping;
import
org.springframework.web.bind.annotation.RequestParam;
import org.springframework.web.multipart.MultipartFile;
```

```
import java.io.File;
import java.io.IOException;
import java.nio.file.Files;
import java.util.List;
import java.util.stream.Collectors;

@Controller
public class FileUploadController {

    @Value("${upload.path}")
    private String uploadPath;

    @GetMapping("/upload")
    public String showUploadForm(Model model) {
        List<String> files = listFiles();
        model.addAttribute("files", files);
        return "uploadForm";
    }

    @PostMapping("/upload")
    public String handleFileUpload(@RequestParam("file")
MultipartFile file, Model model) {
```

```
        if (!file.isEmpty()) {
            try {
                String filePath = uploadPath +
File.separator + file.getOriginalFilename();
                file.transferTo(new File(filePath));
                model.addAttribute("message", "File
uploaded successfully: " + file.getOriginalFilename());
            } catch (IOException e) {
                model.addAttribute("message", "Failed to
upload file: " + e.getMessage());
            }
        } else {
            model.addAttribute("message", "Please select
a file to upload");
        }
        List<String> files = listFiles();
        model.addAttribute("files", files);
        return "uploadStatus";
    }

    private List<String> listFiles() {
        try {
            return Files.list(new
```

```
File(uploadPath).toPath())
                        .map(path ->
path.getFileName().toString())
                        .collect(Collectors.toList());
        } catch (IOException e) {
            return List.of();
        }
    }
}
```

Here,

- **`listFiles()`**: Lists files available in the upload directory.
- Updates the model with the list of files to be displayed in the view.

We have successfully integrated file upload and download handling into our Spring Boot application by following these steps. Our user management system is now more functional, and users can upload and download different types of files as needed.

Integrating Front-End Frameworks

The user experience can be greatly improved by integrating external front-end frameworks with Spring Boot applications. This allows for the creation of dynamic, interactive, and rich user interfaces. Spring Boot's back-end services are fully compatible with popular frameworks like Angular and React, which provide robust tools for developing single-page applications (SPAs). With this integration, the user experience can be enhanced to be more responsive and engaging.

Integrating React with Spring Boot

It is widely known that React is a popular JavaScript library for building user interfaces, and it allows developers to create reusable UI components, manage the application state efficiently, and build complex interfaces with ease.

To begin with, first we need to set up a React project. We will use the Create React App to bootstrap our React application.

```
npx create-react-app my-react-app

cd my-react-app
```

Then, start the React development server to ensure everything is set up correctly.

```
npm start
```

We will then serve the React application from our Spring Boot back-end. This involves building the React app and placing the build artifacts in the Spring Boot static resources directory.

```
npm run build
```

Copy the contents of the **build** directory to the **src/main/resources/static** directory in your Spring Boot project.

Then, ensure that Spring Boot serves the React app correctly by configuring a fallback route for any unhandled requests. The following example demonstrates the configuration of **WebMvcConfig.java**:

```
package com.example.demo;


import
org.springframework.context.annotation.Configuration;

import
org.springframework.web.servlet.config.annotation.ViewCon
trollerRegistry;

import
org.springframework.web.servlet.config.annotation.WebMvcC
onfigurer;


@Configuration

public class WebMvcConfig implements WebMvcConfigurer {
```

```
    @Override

    public void addViewControllers(ViewControllerRegistry
registry) {

        registry.addViewController("/{spring:\\w+}")

                .setViewName("forward:/");

        registry.addViewController("/**/{spring:\\w+}")

                .setViewName("forward:/");

registry.addViewController("/{spring:\\w+}/**{spring:?!(\
\.js|\\.css)$}")

                .setViewName("forward:/");

    }

}
```

Now, add a simple React component to display user data fetched from the Spring Boot back-end. For a better understanding, here is the file **`App.js`**:

```
import React, { useEffect, useState } from 'react';

import './App.css';


function App() {

    const [users, setUsers] = useState([]);


    useEffect(() => {
```

```
        fetch('/users')
            .then(response => response.json())
            .then(data => setUsers(data));
    }, []);

    return (
        <div className="App">
            <header className="App-header">
                <h1>User List</h1>
                <ul>
                    {users.map(user => (
                        <li
key={user.id}>{user.firstName} {user.lastName}
({user.email})</li>
                    ))}
                </ul>
            </header>
        </div>
    );
}

export default App;
```

Start the Spring Boot application and navigate to **http://localhost:8080** to see the React app in action, displaying data fetched from the Spring Boot back-end.

Integrating Angular with Spring Boot

Angular is a platform for building mobile and desktop web applications. It provides a comprehensive framework for building complex, scalable, and high-performance applications.

First, set up an Angular project using the Angular CLI.

```
npm install -g @angular/cli

ng new my-angular-app

cd my-angular-app
```

Start the Angular development server to ensure everything is set up correctly.

```
ng serve
```

Build the Angular app and place the build artifacts in the Spring Boot static resources directory.

```
ng build --prod
```

Now, copy the contents of the **dist/my-angular-app** directory to the **src/main/resources/static** directory in your Spring Boot project.

After this, ensure that Spring Boot serves the Angular app correctly by configuring a fallback route for any unhandled requests. For a better understanding, here is an example configuration of the **WebMvcConfig.java**:

```
package com.example.demo;



import
org.springframework.context.annotation.Configuration;

import
org.springframework.web.servlet.config.annotation.ViewCon
trollerRegistry;
```

```
import
org.springframework.web.servlet.config.annotation.WebMvcC
onfigurer;


@Configuration

public class WebMvcConfig implements WebMvcConfigurer {


    @Override

    public void addViewControllers(ViewControllerRegistry
registry) {

        registry.addViewController("/{spring:\\w+}")

                .setViewName("forward:/");

        registry.addViewController("/**/{spring:\\w+}")

                .setViewName("forward:/");


registry.addViewController("/{spring:\\w+}/**{spring:?!(\
\.js|\\.css)$}")

                .setViewName("forward:/");

    }

}
```

Now, add a simple Angular component to display user data fetched from the Spring Boot back-end by means of **app.component.ts**:

```
import { Component, OnInit } from '@angular/core';
```

```
import { HttpClient } from '@angular/common/http';


interface User {
    id: number;
    firstName: string;
    lastName: string;
    email: string;
}


@Component({
    selector: 'app-root',
    templateUrl: './app.component.html',
    styleUrls: ['./app.component.css']
})
export class AppComponent implements OnInit {
    users: User[] = [];


    constructor(private http: HttpClient) {}


    ngOnInit() {
        this.http.get<User[]>('/users').subscribe(data =>
{
```

```
            this.users = data;
        });
    }
}
```

After that, the Angular application can communicate with the Spring Boot back-end by configuring the proxy in the **angular.json** file.

```
{
    "projects": {
        "my-angular-app": {
            "architect": {
                "build": {
                    "options": {
                        "outputPath": "dist/my-angular-
app",
                        "index": "src/index.html",
                        "main": "src/main.ts",
                        "proxyConfig":
"src/proxy.conf.json"
                    }
                }
            }
        }
```

```
    }
}
```

This proxy configuration ensures that API requests to **`/api`** are forwarded to the Spring Boot back-end.

You have accomplished the integration of React and Angular with your Spring Boot application by following these steps. By integrating with these front-end frameworks, you can take advantage of their robust features, which improve the user experience and make it easier to build dynamic, engaging web apps.

Summary

To sum up all the learnings of this book, very first we explored building web applications using Spring Boot and various front-end technologies. The chapter started with an introduction to Spring MVC, explaining its components such as DispatcherServlet, HandlerMapping, Controller, ModelAndView, ViewResolver, and View. Each component's role in handling web requests and rendering responses was detailed, emphasizing the MVC pattern's significance in creating maintainable web applications. We then delved into creating controllers and views, demonstrating how to manage user interactions and display data using Thymeleaf templates. The process of binding form fields to model attributes and displaying validation errors was explained. This included handling form submissions, processing user input, and validating data to ensure integrity and prevent errors.

WebSocket integration was covered next, highlighting how to configure and establish bidirectional communication between the server and clients. We learned to set up WebSocket endpoints, create controllers to handle WebSocket messages, and build a simple client interface using HTML and JavaScript. This integration enabled real-time updates and notifications in our application. The chapter also covered file upload and download handling, demonstrating how to configure Spring Boot to accept multipart file uploads, process them, and provide download functionality. Examples included creating controllers and views to handle these operations, ensuring a seamless user experience.

Finally, we explored integrating front-end frameworks such as React and Angular with Spring Boot. The steps to set up React and Angular projects, build components to interact with the Spring Boot back-end, and configure the server to serve these applications were detailed. This integration allowed for the development of rich, interactive user interfaces, enhancing the overall functionality and responsiveness of the application.

CHAPTER 8: TESTING SPRING BOOT APPLICATIONS

Chapter Overview

Here in this chapter, we will explore the critical aspect of testing Spring Boot applications to ensure their reliability, functionality, and performance. The chapter begins with an introduction to the essentials of testing, explaining the significance of testing in software development and the types of tests commonly used. We will explore unit testing with JUnit and Mockito, focusing on how to write effective unit tests to validate individual components and their behaviors in isolation. Slice testing will also be introduced, allowing us to test specific layers of the application, such as the web layer or data layer, in isolation.

We will then dive into MockMVC, a powerful tool for testing the web layer of Spring Boot applications. This will include practical examples of testing RESTful services, ensuring that our APIs behave as expected. Testing data repositories will be covered, showing how to validate data access logic using Spring Data JPA and embedded databases. Additionally, we will explore the use of TestContainers for running tests in isolated, reproducible environments.

Lastly, the chapter will introduce performance testing with JMeter, a tool for measuring the performance and scalability of our applications. By the end of this chapter, you will have a comprehensive understanding of how to test different aspects of a Spring Boot application, ensuring its robustness, reliability, and performance under various conditions.

Getting Started with Testing

Background

Testing provides numerous benefits to ensure the quality and reliability of Spring Boot applications and with effective testing, it helps identify bugs and issues early in the development process, thereby reducing the risk of defects in production. It ensures that individual components and the application as a whole work as expected, leading to higher confidence in the software's stability. Testing also facilitates refactoring and code changes, allowing developers to modify the codebase without fear of introducing new bugs. Additionally, comprehensive test coverage can improve the maintainability of the application by serving as documentation that describes how the code should behave.

Types of Testing

Unit Testing

Unit testing involves testing individual components or units of code in isolation. The primary goal is to validate that each unit performs as expected. Unit tests are typically written using frameworks like JUnit and use mocking libraries such as Mockito to simulate dependencies. In Spring Boot, unit testing can be applied to various components, including services, controllers, and utility classes.

Consider the following example of Unit Test:

```
@RunWith(MockitoJUnitRunner.class)
public class UserServiceTest {

    @InjectMocks
    private UserService userService;

    @Mock
    private UserRepository userRepository;

    @Test
    public void whenValidUser_thenUserShouldBeFound() {
        User user = new User("John", "Doe",
"john.doe@gitforgits.com");

Mockito.when(userRepository.findByEmail(user.getEmail()))
.thenReturn(user);
        User found =
userService.findUserByEmail("john.doe@gitforgits.com");
        assertEquals(found.getEmail(), user.getEmail());
    }
}
```

Integration Testing

Integration testing focuses on testing the interaction between multiple components to ensure they work together as expected. Unlike unit tests, integration tests require a more complex setup, often involving a real or in-memory database, application context, and other infrastructure components. Spring Boot simplifies integration testing with its support for loading application contexts and managing dependencies.

Consider the following example of an Integration Test:

```
@RunWith(SpringRunner.class)

@SpringBootTest

public class UserServiceIntegrationTest {



    @Autowired

    private UserService userService;



    @Autowired

    private UserRepository userRepository;



    @Test

    public void whenSaveUser_thenUserShouldBeFound() {

        User user = new User("Jane", "Doe",
"jane.doe@gitforgits.com");

        userService.saveUser(user);

        User found =
userRepository.findByEmail("jane.doe@gitforgits.com");

        assertEquals(found.getEmail(), user.getEmail());
```

```
    }
}
```

Functional Testing

Functional testing verifies that the application functions as intended by testing the complete functionality of the application. It involves testing the application from the end-user's perspective, ensuring that all features work correctly. Functional tests can be automated using tools like Selenium or manual testing.

For a better understanding, here is an example of Functional Test:

```
@RunWith(SpringRunner.class)
@SpringBootTest(webEnvironment =
SpringBootTest.WebEnvironment.RANDOM_PORT)
public class UserControllerFunctionalTest {

    @Autowired
    private TestRestTemplate restTemplate;

    @Test
    public void whenGetUser_thenStatus200() {
        ResponseEntity<User> response =
restTemplate.getForEntity("/users/1", User.class);
        assertEquals(response.getStatusCode(),
HttpStatus.OK);
    }
}
```

End-to-End Testing

End-to-end (E2E) testing ensures that the entire application workflow, from start to finish, works correctly. It tests the application in a production-like environment, covering all integrated components and systems. E2E tests are typically automated and can be executed using frameworks like Cypress or Protractor for web applications.

Given below is an example of E2E Test:

```
describe('User Management E2E Tests', () => {

    it('should display the user list', () => {

        cy.visit('/users');

        cy.get('h1').contains('User List');

cy.get('table').find('tr').should('have.length.greaterTha
n', 1);

    });


    it('should add a new user', () => {

        cy.visit('/users/new');

        cy.get('input[name="firstName"]').type('Alice');

        cy.get('input[name="lastName"]').type('Smith');

cy.get('input[name="email"]').type('alice.smith@gitforgit
s.com');

        cy.get('button[type="submit"]').click();

        cy.visit('/users');

        cy.contains('Alice Smith');
```

```
    });
});
```

Acceptance Testing

Acceptance testing is performed to determine whether the application meets the specified requirements and is ready for delivery. It involves validating the application's functionality against the business requirements and user stories. Acceptance tests are often written in collaboration with stakeholders and can be automated using tools like Cucumber.

Given below is an example of Acceptance Test:

```
@CucumberOptions(features =
"src/test/resources/features")
@RunWith(Cucumber.class)
public class UserAcceptanceTest {

    @Given("a user with email {string}")
    public void aUserWithEmail(String email) {
        // Create a user with the specified email
    }

    @When("the user logs in with email {string}")
    public void theUserLogsInWithEmail(String email) {
        // Simulate user login
    }
```

```java
    @Then("the user should see their profile")
    public void theUserShouldSeeTheirProfile() {
        // Verify user profile is displayed
    }
}
```

Performance Testing

Performance testing evaluates the application's performance under various conditions, such as load, stress, and scalability. It ensures that the application can handle the expected number of users and transactions without degradation in performance. Tools like JMeter and Gatling are commonly used for performance testing.

Given below is an example of Performance Test:

```xml
<testPlan>
    <threadGroup>
        <numThreads>100</numThreads>
        <rampUp>10</rampUp>
        <duration>60</duration>
        <httpSampler>
            <domain>localhost</domain>
            <port>8080</port>
            <path>/users</path>
            <method>GET</method>
        </httpSampler>
    </threadGroup>
```

```
</testPlan>
```

Security Testing

Security testing identifies vulnerabilities and ensures that the application is protected against threats such as SQL injection, cross-site scripting (XSS), and other security risks. Tools like OWASP ZAP and Burp Suite are used for security testing.

Given below is an example of Security Test:

```
zap-cli quick-scan --self-contained --start-options '-config api.disablekey=true' http://localhost:8080
```

Each of the above types of tests serves a unique purpose, from validating individual components to ensuring the entire application works as intended under various conditions. With these, developers can detect issues early, improve code quality, and deliver robust applications that meet user expectations and business requirements.

Unit Testing with JUnit and Mockito

Unit testing is a crucial aspect of ensuring the reliability and functionality of individual components within a Spring Boot application. JUnit is a widely-used testing framework for Java, providing annotations and assertions to write and run tests. Mockito is a popular mocking framework that allows developers to create mock objects for dependencies, enabling isolated testing of components.

Setting up JUnit and Mockito

Adding Dependencies

To use JUnit and Mockito in your Spring Boot application, add the necessary dependencies to your pom.xml.

```
<dependencies>

    <!-- Other dependencies -->

    <dependency>

        <groupId>org.springframework.boot</groupId>
```

```
        <artifactId>spring-boot-starter-test</artifactId>
        <scope>test</scope>
    </dependency>
    <dependency>
        <groupId>org.mockito</groupId>
        <artifactId>mockito-core</artifactId>
        <scope>test</scope>
    </dependency>
</dependencies>
```

The **spring-boot-starter-test** dependency includes JUnit, Mockito, and other useful testing libraries.

Example 1: Unit Testing a Service Layer

In this example, we will write unit tests for a service layer class in our Spring Boot application. The **UserService** class interacts with the **UserRepository** to manage user data as shown below:

UserService Implementation

```
package com.example.demo.service;


import com.example.demo.model.User;
import com.example.demo.repository.UserRepository;
import
org.springframework.beans.factory.annotation.Autowired;
import org.springframework.stereotype.Service;
```

```
import java.util.Optional;


@Service
public class UserService {


    @Autowired
    private UserRepository userRepository;


    public User findUserByEmail(String email) {
        return
userRepository.findByEmail(email).orElse(null);
    }


    public void saveUser(User user) {
        userRepository.save(user);
    }
}
```

UserService Test Class

```
package com.example.demo.service;
```

```java
import com.example.demo.model.User;

import com.example.demo.repository.UserRepository;

import org.junit.jupiter.api.Test;

import org.junit.jupiter.api.extension.ExtendWith;

import org.mockito.InjectMocks;

import org.mockito.Mock;

import org.mockito.junit.jupiter.MockitoExtension;


import java.util.Optional;


import static
org.junit.jupiter.api.Assertions.assertEquals;

import static org.mockito.Mockito.when;


@ExtendWith(MockitoExtension.class)

public class UserServiceTest {


    @Mock

    private UserRepository userRepository;


    @InjectMocks

    private UserService userService;
```

```
    @Test

    public void whenValidEmail_thenUserShouldBeFound() {

        User user = new User("John", "Doe",
"john.doe@gitforgits.com");


when(userRepository.findByEmail(user.getEmail())).thenRet
urn(Optional.of(user));

        User found =
userService.findUserByEmail("john.doe@gitforgits.com");

        assertEquals(found.getEmail(), user.getEmail());

    }


    @Test

    public void
whenInvalidEmail_thenUserShouldNotBeFound() {


when(userRepository.findByEmail("invalid@gitforgits.com")
).thenReturn(Optional.empty());

        User found =
userService.findUserByEmail("invalid@gitforgits.com");

        assertEquals(found, null);

    }

}
```

In the above example,

- **@ExtendWith(MockitoExtension.class)**: Initializes Mockito and JUnit integration.
- **@Mock**: Creates a mock instance of **UserRepository**.
- **@InjectMocks**: Injects the mock **UserRepository** into **UserService**.

Now, to run the tests, execute the following Maven command:

```
mvn test
```

The tests will run, and you should see the results indicating whether they passed or failed.

Example 2: Unit Testing a Controller Layer

In this example, we will write unit tests for a controller layer class. The **UserController** class handles HTTP requests related to user operations.

UserController Implementation

```
package com.example.demo.controller;


import com.example.demo.model.User;

import com.example.demo.service.UserService;

import
org.springframework.beans.factory.annotation.Autowired;

import org.springframework.http.HttpStatus;

import org.springframework.http.ResponseEntity;

import org.springframework.web.bind.annotation.*;


import java.util.List;
```

```
@RestController
@RequestMapping("/users")
public class UserController {

    @Autowired
    private UserService userService;

    @GetMapping
    public List<User> getAllUsers() {
        return userService.findAllUsers();
    }

    @GetMapping("/{id}")
    public ResponseEntity<User> getUserById(@PathVariable
Long id) {
        User user = userService.findUserById(id);
        if (user == null) {
            return new
ResponseEntity<>(HttpStatus.NOT_FOUND);
        }
        return new ResponseEntity<>(user, HttpStatus.OK);
    }
```

```
    @PostMapping
    public ResponseEntity<User> createUser(@RequestBody
User user) {
        userService.saveUser(user);
        return new ResponseEntity<>(user,
HttpStatus.CREATED);
    }
}
```

UserController Test Class

```
package com.example.demo.controller;


import com.example.demo.model.User;
import com.example.demo.service.UserService;
import org.junit.jupiter.api.Test;
import org.junit.jupiter.api.extension.ExtendWith;
import org.mockito.InjectMocks;
import org.mockito.Mock;
import org.mockito.junit.jupiter.MockitoExtension;
import org.springframework.http.HttpStatus;
import org.springframework.http.ResponseEntity;
```

```
import java.util.Arrays;

import java.util.List;


import static
org.junit.jupiter.api.Assertions.assertEquals;

import static org.mockito.Mockito.when;


@ExtendWith(MockitoExtension.class)

public class UserControllerTest {


    @Mock

    private UserService userService;


    @InjectMocks

    private UserController userController;


    @Test

    public void whenGetAllUsers_thenReturnUserList() {

        User user1 = new User("John", "Doe",
"john.doe@gitforgits.com");

        User user2 = new User("Jane", "Doe",
"jane.doe@gitforgits.com");
```

```
        List<User> users = Arrays.asList(user1, user2);

when(userService.findAllUsers()).thenReturn(users);
        List<User> result = userController.getAllUsers();
        assertEquals(result.size(), 2);
        assertEquals(result.get(0).getEmail(),
user1.getEmail());
        assertEquals(result.get(1).getEmail(),
user2.getEmail());
    }

    @Test
    public void whenValidUserId_thenReturnUser() {
        User user = new User("John", "Doe",
"john.doe@gitforgits.com");

when(userService.findUserById(1L)).thenReturn(user);
        ResponseEntity<User> response =
userController.getUserById(1L);
        assertEquals(response.getStatusCode(),
HttpStatus.OK);
        assertEquals(response.getBody().getEmail(),
user.getEmail());
    }
```

```
    @Test
    public void whenInvalidUserId_thenReturnNotFound() {
when(userService.findUserById(2L)).thenReturn(null);
        ResponseEntity<User> response =
userController.getUserById(2L);
        assertEquals(response.getStatusCode(),
HttpStatus.NOT_FOUND);
    }
}
```

Here in this above example,

- **`@ExtendWith(MockitoExtension.class)`**: Initializes Mockito and JUnit integration.
- **`@Mock`**: Creates a mock instance of **`UserService`**.
- **`@InjectMocks`**: Injects the mock **`UserService`** into **`UserController`**.

After this, run the test as done in the previous example, and you should see the results indicating whether they passed or failed.

Conduct Slice Testing for Layer-Specific Tests

Layer-specific testing, also known as slice testing, focuses on testing individual layers of an application in isolation. This approach helps ensure that each layer performs its responsibilities correctly without being affected by other layers. Spring Boot provides annotations to facilitate slice testing, allowing developers to test web, data, or service layers independently.

Understanding Layer-Specific Tests

Layer-Specific Tests

In a typical Spring Boot application, there are multiple layers, such as the web layer (controllers), service layer (business logic), and data layer (repositories). Layer-specific tests target these individual layers, ensuring their functionality in isolation.

- **Web Layer**: Tests controllers and REST endpoints.
- **Service Layer**: Tests business logic and service methods.
- **Data Layer**: Tests repositories and data access logic.

Slice Testing

Slice testing allows testing a specific slice or layer of the application while excluding other layers. This approach uses Spring Boot's test slices, such as **`@WebMvcTest`**, **`@DataJpaTest`**, and **`@MockBean`**, to configure a minimal Spring context for the targeted layer.

To illustrate slice testing, we will perform tests on the data layer and web layer.

Slice Testing for the Data Layer

Setting up Data Layer Tests

We will use @DataJpaTest to configure a minimal Spring context with only JPA components for testing the data layer.

```
package com.example.demo.repository;


import com.example.demo.model.User;
import
org.springframework.data.jpa.repository.JpaRepository;


import java.util.Optional;


public interface UserRepository extends
```

```
JpaRepository<User, Long> {
    Optional<User> findByEmail(String email);
}
```

Creating Data Layer Test Class

For a better understanding, here is an example of **UserRepositoryTest.java**:

```
package com.example.demo.repository;


import com.example.demo.model.User;
import org.junit.jupiter.api.Test;
import org.junit.jupiter.api.extension.ExtendWith;
import
org.springframework.beans.factory.annotation.Autowired;
import
org.springframework.boot.test.autoconfigure.orm.jpa.DataJ
paTest;
import
org.springframework.test.context.junit.jupiter.SpringExte
nsion;


import java.util.Optional;


import static
org.junit.jupiter.api.Assertions.assertEquals;
import static
```

```
org.junit.jupiter.api.Assertions.assertTrue;


@ExtendWith(SpringExtension.class)
@DataJpaTest
public class UserRepositoryTest {

    @Autowired
    private UserRepository userRepository;

    @Test
    public void whenFindByEmail_thenReturnUser() {
        // given
        User user = new User("John", "Doe",
"john.doe@gitforgits.com");
        userRepository.save(user);

        // when
        Optional<User> found =
userRepository.findByEmail(user.getEmail());

        // then
        assertTrue(found.isPresent());
```

```
        assertEquals(found.get().getEmail(),
user.getEmail());

    }


    @Test

    public void whenInvalidEmail_thenReturnEmpty() {

        // when

        Optional<User> found =
userRepository.findByEmail("invalid@gitforgits.com");


        // then

        assertTrue(found.isEmpty());

    }

}
```

Here,

- **@DataJpaTest**: Configures a minimal Spring context with JPA components.
- The tests focus on repository methods, ensuring data access logic works correctly.

Slice Testing for the Web Layer

Setting up Web Layer Tests

We will use @WebMvcTest to configure a minimal Spring context with only web layer components for testing controllers.

```
package com.example.demo.controller;
```

```java
import com.example.demo.model.User;

import com.example.demo.service.UserService;

import
org.springframework.beans.factory.annotation.Autowired;

import org.springframework.http.HttpStatus;

import org.springframework.http.ResponseEntity;

import org.springframework.web.bind.annotation.*;


import java.util.List;


@RestController

@RequestMapping("/users")

public class UserController {


    @Autowired

    private UserService userService;


    @GetMapping

    public List<User> getAllUsers() {

        return userService.findAllUsers();

    }
```

```
    @GetMapping("/{id}")
    public ResponseEntity<User> getUserById(@PathVariable
Long id) {
        User user = userService.findUserById(id);
        if (user == null) {
            return new
ResponseEntity<>(HttpStatus.NOT_FOUND);
        }
        return new ResponseEntity<>(user, HttpStatus.OK);
    }

    @PostMapping
    public ResponseEntity<User> createUser(@RequestBody
User user) {
        userService.saveUser(user);
        return new ResponseEntity<>(user,
HttpStatus.CREATED);
    }
}
```

Creating Web Layer Test Class

Consider the following example of **UserControllerTest.java**:

```
package com.example.demo.controller;
```

```
import com.example.demo.model.User;

import com.example.demo.service.UserService;

import org.junit.jupiter.api.Test;

import org.junit.jupiter.api.extension.ExtendWith;

import org.mockito.InjectMocks;

import org.mockito.Mock;

import
org.springframework.beans.factory.annotation.Autowired;

import
org.springframework.boot.test.autoconfigure.web.servlet.W
ebMvcTest;

import
org.springframework.boot.test.mock.mockito.MockBean;

import
org.springframework.test.context.junit.jupiter.SpringExte
nsion;

import org.springframework.test.web.servlet.MockMvc;

import
org.springframework.test.web.servlet.request.MockMvcReque
stBuilders;



import java.util.Arrays;

import java.util.List;
```

```
import static org.mockito.Mockito.when;

import static
org.springframework.test.web.servlet.result.MockMvcResult
Matchers.*;


@ExtendWith(SpringExtension.class)

@WebMvcTest(UserController.class)

public class UserControllerTest {


    @Autowired

    private MockMvc mockMvc;


    @MockBean

    private UserService userService;


    @Test

    public void whenGetAllUsers_thenReturnUserList()
throws Exception {

        User user1 = new User("John", "Doe",
"john.doe@gitforgits.com");

        User user2 = new User("Jane", "Doe",
"jane.doe@gitforgits.com");

        List<User> users = Arrays.asList(user1, user2);
```

```
when(userService.findAllUsers()).thenReturn(users);


mockMvc.perform(MockMvcRequestBuilders.get("/users"))
                .andExpect(status().isOk())

.andExpect(jsonPath("$[0].email").value(user1.getEmail())
)

.andExpect(jsonPath("$[1].email").value(user2.getEmail())
);
    }

    @Test
    public void whenValidUserId_thenReturnUser() throws
Exception {
        User user = new User("John", "Doe",
"john.doe@gitforgits.com");

when(userService.findUserById(1L)).thenReturn(user);


mockMvc.perform(MockMvcRequestBuilders.get("/users/1"))
                .andExpect(status().isOk())
```

```
.andExpect(jsonPath("$.email").value(user.getEmail()));
    }


    @Test
    public void whenInvalidUserId_thenReturnNotFound()
throws Exception {

when(userService.findUserById(2L)).thenReturn(null);



mockMvc.perform(MockMvcRequestBuilders.get("/users/2"))
                .andExpect(status().isNotFound());
    }
}
```

Here,

- **`@WebMvcTest(UserController.class)`**: Configures a minimal Spring context with only web layer components and the **`UserController`**.
- **`MockMvc`**: Provides a way to perform HTTP requests and verify the responses.

The tests will verify the functionality of repository methods in the data layer, and also validate the behavior of the web layer by testing controller endpoints.

Therefore, by focusing on specific layers, slice testing ensures that each part of the application performs its responsibilities correctly, contributing to the overall reliability and maintainability of the application.

MockMVC for Web Layer Testing

MockMVC is a powerful tool provided by Spring for testing the web layer of a Spring Boot application. It allows you to perform HTTP requests and verify responses without starting a full web server. This section will introduce MockMVC, explain how to set it up in your existing Spring Boot environment, and demonstrate practical examples of using MockMVC for web layer testing.

Introduction to MockMVC

MockMVC is a part of the Spring Test module and is designed to test Spring MVC applications. It enables testing of controllers by simulating HTTP requests and asserting responses. This makes it possible to test the web layer in isolation, ensuring that the controllers behave as expected.

Setting up MockMVC

Adding Dependencies

Ensure that your pom.xml includes the spring-boot-starter-test dependency, which contains MockMVC and other necessary testing libraries.

```
<dependencies>

    <!-- Other dependencies -->

    <dependency>

        <groupId>org.springframework.boot</groupId>

        <artifactId>spring-boot-starter-test</artifactId>

        <scope>test</scope>

    </dependency>

</dependencies>
```

Creating a Test Class

To test a controller using MockMVC, create a test class annotated with **`@WebMvcTest`** and configure MockMVC in it.

Sample Program: Using MockMVC

We will write tests for the **UserController** using MockMVC. This example assumes you have the **UserController** class already set up as shown in previous responses.

Setting up the Test Class

Consider the following example **UserControllerMockMVCTest.java**:

```
package com.example.demo.controller;



import com.example.demo.model.User;

import com.example.demo.service.UserService;

import org.junit.jupiter.api.Test;

import org.junit.jupiter.api.extension.ExtendWith;

import org.mockito.Mockito;

import
org.springframework.beans.factory.annotation.Autowired;

import
org.springframework.boot.test.autoconfigure.web.servlet.W
ebMvcTest;

import
org.springframework.boot.test.mock.mockito.MockBean;

import org.springframework.http.MediaType;

import
org.springframework.test.context.junit.jupiter.SpringExte
nsion;

import org.springframework.test.web.servlet.MockMvc;
```

```
import
org.springframework.test.web.servlet.request.MockMvcReque
stBuilders;


import java.util.Arrays;

import java.util.List;


import static org.hamcrest.Matchers.*;

import static
org.springframework.test.web.servlet.result.MockMvcResult
Matchers.*;


@ExtendWith(SpringExtension.class)

@WebMvcTest(UserController.class)

public class UserControllerMockMVCTest {


    @Autowired

    private MockMvc mockMvc;


    @MockBean

    private UserService userService;


    @Test
```

```
    public void whenGetAllUsers_thenReturnUserList()
throws Exception {

        User user1 = new User("John", "Doe",
"john.doe@gitforgits.com");

        User user2 = new User("Jane", "Doe",
"jane.doe@gitforgits.com");

        List<User> users = Arrays.asList(user1, user2);



Mockito.when(userService.findAllUsers()).thenReturn(users
);



mockMvc.perform(MockMvcRequestBuilders.get("/users")
                .contentType(MediaType.APPLICATION_JSON))
                .andExpect(status().isOk())
                .andExpect(jsonPath("$", hasSize(2)))
                .andExpect(jsonPath("$[0].email",
is(user1.getEmail())))
                .andExpect(jsonPath("$[1].email",
is(user2.getEmail())));
    }

    @Test
```

```
    public void whenValidUserId_thenReturnUser() throws
Exception {
        User user = new User("John", "Doe",
"john.doe@gitforgits.com");



Mockito.when(userService.findUserById(1L)).thenReturn(use
r);




mockMvc.perform(MockMvcRequestBuilders.get("/users/1")
                .contentType(MediaType.APPLICATION_JSON))
                .andExpect(status().isOk())
                .andExpect(jsonPath("$.email",
is(user.getEmail())));
    }

    @Test
    public void whenInvalidUserId_thenReturnNotFound()
throws Exception {

Mockito.when(userService.findUserById(2L)).thenReturn(nul
l);

```

```
mockMvc.perform(MockMvcRequestBuilders.get("/users/2")
                .contentType(MediaType.APPLICATION_JSON))
                .andExpect(status().isNotFound());
    }

    @Test
    public void whenCreateUser_thenReturnCreatedUser()
throws Exception {
        User user = new User("John", "Doe",
"john.doe@gitforgits.com");


Mockito.when(userService.saveUser(Mockito.any(User.class)
)).thenReturn(user);

        String userJson =
"{\"firstName\":\"John\",\"lastName\":\"Doe\",\"email\":\
"john.doe@gitforgits.com\"}";


mockMvc.perform(MockMvcRequestBuilders.post("/users")
                .contentType(MediaType.APPLICATION_JSON)
                .content(userJson))
                .andExpect(status().isCreated())
```

```
                .andExpect(jsonPath("$.email",
is(user.getEmail())));

    }

}
```

Here,

- **@WebMvcTest(UserController.class)**: Configures a minimal Spring context with only the **UserController** and necessary beans.
- **MockMvc**: Injected to perform HTTP requests and verify responses.
- **@MockBean**: Creates a mock instance of **UserService**.

Writing Tests with MockMVC

Each test uses **MockMvc** to perform an HTTP request and assert the response.

1. Testing GET All Users

```
Test

public void whenGetAllUsers_thenReturnUserList() throws
Exception {

    User user1 = new User("John", "Doe",
"john.doe@gitforgits.com");

    User user2 = new User("Jane", "Doe",
"jane.doe@gitforgits.com");

    List<User> users = Arrays.asList(user1, user2);



Mockito.when(userService.findAllUsers()).thenReturn(users
);
```

```
    mockMvc.perform(MockMvcRequestBuilders.get("/users")
            .contentType(MediaType.APPLICATION_JSON))
            .andExpect(status().isOk())
            .andExpect(jsonPath("$", hasSize(2)))
            .andExpect(jsonPath("$[0].email",
is(user1.getEmail())))
            .andExpect(jsonPath("$[1].email",
is(user2.getEmail())));
}
```

Here, this test verifies that a GET request to **/users** returns a list of users with a status of 200 OK.

2. Testing GET User by ID

```
@Test
public void whenValidUserId_thenReturnUser() throws
Exception {
    User user = new User("John", "Doe",
"john.doe@gitforgits.com");


Mockito.when(userService.findUserById(1L)).thenReturn(use
r);


mockMvc.perform(MockMvcRequestBuilders.get("/users/1")
```

```
            .contentType(MediaType.APPLICATION_JSON))
            .andExpect(status().isOk())
            .andExpect(jsonPath("$.email",
is(user.getEmail())));
}
```

This above test verifies that a GET request to **/users/1** returns the user with a status of 200 OK.

3. Testing GET User by Invalid ID

```
@Test
public void whenInvalidUserId_thenReturnNotFound() throws
Exception {

Mockito.when(userService.findUserById(2L)).thenReturn(nul
l);


mockMvc.perform(MockMvcRequestBuilders.get("/users/2")
            .contentType(MediaType.APPLICATION_JSON))
            .andExpect(status().isNotFound());
}
```

This test verifies that a GET request to **/users/2** returns a 404 Not Found status when the user does not exist.

4. Testing POST Create User

```
@Test
```

```
public void whenCreateUser_thenReturnCreatedUser() throws
Exception {

    User user = new User("John", "Doe",
"john.doe@gitforgits.com");



Mockito.when(userService.saveUser(Mockito.any(User.class)
)).thenReturn(user);


    String userJson =
"{\"firstName\":\"John\",\"lastName\":\"Doe\",\"email\":\
"john.doe@gitforgits.com\"}";


    mockMvc.perform(MockMvcRequestBuilders.post("/users")

            .contentType(MediaType.APPLICATION_JSON)

            .content(userJson))

            .andExpect(status().isCreated())

            .andExpect(jsonPath("$.email",
is(user.getEmail())));

}
```

This test verifies that a POST request to **`/users`** creates a new user and returns the created user with a status of 201 Created.

The overall dependability and robustness of the application can be improved by developers through the utilization of MockMVC. This allows developers to guarantee that the web layer functions appropriately and can handle a variety of scenarios.

Testing Data Repositories

Data repositories are a crucial part of any application, responsible for interacting with the database. In Spring Boot, repositories are typically interfaces that extend Spring Data JPA's **JpaRepository** or other repository interfaces, providing CRUD operations and query methods. Testing these repositories ensures that data access logic works correctly and reliably. Different types of repositories include **JpaRepository**, **CrudRepository**, **PagingAndSortingRepository**, and custom repositories. This section will cover the various types of data repositories and demonstrate how to test them.

Types of Data Repositories

JpaRepository

JpaRepository is a JPA-specific extension of CrudRepository. It provides JPA-related methods such as flushing the persistence context and deleting records in a batch.

CrudRepository

CrudRepository provides CRUD (Create, Read, Update, Delete) operations for the entity class that is being managed.

PagingAndSortingRepository

PagingAndSortingRepository extends **CrudRepository** and provides methods for pagination and sorting of records.

Custom Repositories

Custom repositories are interfaces that define additional query methods not provided by the standard repository interfaces. They often include custom implementations.

Sample Program: Testing Data Repositories

We will demonstrate testing for a UserRepository that extends JpaRepository, wherein we setup the User Entity and Repository

```
package com.example.demo.model;



import javax.persistence.Entity;

import javax.persistence.GeneratedValue;
```

```java
import javax.persistence.GenerationType;
import javax.persistence.Id;
import javax.validation.constraints.Email;
import javax.validation.constraints.NotBlank;

@Entity
public class User {

    @Id
    @GeneratedValue(strategy = GenerationType.IDENTITY)
    private Long id;

    @NotBlank(message = "First name is mandatory")
    private String firstName;

    @NotBlank(message = "Last name is mandatory")
    private String lastName;

    @Email(message = "Email should be valid")
    @NotBlank(message = "Email is mandatory")
    private String email;
```

```
// Getters and setters

public Long getId() {
    return id;
}

public void setId(Long id) {
    this.id = id;
}

public String getFirstName() {
    return firstName;
}

public void setFirstName(String firstName) {
    this.firstName = firstName;
}

public String getLastName() {
    return lastName;
```

```
    }

    public void setLastName(String lastName) {
        this.lastName = lastName;
    }

    public String getEmail() {
        return email;
    }

    public void setEmail(String email) {
        this.email = email;
    }
}

//UserRepository.java:

package com.example.demo.repository;

import com.example.demo.model.User;
```

```
import
org.springframework.data.jpa.repository.JpaRepository;


import java.util.Optional;


public interface UserRepository extends
JpaRepository<User, Long> {
    Optional<User> findByEmail(String email);
}
```

Now, we will use **`@DataJpaTest`** to configure a minimal Spring context that includes only JPA components for testing the data layer.

```
package com.example.demo.repository;


import com.example.demo.model.User;
import org.junit.jupiter.api.Test;
import org.junit.jupiter.api.extension.ExtendWith;
import
org.springframework.beans.factory.annotation.Autowired;
import
org.springframework.boot.test.autoconfigure.orm.jpa.DataJ
paTest;
import
org.springframework.test.context.junit.jupiter.SpringExte
nsion;
```

```
import java.util.Optional;


import static
org.junit.jupiter.api.Assertions.assertEquals;

import static
org.junit.jupiter.api.Assertions.assertFalse;

import static
org.junit.jupiter.api.Assertions.assertTrue;


@ExtendWith(SpringExtension.class)

@DataJpaTest

public class UserRepositoryTest {


    @Autowired

    private UserRepository userRepository;


    @Test

    public void whenFindByEmail_thenReturnUser() {

        // given

        User user = new User("John", "Doe",
"john.doe@gitforgits.com");

        userRepository.save(user);
```

```
        // when
        Optional<User> found =
userRepository.findByEmail(user.getEmail());

        // then
        assertTrue(found.isPresent());
        assertEquals(found.get().getEmail(),
user.getEmail());
    }

    @Test
    public void whenInvalidEmail_thenReturnEmpty() {
        // when
        Optional<User> found =
userRepository.findByEmail("invalid@gitforgits.com");

        // then
        assertFalse(found.isPresent());
    }

    @Test
```

```
    public void whenSaveUser_thenReturnSavedUser() {
        // given
        User user = new User("Jane", "Doe",
"jane.doe@gitforgits.com");

        // when
        User savedUser = userRepository.save(user);

        // then
        assertEquals(savedUser.getEmail(),
user.getEmail());
    }

    @Test
    public void whenDeleteUser_thenRemoveUser() {
        // given
        User user = new User("John", "Doe",
"john.doe@gitforgits.com");
        userRepository.save(user);

        // when
        userRepository.deleteById(user.getId());
```

```
        // then
        Optional<User> found =
userRepository.findById(user.getId());
        assertFalse(found.isPresent());
    }
}
```

Here in the above example,

- **`@DataJpaTest`**: Configures a minimal Spring context with JPA components.
- **`UserRepository`** is autowired into the test class to perform data operations.
- The tests cover common repository operations like saving, finding, and deleting users.

After running the test, the tests will:

- Verify that saving a user to the database works as expected.
- Check that finding a user by email returns the correct user.
- Ensure that finding a user by an invalid email returns an empty result.
- Confirm that deleting a user removes them from the database.

Sample Program: Testing a Custom Repository Method

We will add a custom method to our repository and test it.

Adding Custom Method to Repository

Add a method to find users by their first name.

```
package com.example.demo.repository;


import com.example.demo.model.User;
import
```

```
org.springframework.data.jpa.repository.JpaRepository;


import java.util.List;

import java.util.Optional;


public interface UserRepository extends
JpaRepository<User, Long> {

    Optional<User> findByEmail(String email);

    List<User> findByFirstName(String firstName);

}
```

Adding Custom Method Test

Add a test for the custom method.

```
package com.example.demo.repository;


import com.example.demo.model.User;

import org.junit.jupiter.api.Test;

import org.junit.jupiter.api.extension.ExtendWith;

import
org.springframework.beans.factory.annotation.Autowired;

import
org.springframework.boot.test.autoconfigure.orm.jpa.DataJ
paTest;

import
```

```
org.springframework.test.context.junit.jupiter.SpringExte
nsion;


import java.util.List;

import java.util.Optional;


import static
org.junit.jupiter.api.Assertions.assertEquals;

import static
org.junit.jupiter.api.Assertions.assertFalse;

import static
org.junit.jupiter.api.Assertions.assertTrue;


@ExtendWith(SpringExtension.class)

@DataJpaTest

public class UserRepositoryTest {


    @Autowired

    private UserRepository userRepository;


    @Test

    public void whenFindByEmail_thenReturnUser() {

        // given
```

```
        User user = new User("John", "Doe",
"john.doe@gitforgits.com");

        userRepository.save(user);


        // when

        Optional<User> found =
userRepository.findByEmail(user.getEmail());


        // then

        assertTrue(found.isPresent());

        assertEquals(found.get().getEmail(),
user.getEmail());

    }


    @Test

    public void whenInvalidEmail_thenReturnEmpty() {

        // when

        Optional<User> found =
userRepository.findByEmail("invalid@gitforgits.com");


        // then

        assertFalse(found.isPresent());

    }
```

```
    @Test

    public void whenSaveUser_thenReturnSavedUser() {

        // given

        User user = new User("Jane", "Doe",
"jane.doe@gitforgits.com");


        // when

        User savedUser = userRepository.save(user);


        // then

        assertEquals(savedUser.getEmail(),
user.getEmail());

    }


    @Test

    public void whenDeleteUser_thenRemoveUser() {

        // given

        User user = new User("John", "Doe",
"john.doe@gitforgits.com");

        userRepository.save(user);
```

```
        // when
        userRepository.deleteById(user.getId());

        // then
        Optional<User> found =
userRepository.findById(user.getId());
        assertFalse(found.isPresent());
    }

    @Test
    public void whenFindByFirstName_thenReturnUserList()
{
        // given
        User user1 = new User("John", "Doe",
"john.doe@gitforgits.com");
        User user2 = new User("John", "Smith",
"john.smith@gitforgits.com");
        userRepository.save(user1);
        userRepository.save(user2);

        // when
        List<User> found =
userRepository.findByFirstName("John");
```

```
        // then

        assertEquals(2, found.size());

        assertEquals("john.doe@gitforgits.com",
found.get(0).getEmail());

        assertEquals("john.smith@gitforgits.com",
found.get(1).getEmail());

    }

}
```

Here, it adds a test for the custom **findByFirstName** method, and verifies that the method returns the correct list of users with the specified first name. After running the test, it will verify that the custom method **findByFirstName** returns the correct list of users.

To sum up, testing data repositories ensures that the data access logic works correctly and reliably, thereby contributing to the overall robustness of the application.

Testing with TestContainers

TestContainers is a Java library that provides lightweight, throwaway instances of common databases, Selenium web browsers, or anything else that can run in a Docker container. It is particularly useful for integration testing, as it allows developers to spin up a real database instance in a container, perform tests, and then dispose of the container. This ensures that tests run in an environment that closely resembles production.

Setting up TestContainers

To use TestContainers, you need Docker installed on your machine. Follow these steps to set up and use TestContainers in your Spring Boot project.

Add Dependencies

Add the necessary dependencies for TestContainers and your database to your **pom.xml**.

```
<dependencies>
```

```
    <!-- Other dependencies -->
    <dependency>
        <groupId>org.testcontainers</groupId>
        <artifactId>testcontainers</artifactId>
        <scope>test</scope>
    </dependency>
    <dependency>
        <groupId>org.testcontainers</groupId>
        <artifactId>postgresql</artifactId>
        <scope>test</scope>
    </dependency>
    <dependency>
        <groupId>org.springframework.boot</groupId>
        <artifactId>spring-boot-starter-data-
jpa</artifactId>
    </dependency>
    <dependency>
        <groupId>org.springframework.boot</groupId>
        <artifactId>spring-boot-starter-test</artifactId>
        <scope>test</scope>
        <exclusions>
            <exclusion>
```

```
                <groupId>org.junit.vintage</groupId>

                <artifactId>junit-vintage-
engine</artifactId>

            </exclusion>

        </exclusions>

    </dependency>

    <dependency>

        <groupId>org.postgresql</groupId>

        <artifactId>postgresql</artifactId>

        <scope>runtime</scope>

    </dependency>

</dependencies>
```

The above dependencies include TestContainers, PostgreSQL support for TestContainers, Spring Data JPA, and Spring Boot testing support.

Configuring TestContainers

Create a configuration class to set up the PostgreSQL container.

```
package com.example.demo;



import
org.springframework.boot.test.context.TestConfiguration;

import org.springframework.context.annotation.Bean;

import org.testcontainers.containers.PostgreSQLContainer;
```

```java
@TestConfiguration
public class TestContainersConfig {

    @Bean
    public PostgreSQLContainer<?> postgreSQLContainer() {
        PostgreSQLContainer<?> container = new
PostgreSQLContainer<>("postgres:latest")
                .withDatabaseName("testdb")
                .withUsername("test")
                .withPassword("test");
        container.start();
        return container;
    }
}
```

This configuration class sets up a PostgreSQL container with a test database.

Application Properties for Testing

Configure application properties to use the PostgreSQL container for tests.

```
spring.datasource.url=jdbc:tc:postgresql:latest:///testdb
spring.datasource.username=test
spring.datasource.password=test
spring.jpa.hibernate.ddl-auto=update
spring.jpa.show-sql=true
```

These properties configure the Spring Data JPA to connect to the TestContainers PostgreSQL instance.

Writing Integration Tests with TestContainers

We will write integration tests for the **UserRepository** using TestContainers. For a better understanding, here is a detailed example of **UserRepositoryTest.java**:

```
package com.example.demo.repository;


import com.example.demo.TestContainersConfig;

import com.example.demo.model.User;

import org.junit.jupiter.api.Test;

import org.junit.jupiter.api.extension.ExtendWith;

import
org.springframework.beans.factory.annotation.Autowired;

import
org.springframework.boot.test.autoconfigure.orm.jpa.DataJ
paTest;

import org.springframework.context.annotation.Import;

import
org.springframework.test.context.junit.jupiter.SpringExte
nsion;


import java.util.Optional;


import static
org.junit.jupiter.api.Assertions.assertEquals;
```

```
import static
org.junit.jupiter.api.Assertions.assertFalse;

import static
org.junit.jupiter.api.Assertions.assertTrue;


@ExtendWith(SpringExtension.class)

@DataJpaTest

@Import(TestContainersConfig.class)

public class UserRepositoryTest {


    @Autowired

    private UserRepository userRepository;


    @Test

    public void whenFindByEmail_thenReturnUser() {

        // given

        User user = new User("John", "Doe",
"john.doe@gitforgits.com");

        userRepository.save(user);


        // when

        Optional<User> found =
userRepository.findByEmail(user.getEmail());
```

```
        // then
        assertTrue(found.isPresent());
        assertEquals(found.get().getEmail(),
user.getEmail());
    }

    @Test
    public void whenInvalidEmail_thenReturnEmpty() {
        // when
        Optional<User> found =
userRepository.findByEmail("invalid@gitforgits.com");

        // then
        assertFalse(found.isPresent());
    }

    @Test
    public void whenSaveUser_thenReturnSavedUser() {
        // given
        User user = new User("Jane", "Doe",
"jane.doe@gitforgits.com");
```

```
        // when
        User savedUser = userRepository.save(user);


        // then
        assertEquals(savedUser.getEmail(),
user.getEmail());
    }


    @Test
    public void whenDeleteUser_thenRemoveUser() {
        // given
        User user = new User("John", "Doe",
"john.doe@gitforgits.com");
        userRepository.save(user);


        // when
        userRepository.deleteById(user.getId());


        // then
        Optional<User> found =
userRepository.findById(user.getId());
```

```
        assertFalse(found.isPresent());

    }


    @Test

    public void whenFindByFirstName_thenReturnUserList()
{

        // given

        User user1 = new User("John", "Doe",
"john.doe@gitforgits.com");

        User user2 = new User("John", "Smith",
"john.smith@gitforgits.com");

        userRepository.save(user1);

        userRepository.save(user2);


        // when

        List<User> found =
userRepository.findByFirstName("John");


        // then

        assertEquals(2, found.size());

        assertEquals("john.doe@gitforgits.com",
found.get(0).getEmail());

        assertEquals("john.smith@gitforgits.com",
```

```
found.get(1).getEmail());
    }
}
```

Here in this above program,

- **`@Import(TestContainersConfig.class)`**: Imports the TestContainers configuration to the test class.
- The tests perform CRUD operations on the **`UserRepository`** and verify the results.

Run the tests and the test will:

- Start a PostgreSQL container.
- Execute CRUD operations on the **`UserRepository`**.
- Verify that data access logic works correctly with a real database instance.

Using TestContainers, one can ensure that their database-related code works correctly in an environment that closely resembles production, improving the reliability and robustness of their applications.

Performance Testing with JMeter

Performance testing is a critical aspect of ensuring that your application can handle expected load and stress conditions without performance degradation. It helps identify bottlenecks, ensures stability, and verifies that the application meets performance requirements.

Key performance aspects to be tested include:

- **Load Testing**: Evaluates how the application performs under expected user load.
- **Stress Testing**: Determines the application's behavior under extreme conditions.
- **Scalability Testing**: Measures the application's ability to scale with increasing loads.
- **Endurance Testing**: Checks the application's performance over an extended period.

Introduction to JMeter

JMeter is an open-source tool designed for performance testing. It allows you to simulate multiple users interacting with the application simultaneously, providing insights into its performance under various conditions. JMeter supports testing both static and dynamic resources, web applications, and different types of servers (e.g., HTTP, FTP, JDBC).

Setting up JMeter

Download JMeter from the official website and extract the archive to a suitable location on your system. Then, navigate to the **bin** directory inside the extracted folder and launch JMeter as below:

```
jmeter.bat
```

Sample Test Plan

Given below is an example of a more detailed Test Plan for load testing a Spring Boot application:

Create Thread Group Configuration:

- Number of Threads (Users): 100
- Ramp-Up Period: 10
- Loop Count: 10

Add HTTP Requests

- Get Users Request:
    a. Method: GET
    b. Path: /users
- Create User Request:
    a. Method: POST
    b. Path: /users

Body Data:

```
{
  "firstName": "John",
  "lastName": "Doe",
  "email": "john.doe@gitforgits.com"
}
```

Add CSV Data Set Config

- Filename: data/users.csv
- Variable Names: firstName,lastName,email

Add Assertions

- Response Assertion for Get Users:
    a. Field to Test: Text Response
    b. Pattern Matching Rules: Contains
    c. Patterns to Test: User List
- Response Assertion for Create User:
    a. Field to Test: Text Response
    b. Pattern Matching Rules: Contains
    c. Patterns to Test: User created successfully

Add Timers

- Constant Timer:
    a. Thread Delay (in milliseconds): 100

Add Listeners

- View Results Tree:
    a. To view detailed results of each request.
- Aggregate Report:
    a. To view aggregated performance metrics.

To run the test, click the green start button to run the test. After the test completes, review the results in the Listeners: Check individual request and response details. And, review summary statistics such as average response time, throughput, and error rate.

Summary

Overall, the focus of this chapter was on testing Spring Boot applications to ensure their functionality, reliability, and performance. It began with an introduction to the importance of testing, highlighting how it helps identify bugs early, improves code quality, and ensures the stability of applications. Various types of tests were discussed, including unit testing, integration testing, and performance testing, each serving a specific purpose in the software development lifecycle.

Unit testing was covered with detailed examples using JUnit and Mockito, demonstrating how to write and run tests for individual components in isolation. Slice testing was introduced as a method for testing specific layers of an application, such as the web or data layers, in isolation. The use of MockMVC for web layer testing was explained, with practical examples showing how to perform HTTP requests and verify responses without starting a full web server. This approach ensures that the web layer functions correctly and handles various scenarios. The chapter also delved into testing data repositories, explaining the different types of repositories and demonstrating how to perform tests on them. TestContainers was introduced for database integration testing, allowing the use of lightweight, throwaway instances of databases to ensure data access logic works correctly in an environment that closely resembles production.

Finally, performance testing with JMeter was covered, detailing the key aspects of performance to be tested, such as load, stress, scalability, and endurance. The setup and configuration of JMeter were explained, followed by practical examples of creating a test plan, running performance tests, and analyzing results. This comprehensive approach to testing equips developers with the necessary tools and techniques to ensure their Spring Boot applications are robust, reliable, and performant.

CHAPTER 9: SECURITY IN SPRING BOOT

Chapter Overview

Security is a vital component of any web application, ensuring that data and resources are protected from unauthorized access and vulnerabilities. This chapter will explore the various security mechanisms provided by Spring Security, a powerful and customizable security framework for Spring applications.

We will start by exploring the basics of Spring Security, understanding its core features and capabilities. The chapter will teach you through configuring basic authentication to secure your application with simple username and password protection. We will then move on to URL authorization, which allows fine-grained access control over different parts of your application based on user roles and permissions. The chapter will also cover implementing form-based authentication, providing a more user-friendly way of securing web applications. We will delve into advanced authentication mechanisms such as JWT (JSON Web Token) authentication and OAuth2 and OpenID Connect, which are widely used for securing RESTful services and enabling third-party integrations. You will learn how to secure RESTful services, ensuring that APIs are protected from unauthorized access and threats.

Additionally, we will explore integrating Spring Security with LDAP and Active Directory for centralized authentication and user management. The chapter will conclude with a section on customizing security configurations, allowing you to tailor Spring Security to meet the specific needs of your application. By the end of this chapter, you will have a comprehensive understanding of how to secure your Spring Boot applications using Spring Security, ensuring robust protection against various security threats.

Explore Spring Security

Introduction to Spring Security

Spring Security provides a comprehensive security framework including authentication, authorization, and other security features for Java applications, particularly those built with the Spring framework. It is highly customizable and can be configured to meet a wide range of security requirements, from simple authentication to complex enterprise-grade security solutions. At its core, Spring Security offers a robust mechanism to protect applications from common security threats such as unauthorized access, session fixation, cross-site request forgery (CSRF), and more.

Core Components of Spring Security

Authentication and Authorization

Authentication is the process of verifying the identity of a user or system, typically by checking credentials like username and password. Authorization, on the other hand, determines what resources or actions an authenticated user is allowed to access. Spring Security handles both aspects seamlessly. It supports various authentication mechanisms, including basic authentication, form-based authentication, token-based authentication (such as JWT), and integration with OAuth2 and OpenID Connect for third-party authentication. For authorization, Spring Security provides a flexible way to define access control rules using annotations like @PreAuthorize and @Secured, as well as through configuration classes.

Filters and Interceptors

Spring Security leverages a series of filters to process security-related functionality. The core of this is the **FilterChainProxy**, which delegates requests to a list of security filters. These filters include **UsernamePasswordAuthenticationFilter** for processing login requests, **BasicAuthenticationFilter** for HTTP Basic authentication, and **ExceptionTranslationFilter** for handling security exceptions. Filters can be configured to apply to specific URL patterns, allowing granular control over how and when security logic is applied. Interceptors, such as **MethodSecurityInterceptor**, provide security checks at the method level, ensuring that access control is enforced consistently throughout the application.

Security Context and AuthenticationManager

The Security Context is a crucial part of Spring Security, holding the security information of the current user, including their authentication status and roles. The **SecurityContextHolder** is used to access the Security Context, and it is populated by the authentication process. The **AuthenticationManager** is responsible for authenticating users, typically delegating to a series of **AuthenticationProvider**s. These providers perform the actual verification of credentials, supporting different authentication mechanisms. By default, Spring Security provides several implementations, such as **DaoAuthenticationProvider** for database-backed authentication and **LdapAuthenticationProvider** for LDAP-based authentication.

Access Decision Managers and Voters

Once a user is authenticated, Spring Security uses **AccessDecisionManager** to decide whether the user has the necessary permissions to access a resource. The **AccessDecisionManager** delegates to a list of **AccessDecisionVoter**s, each of which votes to grant or deny access based on specific criteria. Common voters include **RoleVoter**, which grants access based on user roles, and **AuthenticatedVoter**, which grants access to authenticated users. This voting mechanism allows for a flexible and extensible way to implement complex access control logic, ensuring that security decisions can be tailored to meet the specific needs of the application.

Password Management

Spring Security provides robust support for password management, including password encoding and validation. Passwords are typically hashed using a **`PasswordEncoder`** before being stored in the database, enhancing security by ensuring that plaintext passwords are never stored. Spring Security supports several encoding algorithms, such as BCrypt, SCrypt, and Argon2, each offering varying levels of security and performance. The framework also supports password policies, such as expiration and complexity requirements, which can be enforced to ensure that passwords meet organizational security standards.

Security Annotations

Security annotations provide a declarative way to apply security constraints at the method level. The **`@Secured`** annotation allows you to specify required roles for accessing a method, while **`@PreAuthorize`** and **`@PostAuthorize`** provide more advanced capabilities, allowing you to define security expressions that are evaluated before or after a method is invoked. These annotations enable developers to enforce security policies directly within their code, ensuring that access control is applied consistently and transparently. By leveraging these annotations, you can simplify security configuration and reduce the risk of security vulnerabilities.

CSRF Protection

Cross-Site Request Forgery (CSRF) is a type of attack that forces authenticated users to submit requests to a web application against their will. Spring Security provides built-in CSRF protection by generating a unique token for each session. This token is included in all state-changing requests (such as POST, PUT, DELETE) and validated on the server side to ensure that the request is legitimate. CSRF protection helps mitigate the risk of unauthorized actions being performed on behalf of authenticated users, enhancing the overall security of the application.

Session Management

Managing user sessions is an essential part of application security. Spring Security offers comprehensive session management capabilities, including session fixation protection, concurrent session control, and session timeout handling. Session fixation protection prevents attackers from hijacking user sessions by ensuring that session identifiers are regenerated upon authentication. Concurrent session control limits the number of active sessions per user, which is useful for preventing account sharing and detecting suspicious activity. Session timeout handling ensures that inactive sessions are terminated after a specified period, reducing the risk of unauthorized access due to forgotten or unattended sessions.

Integration with External Systems

Spring Security can integrate with external authentication and authorization systems, such as LDAP, Active Directory, OAuth2, and OpenID Connect. This integration allows organizations to leverage existing identity management solutions for centralized authentication and user management. For example, integrating with LDAP or Active Directory enables the use of enterprise-wide user directories for authentication, while OAuth2 and OpenID Connect facilitate single sign-on (SSO) and third-party authentication. These integrations provide flexibility and scalability, allowing applications to meet diverse security requirements.

Custom Security Configurations

Spring Security is highly configurable, allowing you to customize almost every aspect of its behavior. Custom security configurations can be implemented by extending core components such as **`AuthenticationProvider`**, **`AccessDecisionVoter`**, and **`Filter`**. Additionally, the framework's configuration DSL (Domain Specific Language) provides a fluent API for defining security settings in a concise and readable manner. This flexibility enables developers to tailor security configurations to the specific needs of their applications, ensuring that security policies are robust, effective, and aligned with organizational requirements.

Spring Security's core components, including authentication, authorization, filters, interceptors, and security context management, provide a solid foundation for securing applications. The framework's support for password management, CSRF protection, session management, and integration with external systems further enhances its capabilities. By using Spring Security, developers can implement robust and flexible security solutions that protect applications from various threats and ensure that access control policies are consistently enforced.

Configuring Basic Authentication

Basic authentication is a simple authentication scheme built into the HTTP protocol. It involves sending a username and password with each HTTP request to verify the user's identity. In Spring Boot, configuring basic authentication involves setting up the necessary security configurations to handle and validate these credentials. We will demonstrate how to configure basic authentication in a Spring Boot application.

Setting up Spring Security

Adding Dependencies

To use Spring Security in your Spring Boot application, you need to add the necessary dependencies to your pom.xml.

```
<dependencies>

    <!-- Other dependencies -->

    <dependency>
```

```
        <groupId>org.springframework.boot</groupId>

        <artifactId>spring-boot-starter-
security</artifactId>

    </dependency>

</dependencies>
```

The **spring-boot-starter-security** dependency includes all the necessary libraries to implement security features in your Spring Boot application.

Creating a Security Configuration Class

Next, create a configuration class to set up basic authentication. This class should extend **WebSecurityConfigurerAdapter** and override the necessary methods to configure security settings. Consider the following example of **SecurityConfig.java**:

```
package com.example.demo.config;



import org.springframework.context.annotation.Bean;

import
org.springframework.context.annotation.Configuration;

import
org.springframework.security.config.annotation.web.builde
rs.HttpSecurity;

import
org.springframework.security.config.annotation.web.builde
rs.WebSecurity;

import
org.springframework.security.config.annotation.web.config
uration.EnableWebSecurity;

import
```

```
org.springframework.security.config.annotation.web.config
uration.WebSecurityConfigurerAdapter;

import
org.springframework.security.core.userdetails.User;

import
org.springframework.security.core.userdetails.UserDetails
Service;

import
org.springframework.security.provisioning.InMemoryUserDet
ailsManager;

import
org.springframework.security.web.authentication.www.Basic
AuthenticationEntryPoint;


@Configuration

@EnableWebSecurity

public class SecurityConfig extends
WebSecurityConfigurerAdapter {


    @Override

    protected void configure(HttpSecurity http) throws
Exception {

        http

            .authorizeRequests()

                .antMatchers("/public/**").permitAll() //
Public URLs
```

```
                    .anyRequest().authenticated() // All
other URLs require authentication
                    .and()
                .httpBasic(); // Enable basic authentication
    }

    @Bean
    @Override
    public UserDetailsService userDetailsService() {
        InMemoryUserDetailsManager manager = new
InMemoryUserDetailsManager();
        manager.createUser(User.withUsername("user")
                .password("{noop}password") // {noop} means
no password encoder is used
                .roles("USER").build());
        manager.createUser(User.withUsername("admin")
                .password("{noop}admin")
                .roles("ADMIN").build());
        return manager;
    }
}
```

Here in this example,

- **`@EnableWebSecurity`**: Enables Spring Security's web security support.

- **configure(HttpSecurity http)**: Configures security settings such as URL authorization and enabling basic authentication.
- **userDetailsService()**: Configures in-memory user details for testing purposes.

Setting up Users and Roles

In the **userDetailsService()** method, we configure an in-memory user store with two users, each having different roles.

- **User.withUsername("user")**: Creates a user with the username "user" and password "password".
- **User.withUsername("admin")**: Creates an admin user with the username "admin" and password "admin".
- **roles("USER")** and **roles("ADMIN")**: Assigns roles to the users.

For production applications, user details would typically be retrieved from a database or another persistent storage.

Testing Basic Authentication

To test the basic authentication setup, create a simple controller with protected and public endpoints. Consider the following example of **TestController.java**:

```
package com.example.demo.controller;



import
org.springframework.web.bind.annotation.GetMapping;

import
org.springframework.web.bind.annotation.RequestMapping;

import
org.springframework.web.bind.annotation.RestController;



@RestController

@RequestMapping("/api")
```

```
public class TestController {

    @GetMapping("/public")
    public String publicEndpoint() {
        return "This is a public endpoint";
    }

    @GetMapping("/private")
    public String privateEndpoint() {
        return "This is a private endpoint";
    }
}
```

Here,

- **`/api/public`**: A public endpoint accessible without authentication.
- **`/api/private`**: A private endpoint that requires authentication.

Customizing Basic Authentication

Customizing the Authentication Entry Point

You can customize the response when an unauthenticated user tries to access a protected resource by defining a custom BasicAuthenticationEntryPoint as shown below:

```
package com.example.demo.config;

import
org.springframework.security.core.AuthenticationException
```

```
;

import
org.springframework.security.web.authentication.www.Basic
AuthenticationEntryPoint;

import org.springframework.stereotype.Component;


import javax.servlet.ServletException;

import javax.servlet.http.HttpServletRequest;

import javax.servlet.http.HttpServletResponse;

import java.io.IOException;

import java.io.PrintWriter;


@Component

public class CustomBasicAuthenticationEntryPoint extends
BasicAuthenticationEntryPoint {


    @Override

    public void commence(HttpServletRequest request,
HttpServletResponse response, AuthenticationException
authEx)

            throws IOException, ServletException {

        response.addHeader("WWW-Authenticate", "Basic
realm=\"" + getRealmName() + "\"");
```

```
response.setStatus(HttpServletResponse.SC_UNAUTHORIZED);

        PrintWriter writer = response.getWriter();

        writer.println("HTTP Status 401 - " +
authEx.getMessage());

    }


    @Override

    public void afterPropertiesSet() {

        setRealmName("myRealm");

        super.afterPropertiesSet();

    }

}
```

Here in this example,

- **`commence()`**: Customizes the response when authentication fails.
- **`afterPropertiesSet()`**: Sets the realm name used in the authentication challenge.

Integrating the Custom Entry Point

Update the security configuration **`SecurityConfig.java`** to use the custom entry point as shown below:

```
@Configuration

@EnableWebSecurity

public class SecurityConfig extends
WebSecurityConfigurerAdapter {
```

```
    @Autowired

    private CustomBasicAuthenticationEntryPoint
authenticationEntryPoint;


    @Override

    protected void configure(HttpSecurity http) throws
Exception {

        http

            .authorizeRequests()

                .antMatchers("/public/**").permitAll()

                .anyRequest().authenticated()

                .and()

            .httpBasic()

.authenticationEntryPoint(authenticationEntryPoint);

    }


    @Bean

    @Override

    public UserDetailsService userDetailsService() {

        InMemoryUserDetailsManager manager = new
InMemoryUserDetailsManager();

        manager.createUser(User.withUsername("user")
```

```
            .password("{noop}password")
            .roles("USER").build());
        manager.createUser(User.withUsername("admin")
            .password("{noop}admin")
            .roles("ADMIN").build());
        return manager;
    }
}
```

This configuration ensures that the custom entry point is used for handling authentication failures.

Just to sum up, we started by adding the necessary dependencies and creating a security configuration class. We then set up in-memory user details for testing and demonstrated how to protect endpoints using basic authentication. Additionally, we covered customizing the authentication entry point to provide a tailored response for unauthorized access attempts. This ensures that your Spring Boot application is secured with at least the basic authentication.

Configuring URL Authorization

URL authorization generally allows you to control access to specific URLs based on user roles and permissions. In Spring Security, URL authorization enables fine-grained access control, ensuring that only authorized users can access certain resources. In this section, we will learn to configure URL authorization, continuing from the basic authentication setup learned earlier.

Setting up URL Authorization

Enhancing the Security Configuration Class

To configure URL authorization, we need to extend our existing SecurityConfig class to specify access control rules for different URLs. Consider the following example of SecurityConfig.java:

```
package com.example.demo.config;
```

```
import org.springframework.context.annotation.Bean;

import
org.springframework.context.annotation.Configuration;

import
org.springframework.security.config.annotation.web.builde
rs.HttpSecurity;

import
org.springframework.security.config.annotation.web.config
uration.EnableWebSecurity;

import
org.springframework.security.config.annotation.web.config
uration.WebSecurityConfigurerAdapter;

import
org.springframework.security.core.userdetails.User;

import
org.springframework.security.core.userdetails.UserDetails
Service;

import
org.springframework.security.provisioning.InMemoryUserDet
ailsManager;


@Configuration

@EnableWebSecurity

public class SecurityConfig extends
WebSecurityConfigurerAdapter {
```

```
    @Override
    protected void configure(HttpSecurity http) throws
Exception {
        http
            .authorizeRequests()
                .antMatchers("/public/**").permitAll() //
Public URLs

.antMatchers("/admin/**").hasRole("ADMIN") // URLs
accessible only by admin

.antMatchers("/user/**").hasAnyRole("USER", "ADMIN") //
URLs accessible by user or admin
                .anyRequest().authenticated() // All
other URLs require authentication
                .and()
            .httpBasic(); // Enable basic authentication
    }

    @Bean
    @Override
    public UserDetailsService userDetailsService() {
        InMemoryUserDetailsManager manager = new
InMemoryUserDetailsManager();
```

```
        manager.createUser(User.withUsername("user")
            .password("{noop}password")
            .roles("USER").build());
        manager.createUser(User.withUsername("admin")
            .password("{noop}admin")
            .roles("ADMIN").build());
        return manager;
    }
}
```

In thet above example,

- **antMatchers("/public/**").permitAll()**: Allows access to URLs starting with **/public** without authentication.
- **antMatchers("/admin/**").hasRole("ADMIN")**: Restricts access to URLs starting with **/admin** to users with the **ADMIN** role.
- **antMatchers("/user/**").hasAnyRole("USER", "ADMIN")**: Allows access to URLs starting with **/user** for users with either the **USER** or **ADMIN** role.
- **anyRequest().authenticated()**: Requires authentication for all other URLs.

Creating Controllers with Role-Based Access

Here, we define controllers with endpoints that correspond to the URL patterns specified in the security configuration. To see how this works in practice, here is an example of **AdminController.java**:

```
package com.example.demo.controller;


import
org.springframework.web.bind.annotation.GetMapping;
```

```
import
org.springframework.web.bind.annotation.RequestMapping;

import
org.springframework.web.bind.annotation.RestController;


@RestController

@RequestMapping("/admin")

public class AdminController {


    @GetMapping("/dashboard")

    public String adminDashboard() {

        return "Welcome to the Admin Dashboard";

    }

}
```

Given below is another example of **UserController.java**:

```
package com.example.demo.controller;


import
org.springframework.web.bind.annotation.GetMapping;

import
org.springframework.web.bind.annotation.RequestMapping;

import
org.springframework.web.bind.annotation.RestController;
```

```
@RestController
@RequestMapping("/user")
public class UserController {

    @GetMapping("/profile")
    public String userProfile() {
        return "Welcome to the User Profile";
    }
}
```

Another example of **`PublicController.java`**:

```
package com.example.demo.controller;

import
org.springframework.web.bind.annotation.GetMapping;
import
org.springframework.web.bind.annotation.RequestMapping;
import
org.springframework.web.bind.annotation.RestController;

@RestController
@RequestMapping("/public")
```

```
public class PublicController {

    @GetMapping("/info")
    public String publicInfo() {
        return "This is a public information page";
    }
}
```

Once done, start the application and test the endpoints using Postman. While doing so, ensure the public endpoint should be accessible without authentication. The user endpoint should require authentication and be accessible with user or admin credentials. And, the admin endpoint should only be accessible with admin credentials.

Customizing Access Denied Handling

Creating a Custom Access Denied Handler

You can customize the response when a user attempts to access a resource they do not have permissions for by defining a custom AccessDeniedHandler as below:

```
package com.example.demo.config;

import
org.springframework.security.access.AccessDeniedException
;
import
org.springframework.security.web.access.AccessDeniedHandl
er;
import org.springframework.stereotype.Component;
```

```java
import javax.servlet.ServletException;

import javax.servlet.http.HttpServletRequest;

import javax.servlet.http.HttpServletResponse;

import java.io.IOException;

import java.io.PrintWriter;


@Component

public class CustomAccessDeniedHandler implements
AccessDeniedHandler {


    @Override

    public void handle(HttpServletRequest request,
HttpServletResponse response, AccessDeniedException
accessDeniedException)

            throws IOException, ServletException {


response.setStatus(HttpServletResponse.SC_FORBIDDEN);

        PrintWriter writer = response.getWriter();

        writer.println("HTTP Status 403 - " +
accessDeniedException.getMessage());

    }

}
```

Integrating the Custom Access Denied Handler

Update the security configuration to use the custom access denied handler.

```
@Configuration

@EnableWebSecurity

public class SecurityConfig extends
WebSecurityConfigurerAdapter {



    @Autowired

    private CustomAccessDeniedHandler
accessDeniedHandler;



    @Override

    protected void configure(HttpSecurity http) throws
Exception {

        http

            .authorizeRequests()

                .antMatchers("/public/**").permitAll()

.antMatchers("/admin/**").hasRole("ADMIN")

.antMatchers("/user/**").hasAnyRole("USER", "ADMIN")

                .anyRequest().authenticated()

                .and()
```

```java
            .httpBasic()
                .and()
            .exceptionHandling()

.accessDeniedHandler(accessDeniedHandler);
    }


    @Bean
    @Override
    public UserDetailsService userDetailsService() {
        InMemoryUserDetailsManager manager = new
InMemoryUserDetailsManager();
        manager.createUser(User.withUsername("user")
            .password("{noop}password")
            .roles("USER").build());
        manager.createUser(User.withUsername("admin")
            .password("{noop}admin")
            .roles("ADMIN").build());
        return manager;
    }
}
```

This above configuration ensures that the custom access denied handler is used to handle authorization failures.

Testing the Custom Access Denied Handler

Test the custom access denied handler by attempting to access resources with insufficient permissions. Use curl as below:

```
# Accessing admin endpoint with user credentials (should
trigger access denied handler)

curl -u user:password
http://localhost:8080/admin/dashboard
```

The response should be:

```
HTTP Status 403 - Access is denied
```

The implementation of URL authorization ensures that only authorized users can access specific resources in your application for an enhanced security and high control over sensitive data and functionalities of your application

JWT, OAuth and OpenID Connect

JWT (JSON Web Token) is a compact, URL-safe means of representing claims to be transferred between two parties. The claims in a JWT are encoded as a JSON object that is used as the payload of a JSON Web Signature (JWS) structure or as the plaintext of a JSON Web Encryption (JWE) structure, enabling the claims to be digitally signed or integrity protected with a Message Authentication Code (MAC) and/or encrypted. JWTs are often used for authentication and information exchange. In this section, we will integrate JWT authentication into our Spring Boot application.

Setting up JWT Authentication

Adding Dependencies

To use JWT in your Spring Boot application, you need to add the necessary dependencies. We will use jjwt for JWT operations.

```
<dependencies>

    <!-- Other dependencies -->
```

```
    <dependency>
        <groupId>io.jsonwebtoken</groupId>
        <artifactId>jjwt</artifactId>
        <version>0.9.1</version>
    </dependency>
    <dependency>
        <groupId>org.springframework.boot</groupId>
        <artifactId>spring-boot-starter-
security</artifactId>
    </dependency>
    <dependency>
        <groupId>org.springframework.boot</groupId>
        <artifactId>spring-boot-starter-web</artifactId>
    </dependency>
</dependencies>
```

Creating JWT Utility Class

Create a utility class to handle JWT operations such as generating and validating tokens.

```
package com.example.demo.util;


import io.jsonwebtoken.Claims;
import io.jsonwebtoken.Jwts;
import io.jsonwebtoken.SignatureAlgorithm;
```

```
import
org.springframework.beans.factory.annotation.Value;

import org.springframework.stereotype.Component;


import java.util.Date;

import java.util.HashMap;

import java.util.Map;

import java.util.function.Function;


@Component

public class JwtUtil {


    @Value("${jwt.secret}")

    private String secret;


    public String extractUsername(String token) {

        return extractClaim(token, Claims::getSubject);

    }


    public Date extractExpiration(String token) {

        return extractClaim(token,
Claims::getExpiration);
```

```
    }


    public <T> T extractClaim(String token,
Function<Claims, T> claimsResolver) {
        final Claims claims = extractAllClaims(token);
        return claimsResolver.apply(claims);
    }


    private Claims extractAllClaims(String token) {
        return
Jwts.parser().setSigningKey(secret).parseClaimsJws(token)
.getBody();
    }


    private Boolean isTokenExpired(String token) {
        return extractExpiration(token).before(new
Date());
    }


    public String generateToken(String username) {
        Map<String, Object> claims = new HashMap<>();
        return createToken(claims, username);
    }
```

```
    private String createToken(Map<String, Object>
claims, String subject) {

        return
Jwts.builder().setClaims(claims).setSubject(subject).setI
ssuedAt(new Date(System.currentTimeMillis()))

                .setExpiration(new
Date(System.currentTimeMillis() + 1000 * 60 * 60 * 10))

                .signWith(SignatureAlgorithm.HS256,
secret).compact();

    }


    public Boolean validateToken(String token, String
username) {

        final String tokenUsername =
extractUsername(token);

        return (tokenUsername.equals(username) &&
!isTokenExpired(token));

    }

}
```

Creating JWT Request and Response Models

Create models to handle the authentication request and response.

```
package com.example.demo.model;
```

```
public class JwtRequest {

    private String username;
    private String password;

    // Getters and setters

public class JwtResponse {

    private final String jwt;

    public JwtResponse(String jwt) {
        this.jwt = jwt;
    }

    public String getJwt() {
        return jwt;
    }
}
```

Creating UserDetailService Implementation

Implement **UserDetailsService** to load user-specific data.

```
package com.example.demo.service;


import
org.springframework.security.core.userdetails.User;

import
org.springframework.security.core.userdetails.UserDetails
;

import
org.springframework.security.core.userdetails.UserDetails
Service;

import
org.springframework.security.core.userdetails.UsernameNot
FoundException;

import org.springframework.stereotype.Service;


import java.util.ArrayList;


@Service

public class CustomUserDetailsService implements
UserDetailsService {


    @Override

    public UserDetails loadUserByUsername(String
username) throws UsernameNotFoundException {

        if ("user".equals(username)) {
```

```
            return new User("user", "{noop}password", new
ArrayList<>());

        } else if ("admin".equals(username)) {

            return new User("admin", "{noop}admin", new
ArrayList<>());

        } else {

            throw new UsernameNotFoundException("User not
found with username: " + username);

        }

    }

}
```

Creating Authentication Controller

Create a controller to handle authentication requests and generate JWT tokens.

```
package com.example.demo.controller;



import com.example.demo.model.JwtRequest;

import com.example.demo.model.JwtResponse;

import com.example.demo.service.CustomUserDetailsService;

import com.example.demo.util.JwtUtil;

import
org.springframework.beans.factory.annotation.Autowired;

import
org.springframework.security.authentication.Authenticatio
```

```
nManager;

import
org.springframework.security.authentication.BadCredential
sException;

import
org.springframework.security.authentication.UsernamePassw
ordAuthenticationToken;

import org.springframework.security.core.Authentication;

import
org.springframework.security.core.AuthenticationException
;

import
org.springframework.security.core.userdetails.UserDetails
;

import org.springframework.web.bind.annotation.*;


@RestController

@RequestMapping("/api")

public class JwtAuthenticationController {


    @Autowired

    private AuthenticationManager authenticationManager;


    @Autowired
```

```
    private JwtUtil jwtUtil;


    @Autowired
    private CustomUserDetailsService userDetailsService;


    @PostMapping("/authenticate")
    public JwtResponse
createAuthenticationToken(@RequestBody JwtRequest
authenticationRequest) throws Exception {
        try {
            Authentication authentication =
authenticationManager.authenticate(
                    new
UsernamePasswordAuthenticationToken(authenticationRequest
.getUsername(), authenticationRequest.getPassword())
            );
        } catch (BadCredentialsException e) {
            throw new Exception("Incorrect username or
password", e);
        }


        final UserDetails userDetails =
userDetailsService.loadUserByUsername(authenticationReque
st.getUsername());
```

```
        final String jwt =
jwtUtil.generateToken(userDetails.getUsername());


        return new JwtResponse(jwt);
    }
}
```

Configuring JWT Authentication Filter

Create a filter to intercept requests and validate the JWT token.

```
package com.example.demo.filter;


import com.example.demo.service.CustomUserDetailsService;

import com.example.demo.util.JwtUtil;

import
org.springframework.beans.factory.annotation.Autowired;

import
org.springframework.security.core.context.SecurityContext
Holder;

import
org.springframework.security.core.userdetails.UserDetails
;

import
org.springframework.security.web.authentication.WebAuthen
ticationDetailsSource;

import org.springframework.stereotype.Component;
```

```
import
org.springframework.web.filter.OncePerRequestFilter;


import javax.servlet.FilterChain;

import javax.servlet.ServletException;

import javax.servlet.http.HttpServletRequest;

import javax.servlet.http.HttpServletResponse;

import java.io.IOException;


@Component

public class JwtRequestFilter extends
OncePerRequestFilter {


    @Autowired

    private CustomUserDetailsService userDetailsService;

    @Autowired

    private JwtUtil jwtUtil;


    @Override

    protected void doFilterInternal(HttpServletRequest
request, HttpServletResponse response, FilterChain chain)

            throws ServletException, IOException {
```

```
        final String authorizationHeader =
request.getHeader("Authorization");

        String username = null;
        String jwt = null;

        if (authorizationHeader != null &&
authorizationHeader.startsWith("Bearer ")) {
            jwt = authorizationHeader.substring(7);
            username = jwtUtil.extractUsername(jwt);
        }

        if (username != null &&
SecurityContextHolder.getContext().getAuthentication() ==
null) {
            UserDetails userDetails =
this.userDetailsService.loadUserByUsername(username);

            if (jwtUtil.validateToken(jwt,
userDetails.getUsername())) {

                UsernamePasswordAuthenticationToken
usernamePasswordAuthenticationToken =
```

```
                        new
UsernamePasswordAuthenticationToken(userDetails, null,
userDetails.getAuthorities());

usernamePasswordAuthenticationToken.setDetails(new
WebAuthenticationDetailsSource().buildDetails(request));

SecurityContextHolder.getContext().setAuthentication(user
namePasswordAuthenticationToken);
            }
        }
        chain.doFilter(request, response);
    }
}
```

Configuring Security Settings

Update the security configuration to use JWT authentication.

```
package com.example.demo.config;


import com.example.demo.filter.JwtRequestFilter;
import
org.springframework.beans.factory.annotation.Autowired;
import org.springframework.context.annotation.Bean;
import
org.springframework.context.annotation.Configuration;
```

```
import
org.springframework.security.authentication.Authenticatio
nManager;

import
org.springframework.security.config.annotation.authentica
tion.builders.AuthenticationManagerBuilder;

import
org.springframework.security.config.annotation.web.builde
rs.HttpSecurity;

import
org.springframework.security.config.annotation.web.config
uration.EnableWebSecurity;

import
org.springframework.security.config.annotation.web.config
uration.WebSecurityConfigurerAdapter;

import
org.springframework.security.config.http.SessionCreationP
olicy;

import
org.springframework.security.core.userdetails.UserDetails
Service;

import
org.springframework.security.crypto.password.NoOpPassword
Encoder;

import
org.springframework.security.crypto.password.PasswordEnco
der;

import
```

```
org.springframework.security.web.authentication.UsernameP
asswordAuthenticationFilter;


@Configuration

@EnableWebSecurity

public class SecurityConfig extends
WebSecurityConfigurerAdapter {


    @Autowired

    private UserDetailsService customUserDetailsService;


    @Autowired

    private JwtRequestFilter jwtRequestFilter;


    @Override

    protected void configure(HttpSecurity http) throws
Exception {

        http

            .csrf().disable()

            .authorizeRequests()

.antMatchers("/api/authenticate").permitAll()

               .anyRequest().
```

```
.anyRequest().authenticated() .and()
.sessionManagement().sessionCreationPolicy(SessionCreatio
nPolicy.STATELESS);
http.addFilterBefore(jwtRequestFilter,
UsernamePasswordAuthenticationFilter.class);

}

@Override protected void
configure(AuthenticationManagerBuilder auth)

throws Exception

{

auth.userDetailsService(customUserDetailsService);

}

@Bean @Override public AuthenticationManager
authenticationManagerBean()

throws Exception { return
super.authenticationManagerBean();

}

@Bean public PasswordEncoder passwordEncoder()

{

return NoOpPasswordEncoder.getInstance();

}

}
```

Here in this above snippet,

- **`csrf().disable()`**: Disables CSRF protection as it is not necessary for stateless

APIs.

- **authorizeRequests()**: Configures URL authorization, allowing unauthenticated access to the **/api/authenticate** endpoint and requiring authentication for all other endpoints.
- **sessionManagement().sessionCreationPolicy(SessionCreationPolicy.STATELESS)**: Configures the application to be stateless, meaning no sessions will be created or used by Spring Security.
- **addFilterBefore(jwtRequestFilter, UsernamePasswordAuthenticationFilter.class)**: Adds the **JwtRequestFilter** to the security filter chain, ensuring that JWT validation is performed before the username and password authentication filter.

The implementation of JWT authentication ensures a highly secure, stateless communication between clients and the server, for enhanced security and scalability of our application.

Setting up OAuth and OpenID Connect

OAuth and OpenID Connect are widely used protocols for authorization and authentication, respectively. OAuth 2.0 is an authorization framework that allows third-party services to exchange information without exposing user credentials. OpenID Connect, built on top of OAuth 2.0, provides a simple identity layer to verify the identity of the user. In this section, we will integrate OAuth 2.0 and OpenID Connect into our Spring Boot application.

Adding Dependencies

Add the necessary dependencies to your pom.xml file to use Spring Security OAuth2 and OpenID Connect.

```
<dependencies>

    <!-- Other dependencies -->

    <dependency>

        <groupId>org.springframework.boot</groupId>

        <artifactId>spring-boot-starter-
security</artifactId>

    </dependency>
```

```xml
    <dependency>
        <groupId>org.springframework.boot</groupId>
        <artifactId>spring-boot-starter-oauth2-
client</artifactId>
    </dependency>
    <dependency>
        <groupId>org.springframework.boot</groupId>
        <artifactId>spring-boot-starter-oauth2-resource-
server</artifactId>
    </dependency>
</dependencies>
```

Configuring OAuth 2.0 Client

Create a configuration file for OAuth 2.0 client settings. This example demonstrates integrating with Google as an OAuth provider.

```yaml
spring:
  security:
    oauth2:
      client:
        registration:
          google:
            client-id: YOUR_GOOGLE_CLIENT_ID
            client-secret: YOUR_GOOGLE_CLIENT_SECRET
```

```
            scope: profile, email
            redirect-uri:
"{baseUrl}/login/oauth2/code/{registrationId}"
            authorization-grant-type: authorization_code
            client-name: Google
        provider:
          google:
            authorization-uri:
https://accounts.google.com/o/oauth2/auth
            token-uri:
https://oauth2.googleapis.com/token
            user-info-uri:
https://www.googleapis.com/oauth2/v3/userinfo
            user-name-attribute: sub
```

Here, in this example,

- Replace **YOUR_GOOGLE_CLIENT_ID** and **YOUR_GOOGLE_CLIENT_SECRET** with your actual Google OAuth 2.0 client ID and secret.
- Configure the redirect URI to match the base URL of your application.

Creating a Security Configuration Class

Update the **SecurityConfig** class to include OAuth2 login configuration.

```
package com.example.demo.config;


import org.springframework.context.annotation.Bean;
import
```

```
org.springframework.context.annotation.Configuration;

import
org.springframework.security.config.annotation.web.builde
rs.HttpSecurity;

import
org.springframework.security.config.annotation.web.config
uration.EnableWebSecurity;

import
org.springframework.security.config.annotation.web.config
uration.WebSecurityConfigurerAdapter;

import
org.springframework.security.core.userdetails.UserDetails
Service;

import
org.springframework.security.crypto.password.NoOpPassword
Encoder;

import
org.springframework.security.crypto.password.PasswordEnco
der;


@Configuration

@EnableWebSecurity

public class SecurityConfig extends
WebSecurityConfigurerAdapter {


    @Override
```

```
    protected void configure(HttpSecurity http) throws
Exception {
        http
            .authorizeRequests()
                .antMatchers("/public/**", "/login",
"/oauth2/**").permitAll()

.antMatchers("/admin/**").hasRole("ADMIN")

.antMatchers("/user/**").hasAnyRole("USER", "ADMIN")
                .anyRequest().authenticated()
                .and()
            .oauth2Login()
                .loginPage("/login")
                .defaultSuccessUrl("/user/profile", true)
                .and()
            .logout()
                .logoutSuccessUrl("/login")
                .permitAll();
    }

    @Bean
    public PasswordEncoder passwordEncoder() {
```

```
        return NoOpPasswordEncoder.getInstance();
    }
}
```

Now in the above program,

- **`oauth2Login()`**: Configures OAuth2 login.
- **`loginPage("/login")`**: Specifies the custom login page URL.
- **`defaultSuccessUrl("/user/profile", true)`**: Specifies the default URL to redirect to after successful login.

Creating a Controller for Login

Create a controller to serve the login page.

```
package com.example.demo.controller;


import org.springframework.stereotype.Controller;

import
org.springframework.web.bind.annotation.GetMapping;


@Controller

public class LoginController {


    @GetMapping("/login")

    public String login() {

        return "login";

    }
```

```
}
```

Creating Login and Profile Pages

Create the **login.html** page for users to select the OAuth2 login option.

```
<!DOCTYPE html>

<html xmlns:th="http://www.thymeleaf.org">

<head>

    <title>Login</title>

</head>

<body>

    <h2>Login</h2>

    <div>

        <a href="/oauth2/authorization/google">Login with
Google</a>

    </div>

</body>

</html>
```

Now, create the **profile.html** page to display user information after successful login.

```
<!DOCTYPE html>

<html xmlns:th="http://www.thymeleaf.org">

<head>

    <title>User Profile</title>
```

```
</head>

<body>

    <h2>User Profile</h2>

    <p>Welcome, <span th:text="${user.name}"></span>!</p>

    <p>Email: <span th:text="${user.email}"></span></p>

    <div>

        <a href="/logout">Logout</a>

    </div>

</body>

</html>
```

Creating a User Model

Create a model to hold user information. Consider the example of **User.java**:

```
package com.example.demo.model;


public class User {

    private String name;

    private String email;


    // Getters and setters

}
```

Creating a Controller for Profile

Create a controller to handle requests to the profile page.

```
package com.example.demo.controller;


import com.example.demo.model.User;

import
org.springframework.security.core.annotation.Authenticati
onPrincipal;

import
org.springframework.security.oauth2.core.oidc.user.OidcUs
er;

import org.springframework.stereotype.Controller;

import org.springframework.ui.Model;

import
org.springframework.web.bind.annotation.GetMapping;


@Controller

public class UserProfileController {


    @GetMapping("/user/profile")

    public String userProfile(Model model,
@AuthenticationPrincipal OidcUser principal) {

        User user = new User();

        user.setName(principal.getFullName());
```

```
        user.setEmail(principal.getEmail());
        model.addAttribute("user", user);
        return "profile";
    }
}
```

Here, **@AuthenticationPrincipal OidcUser principal** injects the authenticated user's details into the controller method.

With this, we have successfully integrated OAuth 2.0 and OpenID Connect into a Spring Boot application using Google as the authentication provider.

Integrating with LDAP and Active Directory

LDAP (Lightweight Directory Access Protocol) and Active Directory (AD) are widely used for managing user authentication and authorization in enterprise environments. Integrating Spring Boot applications with LDAP or Active Directory allows for centralized authentication, user management, and access control, leveraging existing enterprise infrastructure. In this section, we will demonstrate how to integrate a Spring Boot application with LDAP and Active Directory.

Setting up LDAP Integration

Adding Dependencies

To use LDAP in your Spring Boot application, add the necessary dependencies to your pom.xml.

```
<dependencies>
    <!-- Other dependencies -->
    <dependency>
        <groupId>org.springframework.boot</groupId>
        <artifactId>spring-boot-starter-
security</artifactId>
```

```
    </dependency>

    <dependency>

        <groupId>org.springframework.boot</groupId>

        <artifactId>spring-boot-starter-data-
ldap</artifactId>

    </dependency>

    <dependency>

        <groupId>org.springframework.ldap</groupId>

        <artifactId>spring-ldap-core</artifactId>

    </dependency>

</dependencies>
```

Configuring LDAP Settings

Configure LDAP settings in your **application.yml** or **application.properties** file.

```
spring:

  ldap:

    base: dc=springframework,dc=org

    username: uid=admin,ou=system

    password: secret

    urls: ldap://localhost:8389
```

Here, **spring.ldap.base** is the base DN for LDAP queries, **spring.ldap.username** and **spring.ldap.password** are the credentials for connecting to the LDAP server, and **spring.ldap.urls** is the URL of the LDAP server.

Creating a Security Configuration Class

Update the **SecurityConfig** class to include LDAP authentication.

```
package com.example.demo.config;


import org.springframework.context.annotation.Bean;

import
org.springframework.context.annotation.Configuration;

import
org.springframework.security.config.annotation.authentica
tion.builders.AuthenticationManagerBuilder;

import
org.springframework.security.config.annotation.web.builde
rs.HttpSecurity;

import
org.springframework.security.config.annotation.web.config
uration.EnableWebSecurity;

import
org.springframework.security.config.annotation.web.config
uration.WebSecurityConfigurerAdapter;

import
org.springframework.security.core.userdetails.UserDetails
Service;

import
org.springframework.security.crypto.bcrypt.BCryptPassword
Encoder;

import
org.springframework.security.crypto.password.PasswordEnco
```

```
der;


@Configuration

@EnableWebSecurity

public class SecurityConfig extends
WebSecurityConfigurerAdapter {


    @Override

    protected void configure(HttpSecurity http) throws
Exception {

        http

            .authorizeRequests()

                .antMatchers("/public/**").permitAll()

                .anyRequest().authenticated()

                .and()

            .formLogin()

                .loginPage("/login")

                .defaultSuccessUrl("/user/profile", true)

                .permitAll()

                .and()

            .logout()

                .permitAll();
```

```
    }


    @Override
    public void configure(AuthenticationManagerBuilder
auth) throws Exception {
        auth
            .ldapAuthentication()
                .userDnPatterns("uid={0},ou=people")
                .groupSearchBase("ou=groups")
                .contextSource()

.url("ldap://localhost:8389/dc=springframework,dc=org")
                    .managerDn("uid=admin,ou=system")
                    .managerPassword("secret")
                .and()
                .passwordCompare()
                    .passwordEncoder(new
BCryptPasswordEncoder())
                    .passwordAttribute("userPassword");
    }


    @Bean
```

```
    public PasswordEncoder passwordEncoder() {

        return new BCryptPasswordEncoder();

    }

}
```

Here in this above example,

- **ldapAuthentication()**: Configures LDAP authentication.
- **userDnPatterns("uid={0},ou=people")**: Specifies the pattern to search for user DNs.
- **groupSearchBase("ou=groups")**: Specifies the base DN for group searches.
- **contextSource()**: Configures the LDAP server URL and credentials.
- **passwordCompare()**: Configures password comparison and encoding.

Creating a Controller for Login and Profile

Create controllers to handle login and profile requests, as shown in previous examples.

```
package com.example.demo.controller;


import org.springframework.stereotype.Controller;

import
org.springframework.web.bind.annotation.GetMapping;


@Controller

public class LoginController {


    @GetMapping("/login")
```

```
    public String login() {
        return "login";
    }
}

//UserProfileController.java:

package com.example.demo.controller;


import com.example.demo.model.User;
import
org.springframework.security.core.annotation.Authenticati
onPrincipal;
import
org.springframework.security.ldap.userdetails.LdapUserDet
ails;
import org.springframework.stereotype.Controller;
import org.springframework.ui.Model;
import
org.springframework.web.bind.annotation.GetMapping;

@Controller
public class UserProfileController {
```

```java
    @GetMapping("/user/profile")
    public String userProfile(Model model,
@AuthenticationPrincipal LdapUserDetails principal) {
        User user = new User();
        user.setName(principal.getUsername());
        user.setEmail("N/A"); // Adjust as per your LDAP
schema
        model.addAttribute("user", user);
        return "profile";
    }
}
```

`@AuthenticationPrincipal LdapUserDetails principal` injects the authenticated LDAP user's details into the controller method.

Integrating with Active Directory

Configuring Active Directory Settings

For Active Directory, configure the necessary settings in your application.yml file.

```yaml
  ldap:
    urls: ldap://<AD_SERVER>:<PORT>
    base: dc=example,dc=com
    username: cn=admin,dc=example,dc=com
    password: admin_password
```

Updating Security Configuration Class

Update the **SecurityConfig** class to include Active Directory authentication.

```
package com.example.demo.config;


import org.springframework.context.annotation.Bean;

import
org.springframework.context.annotation.Configuration;

import
org.springframework.security.config.annotation.authentica
tion.builders.AuthenticationManagerBuilder;

import
org.springframework.security.config.annotation.web.builde
rs.HttpSecurity;

import
org.springframework.security.config.annotation.web.config
uration.EnableWebSecurity;

import
org.springframework.security.config.annotation.web.config
uration.WebSecurityConfigurerAdapter;

import
org.springframework.security.crypto.bcrypt.BCryptPassword
Encoder;

import
org.springframework.security.crypto.password.PasswordEnco
der;
```

```
@Configuration

@EnableWebSecurity

public class SecurityConfig extends
WebSecurityConfigurerAdapter {


    @Override

    protected void configure(HttpSecurity http) throws
Exception {

        http

            .authorizeRequests()

                .antMatchers("/public/**").permitAll()

                .anyRequest().authenticated()

                .and()

            .formLogin()

                .loginPage("/login")

                .defaultSuccessUrl("/user/profile", true)

                .permitAll()

                .and()

            .logout()

                .permitAll();

    }
```

```
    @Override
    public void configure(AuthenticationManagerBuilder
auth) throws Exception {
        auth
            .ldapAuthentication()
                .userDnPatterns("uid={0},ou=users")
                .groupSearchBase("ou=groups")
                .contextSource()
.url("ldap://<AD_SERVER>:<PORT>/dc=example,dc=com")
.managerDn("cn=admin,dc=example,dc=com")
                    .managerPassword("admin_password")
                .and()
                .passwordCompare()
                    .passwordEncoder(passwordEncoder())
                    .passwordAttribute("userPassword");
    }

    @Bean
    public PasswordEncoder passwordEncoder() {
        return new BCryptPasswordEncoder();
```

```
    }
}
```

In the above code snippet,

- Replace **<AD_SERVER>** and **<PORT>** with your Active Directory server details.
- Adjust the user DN patterns and group search base according to your Active Directory schema.

And as shown in the previous examples, create controllers and views for handling login and profile requests. The integration with LDAP and Active Directory has enabled centralized authentication and user management, and as a whole utilizes existing enterprise infrastructure to enhance the security and manageability of our application.

Summary

So, just to sum up, the chapter began by exploring Spring Security, detailing its core components such as authentication, authorization, filters, interceptors, and security context management. It then moved on to configuring basic authentication, showing how to set up security configurations to handle and validate credentials using in-memory user details.

The next section covered URL authorization, demonstrating how to control access to specific URLs based on user roles and permissions. This was followed by form-based authentication, which provided a user-friendly way for users to log in via a custom login form. The implementation included creating login and profile pages and setting up the security configuration to handle form submissions and user sessions. JWT (JSON Web Token) authentication was then introduced, explaining the process of generating and validating tokens for stateless authentication. The setup involved creating a JWT utility class, authentication controller, and JWT filter to secure API endpoints.

The chapter also included OAuth and OpenID Connect integration, enabling secure authentication using external identity providers like Google. This involved configuring OAuth2 client settings, updating security configurations, and creating login and profile pages to handle the OAuth2 login flow. Finally, the chapter addressed integrating with LDAP and Active Directory for centralized authentication and user management. This section detailed the configuration of LDAP settings, security configurations for LDAP authentication, and the creation of controllers and views for handling login and profile requests. The integration allowed leveraging existing enterprise infrastructure for enhanced security and manageability of the Spring Boot application.

Index

Y

Epilogue

Here at Spring Boot 3.0 Crash Course, I'd like to take a second to appreciate all that we've accomplished as a community. Writing this book and sharing my experiences with you has been really fulfilling. I'm Kit Harrington, and I've made it my mission to teach you what you need to know to create safe, scalable, and reliable Spring Boot apps.

Throughout this book, we've covered everything from configuring your development environment to deploying applications on cloud platforms and Kubernetes. We've looked at the main elements of Spring Boot, advanced customizations, and critical areas of security and data access. We've learned how to use technologies like JMeter to manage form submissions, validate user inputs, integrate front-end frameworks, and improve performance. One of the most important lessons from this book is the power and flexibility that Spring Boot provides. You may streamline your development process, cut down on boilerplate code, and concentrate on creating excellent products by taking advantage of its advantages.

Security has been a major concern throughout this work. You may implement Spring Security's authentication and authorization features, set up JWT tokens, integrate OAuth2, and OpenID Connect, and your apps will be secure, allowing your users to rest easy. Another key component we've looked into is data access. You learned how to properly manage data sources, conduct CRUD operations, and handle transactions with Spring Data JPA. Integrating with solutions like as Liquibase and Flyway allows you to manage database migrations smoothly, ensuring that your data layer remains consistent and trustworthy.

Now that you know what to expect, deploying apps to production environments isn't as scary as it once was. From generating Docker images to deploying on cloud platforms like Kubernetes, you've seen how to easily package and deploy your Spring Boot apps while assuring scalability and stability. A developer's toolbox should always include performance optimization and debugging techniques. You can make sure your apps work well and give users a good experience by learning to find bottlenecks, optimize your code, and fix frequent problems.

As you go, I encourage you to keep trying, creating, and learning. The world of software development is always growing, and there is always something new to uncover. Use everything you've learned in this book as a basis to take on new challenges and create even more outstanding apps. I hope you've found this book as enlightening as I did when writing it. Remember, practice and dedication are essential for mastering any technology. Continue to code, explore, and push the edges of Spring Boot 3.0's capabilities.

Happy coding!

Thank You

www.ingramcontent.com/pod-product-compliance
Lightning Source LLC
Chambersburg PA
CBHW080207170726
48282CB00030B/1032

9788119177387